BEGINNING WOODCARVING

• PROJECTS • TECHNIQUES • TOOLS •

BEGINNING
WOODCARVING

• PROJECTS • TECHNIQUES • TOOLS •

GUILD OF MASTER CRAFTSMAN PUBLICATIONS

This collection first published in 2001 by
Guild of Master Craftsman Publications Ltd
Castle Place, 166 High Street,
Lewes, East Sussex BN7 1XU

Reprinted 2003

ISBN 1 86108 280 0

British Library Cataloguing in Publication Data.
A catalogue record of this book is available from the British Library.

A catalogue record for this book is available from the British Library.

Printed and bound in Hong Kong by CT Printing Ltd

Cover designed by Ian Smith at GMC Publications Studio
Cover photograph by Anthony Bailey

CONTENTS

INTRODUCTION

Welcome to the wonderful world of carving – a rich and rewarding hobby that stimulates both the mind and one's abilities. It is difficult to express how much enjoyment can be gained from creating work with your own hands, and especially from carving. Since you are reading this, you are already on the fascinating path of exploring this for yourself.

There are many aspects of carving to tackle (lettering, panelling, portraits, bodywork, bird carving, architectural work and much more), but how do you get started? The thirst for easy-to-follow information is almost unquenchable, and it explains why this book has been created.

We use a variety of authors – all experts in their field – to guide you progressively to a firm understanding of the fundamental principles involved in turning that initial block of wood into an attractive work of craftsmanship. Each of the articles is richly illustrated with pictures and diagrams, and is written in a style that is both concise and easy to understand.

The techniques demonstrated in these pages show you how to choose, use and sharpen carving tools, help you select the best timber and instruct you on how to cut and hold it. The articles also take a look at a wide variety of projects that you can tackle (using both hand and power tools), and deal with the inevitable problems that will occasionally arise.

You will have great fun practising the techniques shown and discovering what can be done. In reality carvers never stop learning, but armed with these new skills you will be able to develop quickly as you explore the wonderful array of opportunities open to you.

There are other books available from GMC that will help you explore additional techniques and aspects of carving, while *Woodcarving* magazine will further help you to develop your skills.

Mark Baker

Group editor, Woodworking magazines

The first carving
that Geoff Dixon
completed,
Desmond the Cat

GEOFF DIXON

Some beginners prefer to find their own way, others flourish in groups under guidance.

The self-taught woodcarvers are justifiably proud. They have developed their skills through years of practice. Facing countless problems and untold frustrations, all of which have been overcome by dogged resourcefulness and determination. For this alone they are to be admired.

An alternative approach is to enrol with a woodcarving course. I was fortunate to have a weekly class held nearby. After attending these classes for a year I can now look back and compare my self-taught experience with that of the instruction I have received.

Starting to carve

I started out, probably like most woodcarvers, intending to teach myself. The only help I could find was from the wealth of books available. Although good, so many books were of a similar style and covered much the same ground. Advice on subjects such as which gouges to purchase was often cursory and confusing. What to look for in the quality of a gouge was rarely mentioned. As a result, I purchased a set of gouges which I later discovered were of poor quality and some of which are unlikely ever to be used.

Whilst struggling to write this article I realised how difficult it is to explain ideas and thoughts in words. So it must have been

Geoff's second piece, *Lyn*

Sld is Geoff's third piece showing much improvement in modelling, detail and finish

for the authors of my books. They advised, quite rightly, to ensure that gouges are sharp before commencing work. Their descriptions of sharpening, however, left a lot to be desired and I now realise that their methods of sharpening and honing, whilst probably eminently suitable for an expert, were far too demanding for a beginner. I struggled with various stones and slips for two days before my gouges were anything like sharp.

I shall never forget my first efforts at producing a drawing for a carving of a small owl. Rembrandt could not have put more effort into a single pencil drawing than I did, and I am sure he never ended up with such a miserable result. This was followed by hour after hour of tentative chipping away at a poor beleaguered piece of teak. 'Oh what a lovely budgie!' people said when confronted by my woodcarving. I felt dispirited. I was sure my woodcarving days were over. I did not think that I had the determination a self-taught carver requires.

Teaching experience

Then I discovered a local woodcarving class which was held every Tuesday evening. This appeared to be the answer to my dreams. However, it was over 20 years since I had undertaken any form of education and I had hoped my days of schooling were well and truly over. I had a vision of being reprimanded for mistakes. I had never

TAUGHT OR

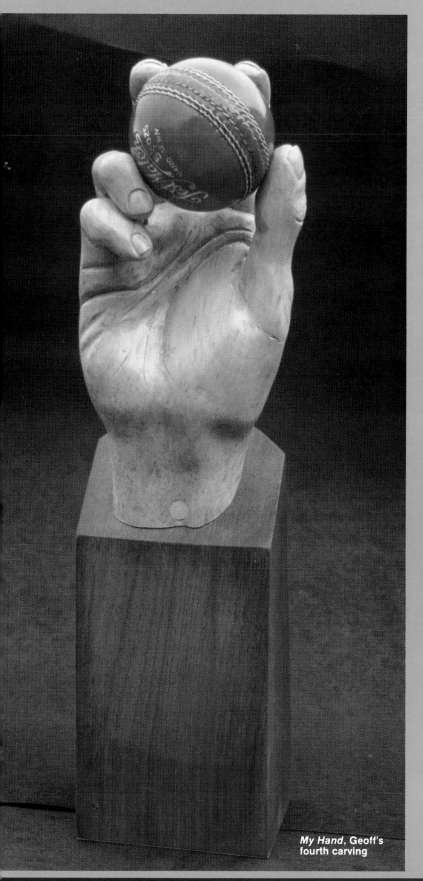

My Hand, Geoff's fourth carving

worked well when people peered over my shoulder. Surely I would freeze and the gouges become unmanageable when the tutor came to inspect my work. After several weeks of dithering, my wife persuaded me to get in touch with the instructor concerned, and before I knew it I was nervously arriving for my first class.

What a surprise! Everybody was so pleasant and helpful. I was encouraged every step of the way. I was allowed to carve any subject I fancied, so that the very small amount of artistic flair I possessed was nurtured and developed. I never had to follow a set course or work on set themes as I had feared. I was surrounded by examples of other people's work, both beginners and experts. These gave me plenty of encouragement and inspiration, but most of all it was the professional advice and guidance available which resurrected my woodcarving. I was introduced to better quality tools and, to my great relief, machine honing. Gone were the hours toiling over a stone, replaced by minutes on a machine to produce a far sharper edge than I could otherwise have achieved.

'I am sure he never ended up with such a miserable result.'

No longer do problems, which any carving can present, seem insurmountable. No longer am I faced with agonising indecision about which way to proceed, fearing that a wrong choice will lead to a ruined piece of work. I can take advantage of someone else's years of experience. Not only this, but I am in an environment where discussions on woodcarving and art are natural. Ideas seem to flow thick and fast in this heady atmosphere. No longer do I scratch my head and wonder what to carve next or wonder if it is within my capability. Now I wonder if I will ever find all the time I need for my woodcarving.

With the benefit of hindsight I am sure that my carving skills would never have developed so quickly, and so painlessly, if I had struggled on alone. The self-taught woodcarver is still someone I much admire and respect. However, I am very glad I short-circuited the learning experience and saved myself from the years of struggle I otherwise faced. ■

ELF-TAUGHT

Jean Gordon proves
it is never too late to
start carving

VINTAC

I am an 81-year-old amateur woodcarver. I started carving when I was nearly 70, so I am the proverbial late starter. Wanting to do something different, I looked down the list on offer at the local further education classes and boldly decided on woodcarving. My knowledge of wood was nil, and I just about knew one end of a chisel from the other. To give the instructor Ivor Fountain his due, his welcoming smile didn't falter.

I was asked to get a piece of soft wood, about 9 x 3 x 2in, 230 x 75 x 50mm, plus a smaller block of wood. Seeing other women registering made me feel less nervous. All 15 of us turned up the following week, and I was encouraged to see that although I was the oldest, I wasn't the only novice.

The first evening was spent learning the skill of tool sharpening. I soon found men were much more at home at this, taking gouges and skew chisels in their stride. The advantage of starting out in a class like this was we didn't have to go to the expense of buying tools, sharpening stones etc, if we decided carving was not our thing.

Fish tale

The next step in our lesson was to draw the outline of a fish (supplied) on our piece of wood and screw the oblong block underneath. Then we inserted this in the vice, before picking up our newly sharpened tools to attack the fish.

We soon realised what an excellent choice this was for a beginner. We learned to use our tools, working down the side of the fish. We left a base of about ½in, 13mm, which gave us the idea of relief work.

Rounding the top surface, we got a feeling for shape. We undercut until the fish was attached to the base by only a small area under the body, and lo and behold a three-dimensional carving!

Thinning down and shaping the fins and tail was quite a step forward. Putting in the eyes and mouth was also

Top **Relief carving of Henry VIII and his wives**
Above **Japanese lady and Chinaman**

covered, and the least interesting but important task of sanding down. Finally came the polishing.

There was laughter when we assembled our masterpieces together. All were different and it was difficult to believe we had all begun with the identical drawing. We also wondered why some fish looked as if they were actually swimming and others looked stranded on the beach.

My fish has pride of place on my sideboard, and I wouldn't part with it for the world.

I lost no time in enrolling for the next term. I had some soft wood left over from the fish, so I copied a model of a porcelain dog. I think it is quite useful for a beginner to copy a model as it helps you to see in the round.

My next few projects were taken from illustrations in carving books, complete with instructions. The men usually had wood lying about in their sheds or workshops and I

VERSATILITY

relied on their generosity to keep me supplied. With their help, I carved a pair of leopards in mahogany (*Swietenia macrophylla*), a bird in teak (*Tectona grandis*), a heron in walnut (*Juglans spp*), and owls in everything.

I now felt confident enough to buy myself a straight and skew chisel, a couple of gouges of different sizes, a V-tool and a mallet.

Just in lime

One day, a fellow carver brought me a branch of lime (*Tilia spp*), about 4in, 100mm in diameter. This became a Chinaman and so began my gallery of figures. These include a Japanese lady, an Indian dancer, a Grecian lady and also one of my violinist daughter. Some of my more recent carvings have been of double figures with a humorous twist. As lime has a close grain and takes fine detail, I always use it for my figures. I see a picture or a drawing I like on a calendar or magazine and have it photocopied to the size I use, which is 14½in, 368mm tall including base.

Next, I draw this onto the wood, roughly bandsaw the front profile and then work my way back with a mallet and chisel. It is great to see the figure emerging, assuming I have visualised the sides and backs correctly, or I have to re-think. A woodcarver never makes mistakes, only adjustments.

For a change, I carve simple stylised carvings in more unusual woods, and find this very relaxing.

I've nothing against power tools and think they have their place, but I prefer to use hand tools. I find the new palm (Micro) tools, by Robert Sorby of Sheffield, give me the best control when putting folds in clothes. For very fine work, I use the micro tools from Tilgear in Cuffley.

Exclusive equipment

I do not have a workshop. I carve happily in my home. I have set up my Workmate in the kitchen with a large

Top **Spirit of the Wind**
Above **Indian dancer**
Left *Interlude*

Above **The 'Sit on Workhorse'**
Below *Sweet Nothings*

wooden vice bolted on to it. This is one of two extremely useful pieces of equipment made for me by Brian Williams, with the help of a friend.

It has bed irons welded on to the sides for strength, and a screw from a discarded swivel chair. This copes with all my chisel and mallet work. When I've finished sending wooden chips round the kitchen, I retire to my sitting room where I spread a ground sheet over the carpet and sit down at my second piece of equipment.

My custom-built 'Sit on Workhorse' has a frame made from 1in, 25mm box iron, with a stand at one end. Bolted on to this is a carpenter's vice mounted on a ball joint arrangement. This enables me to rotate my carving through 360° and from the vertical through 90° to the horizontal. A typist's chair, with inverted angle irons welded underneath, allows me to move backwards and forwards. There is also a roller at one end so I can wheel it out or park it.

As I usually have this set up alongside my dining table, I have a handy place for my tools, but can also swivel the chair to face the table and have a meal, or use the computer.

It is not the intention of this article to teach anyone how to carve, rather to point out it is never too late to start. Don't be nervous, have a go and you might surprise yourself!

I belong to the Waterside Guild of Woodcarvers in Hythe, Southampton. We have a monthly social evening, with a speaker, when all visitors are welcome.

As guild members, we visit fairs throughout the county, exhibiting and demonstrating our work. We are often asked how long we have been carving, what type of wood we use and how long the carving process takes.

I also belong to two clubs, one of which meets twice a month in Hythe. We admire and criticise each other's work, have a cup of tea and enjoy ourselves. The other club meets in Southampton. Everyone is warmly welcomed, from absolute beginners to experienced carvers. ●

Jean Gordon was born in India in 1914. When she came to England at age 18, she trained as a chiropodist. After marrying in 1937 she spent the next 20 years as a housewife. After she was widowed, she realised she should get out of the house to meet people. She learned to swim, gaining her 1500m badge, and has tried badminton, table tennis and short tennis at the over 50s club. Jean took up woodcarving by chance when she was 69. She now has many friends and leads a very active social life.

If you would like to join the Waterside Guild, contact Richard Colebrook, Tel: 01703 846637.
For the woodcarving club in Southampton, ring Brian Williams on 01703 843573

es Jewell served an
■ apprentice-
with an
nationally well-
∪n ecclesiastical
in Exeter,
∋n.
∍ the exception of
∪ar years, when
∍rved with the
∍l Engineers in
h Africa and in
, he has been
tantly employed
carver and
∋tor. He has
∢ in very many
ches in the UK
∢broad, notably
∩erica, in
hington DC and
∍land, Ohio. In
∃ he gained the
tsman of the
⌐ Award for his
in the
∋ration of St.
's Cathedral in
∟sonville, Florida.
∍ a member of
Master Carvers,
∍ldest body of
∍ssional carvers
∍culptors in
t Britain.
∩as also had
∍ss with his
∨life sculpture,
∩g awards in
⌐ent years at the
∍l West of
∩nd Academy.
∍ a teacher with
∋evon Education
∋rity, taking
∩g classes
ly with adults.
∨so lectures to a
selection of
∍nces and is a
ber of the
∍h Woodcarvers
∍ciation.

I would like to donate this article to the absolute beginner; the one who has always wanted to carve something but hasn't a clue how to start. I know there are a lot of these people, because every year I have some in my classes, male and female, and once they have got confidence, it's amazing how soon they are producing a piece of carving.

Tools

I get mildly irritated when someone talks about carving chisels. A chisel is a straight piece of metal, whereas a carving kit consists of many different shapes, V-tools, gouges, bent gouges, fluters, veiners and many more. In fact almost the only time I use chisels is when I am cutting letters.

I won't spend much time on tools; six gouges and one V-tool ranging from a ¼" 6mm to 1" 25mm will do nicely for the start. They can be added to later on. The one 'must' in my kit is the V or 'parting tool', known as the 'carver's pencil'. Its uses are manifold, from feathering and furring it can be used to lightly 'set in' a drawing on wood, which would disappear in the handling if it were just pencil marks.

BEGINNER'S LUCK

LES JEWELL

UNDER PRESSURE FROM STUDENTS AND FRIENDS LES JEWELL HAS DEVISED A PROJECT THAT SHOULD LEAD TO GREATER THINGS.

The seven tools used

Sharpening gouges

Sharpening gouges

Carvers have different methods of sharpening gouges. I always rotate mine backwards and forwards along the whole length of the oilstone, rolling it as I go. Of course, the deeper the tool the more you tip it over, if you take care and watch what you are doing you will obtain a uniform bevel on the edge of the tool.

Sharpening V-tool

Sharpening V-tools

The V-tool is given an edge by treating it as if it were two chisels; putting one side of it on the stone at a time until you have an equal bevel on both sides. Make sure you eliminate the little 'nib' that sometimes occurs on the bottom as with this it will never cut.

Rubbing out with slipstones

It is essential to use a slipstone the exact shape of the interior of the tool for the next stage, known as 'rubbing out'. The slipstone is tipped slightly downwards and sideways to form a small inside bevel. This will enable the throat

Rubbing out with a slipstone

of the tool to cut cleanly when entering the wood. With all tools a perfect fit with the slip ensures the shape remains unaltered. With straight tools work it away from you; this eliminates the chance of cutting yourself.

Stropping on dressed leather

Stropping

When you are reasonably sure the tool is well honed you should strop it as you would a razor. A strop is a piece of fine leather coated with a slight abrasive. I always use crocus powder with tallow, mixed into a paste and rubbed into the surface of the strop. Press the tool down firmly and draw it steadily towards you, then fold the leather and apply it to the inside. Stropping removes the final little burr from the edge.

Testing

When testing the sharpness, do not use your thumb. If the tool is really keen you will end up with a thumb looking like a moonscape, and a leaking digit paints the wood in a horrible way. Instead secure a piece of softwood to the bench and push the tool across the grain. If it cuts crisply and cleanly, without leaving scratch marks in the groove, then you have something to be proud of!

Grinding

After a lot of sharpening a tool will thicken up. This means having to grind some metal off the back. Try to use a water whetstone or a flat oil wheel. A carborundum wheel running at high speed will take the temper out of a tool in seconds. If it turns blue at the tip you are in trouble, and although you can put the temper back, it is better not to lose it in the first place! Never grind right out to the edge, as the ragged end this makes is much harder to get out when you put the bevel back.

Mallet

I advocate the carver's mallet as it is round in shape. This enables it to be used in comfort as it has a better grip and what is more, to the point, its contact with the tool handle is only in the middle of the top. This stops that horrible splitting of the handle and turning over of the edges, which is so typical of the effect of the carpenter's square mallet — not a pretty sight!

The mallet

The model, an ivy leaf

The first piece of carving

The first piece of carving I set my students is taken from something available in most gardens, certainly in mine! An ivy leaf in fact. I choose this as I assume most people want to carve just for the joy of it, and so as not to get bogged down by mechanical designs, I go back to nature. Before you do anything at all, take the leaf and study it. A big percentage of carving is using your eyes, and what is more important, understanding what you are looking at.

Setting out

Take a piece of wood 7″ x 5″ x 1″ 178 x 127 x 25mm; I prefer lime. The final size will be 5″ 127mm square, but I have allowed the extra 2″ 51mm space for holding with G-cramp. This will allow you to work in comfort without the risk of blunting your tools on the cramp. You will find that few ivy leaves are symmetrical, so you may have to help it a little. Draw the outline of the leaf on the wood and set it in with your V-tool.

Setting down

With a marking gauge, scratch a line all around the wood ½″ 12.5mm down, exactly half the thickness of the wood. Now chop away the top surface, all round the leaf, down to the gauge line, until you have the leaf raised in silhouette. It is important to cut straight down absolutely vertically; if you don't the shape of the leaf will alter as you carve it. The stem is the weakest part, and this is where most people have trouble, so keep it strong and much thicker than it will be at the finish. It is not essential to have the background completely level and clean but try, and take it as a plus if you succeed.

Carving the leaf

Start now to carve the leaf, keeping the natural one in front of you, studying it all the time. You

Putting in the central vein

will be surprised what you find. Remember that although you have to 'throw' the carving about to get some life into it, you must keep some section of the surface up to the ½″ 12.5mm projection, or else all that work you put in to sinking it down has been wasted.

There is a paradox that, to a carver, a dead leaf is a 'live' leaf. All those exaggerated hollows and bumps that you see in this example do occur as the leaf dies.

Putting in the veins

If you look closely at the middle vein you will see that it is thicker than the others, so for this you treat it as a continuation of the main stem. Take your V-tool and cut a double line so that the vein has a thickness and is standing up.

With the V-tool, finish the leaf

The finished leaf, the stalk thinned at last

by putting in all the subsidiary veins. Take your time over this, if necessary pencil them in first. A bad line will spoil the look of the leaf, so make sure they are right. Set down the main stem and cut it back to its proper size, as its projection now is much less, there should be no chance of breaking it off.

Undercut all the high projections; this will help the final appearance. Cut off the spare clamping wood, so that the leaf finishes 5″ x 5″ 127 x 127mm. Put a fastening on the back, and hang it on the wall where you can always see it. You can judge your future progress from this piece.

As wood gets dirty if left in its natural state, it needs protection. I always seal my carvings with a matt varnish and use beeswax to get a more refined finish. A high gloss will spoil the appearance of most carving.

The Thrushes' Anvil in lime, backboard in oak, by Les Jewell

Detail of *The Thrushes' Anvil,* by Les Jewell, based on wild dog rose

Carving a plaque

Now that you have started, take it further! What you have learned from the ivy leaf can be used to good effect. My plaque *The Thrushes' Anvil* will give you an example of what can be done. Try your hand at designing one, after all, it's only a case of putting together a number of leaves instead of one.

Draw your design on paper first – don't try to be too elaborate – then transfer it to the wood. With a pierced design perforate all the holes, but don't cut dead on the line, leave quite a bit of waste. If you want to alter something that doesn't look right, you need to have the wood to do it. For carving fix the work to a backboard. This has to be expendable as it will be badly marked when you pare through the carving. Secure the carving to the board by screwing through the back. Pick the highest projections of the carving to screw into, as you don't want to hit a screw with your carving tools.

When you have finished the carving on the face, detach it from the board and undercut. Only undercut after all surface carving is finished: this will try your patience but if you undercut first you won't be able to 'throw the foliage about'. Now find a nice contrasting piece of wood for the back and join them together.

My carving, *A Hunter's Moon,* shows what you could eventually do. I have used a combination of vegetation and field mice, with a hunting barn owl to make up this design. As before, you can see how important it is to finish the carving before you undercut, or back off as it is called. Although it is considerably bigger than *The Thrushes' Anvil,* the system used is the same. ∎

Detail of *A Hunter's Moon,* by Les Jewell, showing harvest mice, wheat, and wild convolvulus

A Hunter's Moon, by Les Jewell, in lime, 29" x 22" x 4"

When I was commissioned to create a three-dimensional carving of a family crest, for reference I was given a drawing no bigger than a large postage stamp. From that I had to carve an accurate representation of a bird with a wingspan of about a metre. Like many of the devices used in heraldry, the bird did not conform exactly to any living species, but it was based in very broad terms on an osprey.

The first task was to enlarge the drawing with a photocopier. There was some loss of clarity but it remained reasonably distinct when taken up to half the final size. From this it became clear that the design might not lend itself readily to three-dimensional treatment. The problem was the position of the wings relative to the body line, and the fact that one wing seemed to droop. The tail would also need to be joined to the plinth to provide extra strength.

A MODEL EXAMPLE

MAKING A CLAY MODEL FIRST
CAN HELP TO SOLVE MANY
CARVING PROBLEMS WITHOUT
WASTING TIMBER.
JEREMY WILLIAMS EXPLAINS
THE TECHNIQUES USED ON A
RECENT PROJECT – AN UNUSUAL
HERALDIC BIRD IN ELM

So I opted to start with a maquette – a clay model. Using clay can help to overcome a mental block when trying to visualise a shape, and also allows a carver to explore a form without wasting valuable timber. Fine grade pottery clay is suitable: it's cheap and can be re-constituted by soaking in water so it can be re-used time and again. Some model-makers prefer to use oil-bonded clay such as Plasticine, which is more expensive.

Not many tools are needed for simple modelling: a spatula made from a strip of wood, and maybe a piece of old hacksaw blade, for shaping; and a loop made from a wire coat-hanger for hollowing. Generally your fingers do most of the work. A sponge and water will be needed to keep the clay pliable and your hands clean. A house-plant spray is also useful.

If you wish to keep the model for any length of time, it may need to be hollowed out when 'leather

Finished carving of a heraldic bird, before staining, in front of the clay maquette

11

hard', ie, not quite dry, to prevent cracking. Coating it with acrylic varnish when fully dry will give the maquette extra strength and stop the dry clay crumbling.

Support structure

Small maquettes can be modelled without being reinforced, but large subjects will need the support of an internal wire frame, known as an armature. This must be robust enough to carry the considerable weight of the clay.

Use stiff wire – welding rod is ideal – or aluminium rod, which will not stain, and work on a good sized platform to prevent the model tipping over. Once the basic framework has been made, gaps can be filled in with wire netting.

Then bandage the whole armature so that the wire doesn't cut through the clay. Use ordinary first-aid bandages, strips of old cloth or hessian. Decorator's reinforced paper tape soaked in wallpaper paste also works well and gives added strength when dry; or you can use cloth impregnated with plaster of Paris.

Body building

Start by applying small lumps of clay flattened in the palm of your hand and then pressed onto the bandage. If at this stage the bandage is not totally dry, so much the better as the armature shape can be adjusted if necessary.

Don't make the clay too thin – 5mm, ¼in is about the minimum – or it will crack as it dries. Build up

From top to bottom
Maquette in the making: the armature, a supporting framework of wire and wood. Gaps are filled in with wire netting

Bandages are wrapped around the armature

Small flattened lumps of clay are pressed on to the bandages, with fingers and a wooden spatula, to gradually build up the shape

Shaving off small amounts of clay with a piece of hacksaw blade. A house-plant spray is useful to keep the clay moist

A wire loop is ideal for removing larger amounts

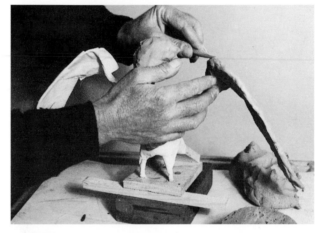

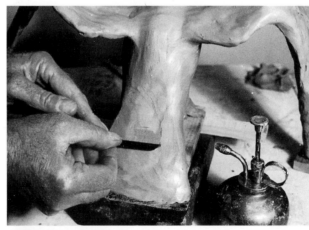

the shape, and smooth th surface with a damp sponge. between modelling session: cover the maquette with a dam cloth. In very hot weather spra with water from time to time, b never so much as to dissolve th clay.

If the maquette is just t establish general shape and siz fine details can be omitted. But the detail will need addition wood when it is carved, such a the harness on a horse f example, then it is best to inclu it in the maquette. Callipers a useful for accurate measurement

Shaping and sizing

Shave off small amounts o excess clay with a piece hacksaw blade. To remove larg amounts a wire loop works we though specially made tools ca be bought at art shops.

The model doesn't have to the same size as the final carvin but it helps if it is worked to definite scale – half size, quart size or whatever. Dimensions ca then be transferred to the wood simple measurement, or by usir a point-to-point pantograph.

My clay model was primari used to judge the size, shape ar position of the wings, since th were the dominant feature of th design. Aspects such as surfac texture were of secondary interes With the pasted bandage still n quite dry, it was possible to jigg the wings about, even with son clay on them, until the rig position and angle were found.

Carving and fixing

The following aspects construction apply to any larg bird carved with outstretche wings. Generally the bas method of carving from bandsawn shape is the same, b to minimise waste and provid structural strength the wings we worked separately and then joine to the body.

I chose to fix the wings wit dowels, not mortise and teno joints. This meant that if ther was any need to change the wir position, it would only be a matt of drilling new dowel holes ar filling in the old ones.

With the wings rough-cut,

Top
**Setting in the eyes.
Dowels are in
position to fit the
wings**

Centre
**All trussed up.
Wings are glued
into position**

Below
**Finished bird,
clutching
parchment scroll**

plotted where to mount them on the body. A generous area was marked on either side of the body to ensure enough timber would be retained during body shaping to blend in the joints. It is a good idea to cover these areas with masking tape, to remind you not to chop into them.

When shaping the wings, plenty of spare wood was left where the dowel holes would be drilled. This may seem obvious but it is often overlooked, with the result that the wings look unnatural. For a life-like bird

carving the wings would probably be raised or outstretched. But for my heraldic carving it was more a matter of following the prescribed design than positioning the wings naturally.

Before they could be drilled, the wing-ends had to be cut and sanded to the correct angle. This meant testing them against the body 'flats'.

It is safer to drill the dowel holes first in the wings. This can be a two-person job: one to drill, the other to check the alignment. Then, with centring caps fitted into these holes, corresponding ones can be marked on the sides of the body. I found it best to dry-fix one wing in place before tackling the other. This helped to check the angle of alignment.

Down to detail

Gouges were used to shape the underside of the wings. Only then, when this concave form was set, were the upper surfaces tackled. They were shaped with a Black & Decker Power File and then finished off by hand with rifflers and abrasive paper. Feather lines were incised with a v-tool. Eyes were a striking feature, and were set in with a hollow punch.

The crest shows the osprey clutching a scroll. The wood for this was turned as a separate piece to a prescribed diameter, then finished by hand to simulate parchment rolled up. It was then cut into two equal parts, and the pieces fitted into recesses drilled in the sides of the feet.

Trussed up

Gluing up the carving proved an interesting operation. A dummy run was carried out, just to check what clamps would be needed to hold everything in place. You don't want to be rushing off to borrow an extra clamp with the glue setting! The bird was well trussed up with a couple of sash clamps, four G-clamps and two rope Spanish windlasses. It was left standing for 48 hours for the Cascamite glue to cure.

Finally the carving was treated with three coats of microporous wood stain, to give good protection out of doors. ∎

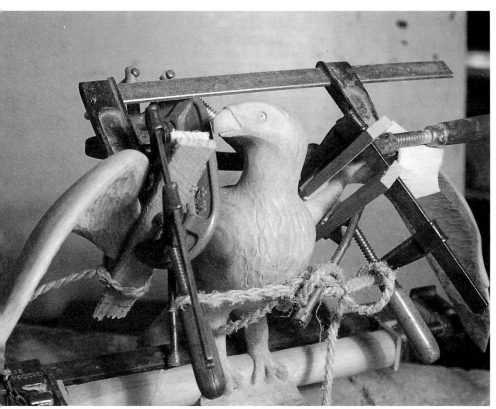

**Jeremy Williams
started carving at
the age of 14, over
40 years ago. He
has had extensive
experience as a
teacher, and since
1982 has run his
own courses in
woodcarving. He
contributes to
several woodworking
magazines, and has
also written a book,
_Decorative
Woodcarving_,
published by
GMC Publications**

BERTIE SOMME

A SIMPLE SPOON CAN BE A GOOD WAY TO START CARVING WITH A FEW TOOLS.

There is a tremendous urge in most of us to be creative. Some of us even dream about carving, but somehow the difficulties involved are too much. Perhaps it is because the tools are difficult to sharpen well (a complete skill in itself). Perhaps the original subject of the carving is just too complex, and for many, not knowing the first thing about carving doesn't help either. I have faced this problem myself and I evolved the technique which follows.

The importance of this technique lies in its simplicity and its cheapness in terms of tools, materials and space. I have carved in front of the fire in the living room, on a cold winters night, just as easily as in a well equipped workshop.

Many experienced carvers have expressed doubts as to the safety of my technique. To those I say, try it before you criticise it, and if you still feel unhappy about it let me know, because so far it has passed every test with flying colours and is regularly and successfully taught in my workshop in Devon. Yes, the technique can be dangerous, but only if you don't follow the rules closely, so please read, learn, and inwardly digest.

Why spoons?

Initially, I felt that spoon carving was very undervalued and that traditions blanketed the possibilities hidden in what could become an art form. Making up to 30 new designs a year I have yet to feel that I am wrong.

The great thing about spoon carving is that it is a wonderful way of learning to carve — with convex and concave shapes — coupled with this, who is to say that the spoon you are making is wrong in design. Provided that it is well presented and finished, even asymmetry is not at all out of place. My pupils all use spoon carving as a touchstone — it helps them to understand and comprehend shape. It also provides them with something to make quickly and well, and even to try out an idea and then to see how far it can go.

To go further still, the development of my spoon carving abilities has helped me enormously with my furniture making. The same techniques and methods have helped me to shape components in ways I would have ignored before, and my understanding of the behaviour of wood has increased as well.

So far, all my pupils have expressed astonishment and satisfaction at what they have achieved. This has made me feel that here is something really worthwhile that can give others the joy and satisfaction that it has given me.

Shaping a spoon

To start with I usually make a pattern. If it is a shape that I think I will use several times I make the pattern in hardboard, otherwise card will do. If the spoon is to be symmetrical I only make a half pattern. I have borrowed a jewellers technique for cutting the patterns, using a board with a vee cut in it to support the pattern while cutting with a coping saw blade in a fretsaw frame held vertically. This way I can cut to a line easily, moving saw and pattern quickly to follow the curves.

The wood for a spoon usually starts about ¾in 19mm thick, though it could be thinner, and I prefer woods that are easy to carve (the example in the photographs is pear wood). Draw a centre line for the spoon, then draw round one side of the pattern and flip it over for the

Sawing out a hardboard half pattern using a support board a a coping saw blade in a fretsa

The sawn half pattern, showin the vee in the support board

The spoon is c out in the same way as the hardboard patt

Below
Rounding the spoon handle with a round bottomed spokeshave; it can be used cutting away from you . . .

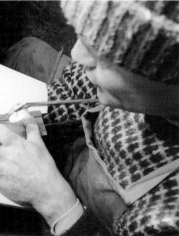

other side of the spoon. In this way you get a symmetrical spoon without having to make a symmetrical pattern. I use the same method to cut out the spoon as I do for the hardboard patterns.

With the blank cut out I can start to carve the spoon. The handle can be shaped using a

spokeshave, which I think is a marvellous tool as it can be used with equal facility cutting towards or away from you. I use a round bottomed spokeshave to get as far round the junction between handle and bowl as possible.

. . . or cutting towards you

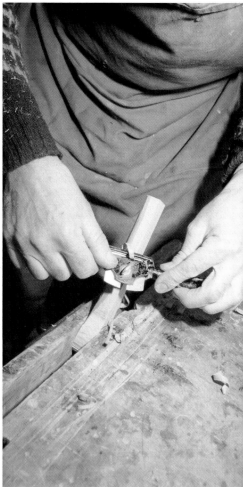

Using a knife to round the spoon handle; the wrists locked, the right arm pivots from the elbow. A cut that quickly removes waste, but be careful of others around you

Cutting towards you safely; thumbs locked, only the fingers move. Note that the handle of the knife hits the right-hand thumb before the blade cuts either hand

You could also use a knife to shape the handle, using what I call the power cut because it removes a lot of waste quickly. When using this cut don't use your wrists — they are locked solid — your arm should pivot at the elbow. The knife is easy to control and you should not waste effort bringing it back to the work, the knife should have a very limited amount of travel. Learn this technique well, as using this technique without care is dangerous to others near you and to yourself. The knife should have a relatively thick blade, so that it doesn't bury itself in the wood easily, and of course it should be razor sharp.

The fine shaping of the handle and the outside of the bowl is done with a series of controlled paring cuts with a knife. These cuts are made close to the body and hands, and in some cases you will be cutting towards yourself. The secret of doing this safely is to follow the cut through with your mind first, if the blade is going to meet flesh at the finish of the cut you are doing it wrong.

Some carvers don't like to see others cutting towards their bodies or hands, but it can be done safely. I use, and teach, a paring cut I have developed where you are deliberately cutting towards yourself. In this cut the thumbs are locked against each other so that the hands don't move in relation to each other. The movement is from the fingers and the knife is held so that the knife handle hits the thumb of the right hand before the blade can cut the fingers. It is safe if done properly.

A similar cut is used round the end of the spoon handle and, although the hands are in a slightly different position, the knife handle hits the thumb preventing the blade from cutting the carver. The easiest cut I use is also one of the most powerful and the most controlled — the thumb push. The thumb of the hand holding the spoon simply pushes the blade forward (away from the carver and the hands), the other hand holds the knife and guides the direction and depth of the cut. This may sound awkward, but look at the photograph and you will see how easy it actually is; the blade only moves about ½in 13mm and is guided all the time.

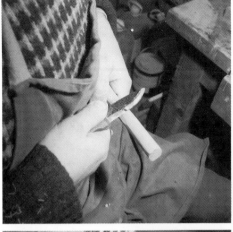
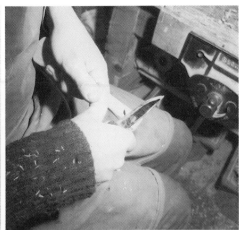
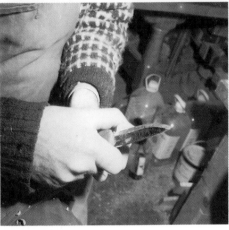

Trimming the end of the handle, again the thumb acts as a stop against the handle of the knife

The thumb-push cut, the thumb of the left hand pushes, the right hand controls the cut

The outside of the spoon shaped with the knife

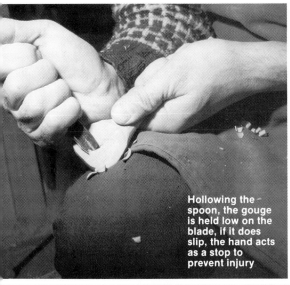

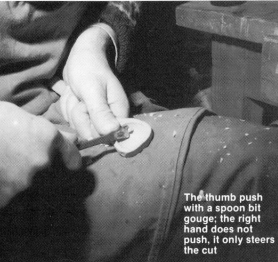

Hollowing the spoon, the gouge is held low on the blade, if it does slip, the hand acts as a stop to prevent injury

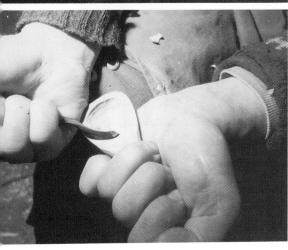

The thumb push with a spoon bit gouge; the right hand does not push, it only steers the cut

looks angerous, but the de of the hand is gainst the edge of e spoon — the avel of the gouge strictly limited

The bowl

The outside of the bowl is carved with the knife, but the hollow must be cut with a gouge. I start off with a straight gouge then move on to a spoon bit gouge as the hollow gets deeper. You could actually do away with the straight gouge if you're on a tight budget, and carve the whole of inside the bowl with a spoon bit gouge. For this operation I sit down and use my knees and thighs as rests for the work. I do not have any holes in my knees as I use a similar method of cutting as I do with the knife.

Hold the gouge well down on the blade, so that it can only travel so far then it is stopped by the side of your hand coming up against the work. The gouge should only be able to travel a short distance. Again follow the cut through in your mind and if the cut finishes in flesh it is going too far.

The first cuts into the bowl are across the grain and you should deepen the bowl from either side; the cuts are short and controlled. As the bowl get deeper you will have to change to the spoon bit gouge, which is used in the same manner as before, holding it well down the blade. Another useful cut when you get down into the bowl is a variation of the thumb push. The thumb of the hand that is holding the spoon is used to push the blade into the cut. The other hand holds the tool in contact with the wood and directs the cut, it should not push the blade at all, as this could follow through into the leg of the carver.

As you get lower in the bowl of the spoon change over to carving with the grain, and finish carving by taking small fine cuts, leaving very few bumps to be sanded away.

These paring cuts can be used to carve the spoon handle into any shape desired. Spoons can be functional — kitchen spoons or salad servers — highly decorative and sculptural, or anything in between. The example shown is simply to demonstrate the technique, but there is really no limit to the shapes you can carve using this method.

Carving finished the spoon only needs to be sanded and oiled

Finishing

I start sanding with 80 grit aluminium oxide abrasive; this flattens any bumps, providing a regular finish in no time. In fact it can work like a file, as it is so coarse. Abrasives are quite a complex subject, but one important thing to remember is what 'sandpaper' actually is; simply put abrasives are crystals glued on to paper or cloth. If you fold it up and wrinkle it too much the glue will crack and the crystals will fall off. The glues are also affected by damp, and this can be another cause of the migration of crystals. Try to keep abrasive papers as flat as possible when in use. There are flexibly backed abrasives, and waterproof ones too, they are good but more expensive.

After the 80 grit abrasive I move on to a 150 grit silicon carbide paper, then 240 ending with 320 or 500 grit. If sanding has blurred a feature I often re-carve carefully, and follow with 150 or 240 grit abrasive. I suppose that all the grades after the 80 grit are used to remove the sanding marks it leaves.

If the spoon is not to be used with food I finish it with Danish oil - I leave it to harden for about 20 minutes, then give it a vigorous buffing. If you do want to cook or eat with the spoon, you can leave the wood 'raw', as most commercial wooden spoons are, or you could finish it with walnut oil, which takes a while to dry, and will need renewing every now and again. ∎

VICKI OTTÉ

'Every artist, musician and dancer translates his understanding of life through expression, humour, beauty and joy, revealing himsel[f] in his thoughts, in sound, in line and in colour. For me, painted woodcarvings are the vehicle.'

icki Otté lives and works in the village of Kimpton in Hertfordshire. Here she makes her unusual and original painted woodcarvings.

Her early talent took her to an art school in Norfolk, where close contact with the seaside scene combined her enthusiasm for colour, the bizarre and the fascination of the human form. Her wooden figures are odd, different, endearing, ugly, just like most ordinary people in fact.

The completion of a single small carving occupies about two days' work. She tends to have several going at the same time in various stages of completion. She enjoys the challenge of special commissions, reading widely and watching for fresh ideas.

Vicki Otté regularly exhibits around the country and her work is represented in the Hertfordshire and Bedfordshire Schools Loan Service. She recently appeared on the George Melly 'Moving Art Show' in October and has exhibited in the Open Art Exhibition two years running.

Vicki Otté is married with one daughter.

I started 'playing around with wood' some 20 years ago, making families of peg dolls for my small daughter, occasionally exhibiting in craft shops and selling to friends and friends of friends. Anyone can make little figures — there is no set pattern to follow — and perhaps that's the joy of it. You have to find out for yourself what you can do. Sometimes I start out with an idea but quite often it develops itself unplanned. A Special Sort of Magic.

I began by using branches blown down by the wind, favouring beech, a straight-grained hardwood fairly easy to work. Birch, a yellowish white wood often used for making walking sticks, and fruit-bearing wood — apple, pear and cherry — together with lime, a favourite among great woodcarvers like Grinling Gibbons, were subsequently used.

Many years on and two arm operations later I decided a softer more pliable wood was in order and now buy van loads of geleton, a lightweight wood from a tree grown in Borneo. It is easy to cut and sand and takes paint very well. Much easier on the joints!

When selecting wood for a project, care must be taken to ensure the grain runs in the right direction to prevent it splitting. It is important also to use only wood that has properly dried out.

Whittling, the humble brother of the mightier woodcarving, is the oldest craft in the world and one which anyone can master. Being able to draw is an advantage but there are ways to get round this problem. Getting an outline is the first step. If you have difficulty in drawing, why not trace to begin with and then advance to free-hand drawing when you feel you have the confidence.

The difference between the whittler and th[e] woodcarver, is that the former relies solely on [a] sharp knife and sandpaper and perhaps a larg[e] supply of plasters. The woodcarver, while st[ill] needing the sandpaper and plaster, moves on to [a] higher plane, experimenting with a wide variety [of] equipment. Whole books are written on the variou[s] mallets, chops, chisels of bewildering shapes an[d] sizes, saws and a multitude of complicate[d] machinery.

Heaven-sent

High-powered grinders, routers and drill[s] deserve a great deal of respect safety-wise. The[se] are tools which I find frighteningly aggressiv[e] although I recently acquired my one and on[ly] piece of electrical equipment, a 14" 3-whe[el] bandsaw which I use with a prayer and fin[d] heaven-sent. It skims through large chunks [of] wood which, with a handsaw, would have taken [...]

2.

5.

A SPECIAL S[O]

whole morning to assume a manageable shape and size. It enables me to get down to the skill stage and details in half the time.

Geleton can be obtained from most sawmills (smaller wood yards may not stock it; it's best to telephone first to make sure). I buy it in 6ft planks from Atkins & Cripps, Bishops Stortford.

If I have a preconceived idea of a design it is drawn first and cut out as in photographs of supple dancers. (The Aerobics Class, Photo 1.)

Most of my orders are by word of mouth or from work seen in exhibitions. The same customers turn up year after year for personalised birthday, anniversary or Christmas presents. 'My husband plays golf, drinks Port, belongs to the Masons, what can you do?' 'My boyfriend plays the guitar, is ginger, has big ears' (Photo 2).

Chess Sets

Some years ago I was given a large supply of old school desk legs made from beech. Over the months, they were transformed into a chess set depicting the Wars of the Roses faithfully coloured in the York-Lancaster battle colours. Being thus inspired, there followed armies of soldiers, both French and English. Sets of historical figures, such as Henry VIII and his poor wives, Queen Elizabeth and Cromwell followed as, later, did institutions — Mothers' Union, Brigades, Chelsea Pensioners — Nuns and Monks.

A selection of work is kept on shelves for sale or exhibitions. These are mostly just 'Happenings'

as in the case of the Wedding Couples, Photo 3. They simply evolved.

Publicity

I was lucky enough to gain quite a bit of publicity from advertisements for Winsor & Newton paints in an art teachers journal in the eighties. Also for helping to advertise Guinness in the glossy magazines *SHE* and *Good Housekeeping* with the theme *'Drink Guinness and you too can hack enormous tree trunks into miniature wooden humans'*.

Ideas are everywhere. Enormous ladies at the Tesco checkout — swollen ankles, double chins. Girls with stick legs and huge boots. The Ridiculous, The Ghastly and above all The Humorous. A certain expression on a weary exasperated father's face; rush hour; the Salvation Army; births; deaths; marriage. There are endless possibilities, including a colourful circus group, Photo 4.

Once a piece is carved the subject itself will dictate how much finished sanding you do. For example, a mermaid may be finished stain-wise to a glossy sheen with all the tool marks sanded off. Leaving the tail textured, with crisp tool marks and painted in thick textured strokes, creates an interesting colour texture contrast. (Mermaid Photo 5.)

After sanding, the image is varnished and allowed to dry before painting with a variety of oil and water-based paints, choosing those that dry fairly quickly. Light water colours can be used for the faces depending on the subject — colourful clown or fragile delicate ballerina. Having changed the expressions several times until satisfied, seal again with matt varnish.

But the technique of How — How to Cut, What to Cut, How to Paint — is not the satisfaction. The satisfaction is to mimic the gesture of a human smile on a satyr's face or that Tesco Exhaustion on a mermaid's frown . . . to be completely obsessed by wood, paint and human quirks. ∎

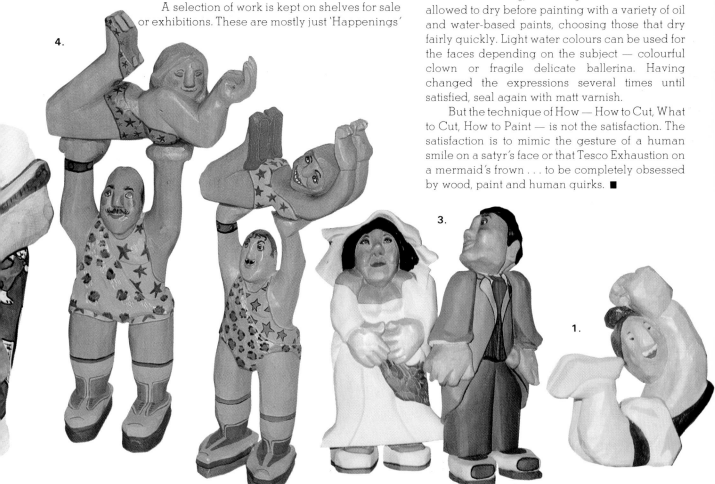

4.

3.

1.

RT OF MAGIC

Victor Stok is a professional artist who has been in the education service for 34 years. Though he retired in 1989 he still runs a carving class in wood and stone at Yeovil College in Somerset, on Monday evenings. Eventually trained as a painter, he taught himself to carve when he was 14 years old.

His time is now divided between doing his own work as a painter and sculptor and serving on two committees – The Friends of the Museum of South Somerset as chairman, and the Act for Hospitals Committee in Yeovil.

Victor's hobbies contrast effectively with his work, though he does get influenced by some aspects – natural history, bird watching, fish keeping, collecting penknives and china cats, and the history of submarines, with last but not least creative cookery!

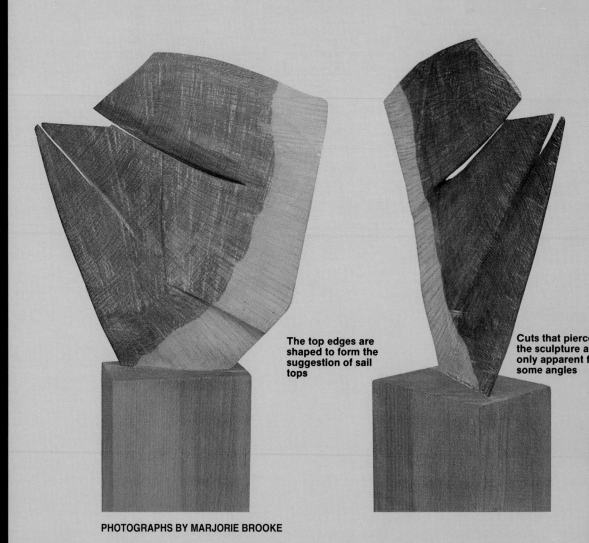

The top edges are shaped to form the suggestion of sail tops

Cuts that pierce the sculpture a only apparent f some angles

PHOTOGRAPHS BY MARJORIE BROOKE

A SUGGESTION O

VICTOR STOK STUMBLED OVER A PIECE OF WOOD WHICH HE MADE INTO A SCULPTURE INSPIRED BY SAILS

The West Country is a marvellous place for discovering things in nature, as much of it is still unspoiled. As a keen amateur naturalist I was wandering about in the woodlands near Turn Hill, admiring the flowers and keeping an eye open for birds, when I almost tripped over a piece of flat oak. It had been sawn off the end of a trunk, and had lain, for goodness knows how long, half buried beneath leaves and soil. The piece was not more than an inch thick anywhere, but something moved me to pick it up and take it home.

I make sculpture in stone and wood — the two seem to be related — stone the skin of the earth, wood the hair upon it. I do

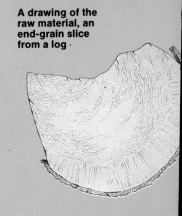

A drawing of the raw material, an end-grain slice from a log

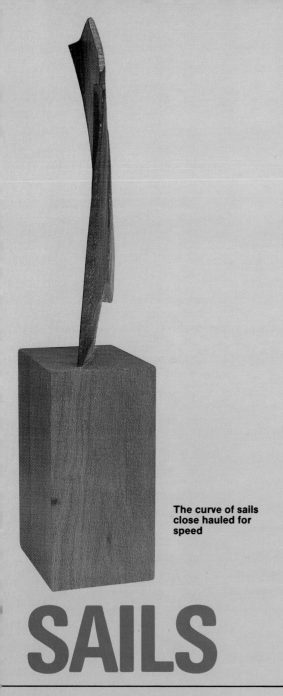

The curve of sails close hauled for speed

SAILS

Each form in nature has an underlying geometric structure and each abstract form has organic roots in nature.

The very thinness of the piece I had picked up became a source of attraction and challenge — how to produce a form that would 'move' inside the constraints of the block. The first thing to do was to take off the bark around the edge of the wood.

Concept

It was impossible to use any of the usual cutting tools, as the impact of mallet and gouge would shatter this end grain piece. Here I must digress for a moment. When shaping a form I go about it in one of two ways.

Drawings can shape up and crystallise an idea. Then the drawing is put to one side and direct cutting is the order of the day, with minimal or no marking up of the block. Alternatively direct cutting starts the ball rolling and things develop accordingly — the relationship of planes and masses extracted leading again to the crystallisation of an image. It is amazing how quickly an idea is clearly established in the latter case — and then fully and deliberately developed.

A tiny painting, the result of watching offshore sailing races at Lyme Regis, gave me an idea. Sail shapes, not billowing out but close hauled for speed, became my theme. But, how to realise this was the challenge.

Execution

I had at the time a Black & Decker drill with some basic bits and pieces — to make me the 'handyman about the house'. For one of these jobs I had found a Cintride disc a particularly useful abrasive tool to smooth a surface.

If it was able to smooth a surface, then it could shape a chunk of wood. By tilting the drill, the edge of the disc could make lines on a surface, thereby cutting into it — and an idea was born!

I placed the oak piece in the wooden chops, then I started to work my way into the form. The Cintride disc was simply rocked from side to side to make the first cut, from which the other shapes would evolve. These were drawn in directly with the edge of the disc and then shaped up until all the 'sail' shapes were completed.

When seen from above, the planes created were slanted appropriately within the limitations of the block. Then the top edges were shaped — as shown in the photographs — to form the suggestion of sail tops and take away the confining original block shape.

Next it had to be placed on a base and I found a good block of beech for this. A tight fitting slot was cut into this and the carved form inserted with casein glue.

Finishing

Then followed a very important part of the operation, the polishing of the sculpture and its base. For this I just used the Cintride disc itself, then a finer version, to be followed by three stages of ever finer abrasive paper. When the hand can slide over a carved form and feel that ineffable sensation of sympathy, it is ready for a protective finishing coat.

It is a personal foible that I detest varnish in any shape or form on sculpture. I prefer the quality that real beeswax gives to a sculpture. It is applied with the hand, so that the warmth of the palm of the hand is instrumental in rendering a surface that is a complement to the wood. A little final buffing with a soft cloth can give a glow to the wood — but not a high gloss shine.

The sculpture was fixed at a slight angle on the base to preserve the spirit of close hauled sails. ■

ft

is small painting sailing boats cing gave the ea for the ulpture

low

ing the edge of e Cintride disc to ape the wood

not like pieces of stone or wood which half suggest a subject to me. Rather, I seek lumps of stone or wood from which I extract the ideas I have in mind. These may be abstract or representational — each being dependent on the other for successful realisation.

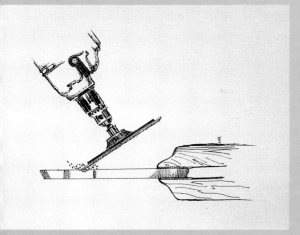

Regatta, inspired by sails but not a simple representation of them

MASTERING YOUR MALLET

IN THE FIRST OF TWO ARTICLES ABOUT HANDS AND TOOL HANDLES, GRAHAM BULL EXAMINES THE MALLET

One of the unfortunate things about woodworking books and classes is that they cover the ins and outs of the things we can make and how we should do it, the tools to use and how to use them and a host of other 'hands on' hints, but there is rarely any discussion of hands and tool handles.

Of all the things that need to 'connect' to achieve good quality woodwork, these are two of the most important. There seems to be an assumption that a handle is a handle and a hand is a hand and that's that. But the reality is quite different.

HOW HANDS WORK

Before we look at mallets, let's look at hands and what they are connected to. Between your neck and the tip of your middle finger are 32 bones, all surrounded by blood vessels, muscles, nerves, fat, skin and other tissue.

Messages from your brain activate the muscles that move the bones. When you wrap your fingers around the handle and pick up the mallet a whole system of 'levers' is activated. This system, in conjunction with your eyes, weighs and measures the mallet, sending a message to your brain with an assessment of whether it believes your particular system can handle it.

It doesn't matter if your hand is big, little, fat, thin, strong, weak or arthritic. An assessment will be made and a message will get through. What does matter is that every hand will make a different assessment, even your left and right ones will vary.

This assessment depends not only on the characteristics of your mechanical (motor) system and how it relates physically to the mallet, but also your history of previous experiences in handling mallets. If you are right-handed, it will feel funny in your left

A collection of different mallets

Top **A light-weight mallet with hollow for the thumb and index finger**
Above **This polthead mallet is quieter and jar-free with a long life**

enough, and in the right direction. You need a mallet of the right design configuration to give the correct combination of control and power for the activity you want to achieve. This combination of control and power will be determined by your personal characteristics.

When you are carving, you are probably chiselling in a curve, unlike a carpenter, who works mostly in straight lines. You should be using a lot of hand and wrist movement with the centre of your swing generally from the elbow, so you need a mallet which can cope with hitting the end of your chisel accurately from any direction.

The hitting surface of your mallet must always present itself in the same way to the chisel handle, irrespective of the direction it is coming from. Basic geometry indicates this surface should be curved, and not flat. This is why a carver's mallet is round in cross section and tapered longitudinally. Round to cope with a twist of the wrist, and tapered (cone shaped) to cope with the arc of the strike.

hand and vice-versa. The important point is that everyone is different.

HAND HELP

The mallet was invented to help the hand push a chisel through wood. The two fundamental questions are, why do we need it and what should its design be?

Let's go back to hands and arms. Experience tells us the drawing of a straight line is foreign to the operation of our mechanics. This is not necessarily because we aren't capable of doing it, but most likely because we haven't trained our brain to control our mechanics to operate in a straight line.

The key word is control. If you push your carving chisel across the wood and you aren't in control, it will go in the wrong direction, you will slip, and probably damage your carving. Instead of holding the chisel in one hand and pushing it with the other, you can tap it with a mallet.

The harder or softer you hit it, the more or less it will move. Once you are in control, the more power you apply, the greater the cut. Power is the other main benefit of a mallet.

The trick, then, is to have a mallet that helps move the chisel both far

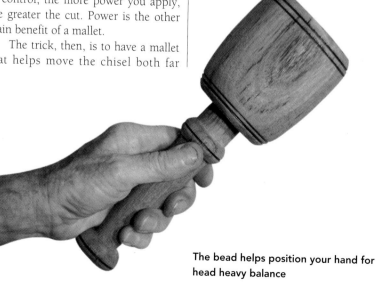

The bead helps position your hand for head heavy balance

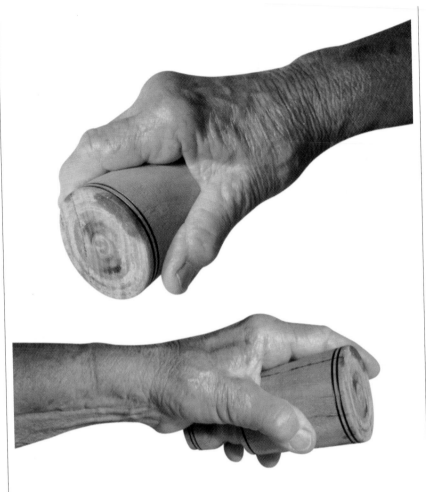

Top **A small palm mallet**
Above **A hollow made for the little finger makes the palm mallet easier to hold**

WEIGHT DISTRIBUTION

If you need great power, to carve a large hardwood sculpture for instance, you need heavy weight delivery unrestricted by your hand and arm movements. The balance (weight distribution) of the mallet when you are holding it needs to be skewed towards the head and away from your hand, so it feels a bit top heavy.

If you need great control, the weight needs to be less heavy, and the centre of balance closer to the hand which is controlling the mallet's movements. It is worth noting that a top heavy mallet will be a hindrance to achieving maximum control.

MADE TO MEASURE

Blending the right combination of your personal characteristics to choose the curve and taper of the mallet head, its weight and balance, will help you tremendously in your work.

Mallet weight is determined by the amount and kind of material used for its production. If it is turned from wood, as most are, then select the density to suit the purpose. High density (weight per unit volume) for heavier mallets, lower for lighter. Choose a hard timber that has a high resistance to wear and marking. In Australia, for example, good woods are tallow, jarrah (*Eucalyptus marginata*), myall (*Acacia spp*), and brush box.

The density will help determine the general size of the mallet, but you must remember that the diameter of the

handle will largely depend on the size and strength of your hand. The greatest flexibility for size is in the head itself. There is nothing more uncomfortable than trying to hold on to a handle that is too thick for your hand and it is surprising how much difference just a millimetre or two can make!

So it's best to get the handle right and adjust the weight of the head, by altering its diameter and/or its length. You could also use a combination of different density woods for the head and the handle to find the correct balance.

MAKING MALLETS

Here are some guidelines to help you make your own mallets:

Handle length – no less than the width of your hand (including your thumb) when all your fingers are together. The longer the handle, the further away from the head you can grip it, making it top heavy, if you wish.

Handle diameter – place the tip of your index finger on the tip of your thumb and measure the internal diameter of the circle formed.

Length of the head – approximately 4in, 100mm is usually about right. Too much shorter and it is too easy to miss, and too much longer makes it too cumbersome.

Amount of taper – make the smaller diameter about 15% less than the larger end.

Here are a few suggestions to help you make mallets for some common situations:

If you have a small hand, are not particularly strong and want to do fine relief carving for furniture or boxes, I would recommend using a mallet weighing 400 to 450 gms. Have the centre of balance as close to your hand as possible. To help achieve this, make a hollow for your thumb and index finger close to the head. The head will be about 3¼in, 85mm long, with a diameter tapering from 2⅜ to 2in, 60–50mm, with a handle about 4in, 100mm long and 1⅛in, 28mm thick.

A fairly robust person wanting to do medium to large carving in the

not looking for power so you should use your palm mallet with finer chisels and softer wood such as jelutong (*Dyer costulata*). Consult your Doctor if you have any doubts.

INJURY WARNING

Other conditions such as RSI (Repetitive Strain Injury) and Tennis Elbow can be introduced or worsened by the use of the wrong kind of mallet. A mallet that is too heavy for your personal characteristics will place unnecessary strain on your system, while one that is too light for the work will cause you to hit it too hard, and could equally cause injury.

I would recommend a mallet of around 550–600 gms for carvers of average size and strength, wishing to work on relief and round carving, for furniture and small to medium ornaments. The centre of balance should be as close to your hand as possible, with the head about 4in, 100mm long tapering from 3⅛in, 80mm to 2⅜in, 65mm. The handle will be about 4in, 100mm long and 5⅛in, 130mm thick with a finger hollow about ¾in, 20mm from the head. Note that despite the taper, it is still possible to strike a glancing blow. ●

round, or garden sculpture, could try a mallet weighing about 600–650gms. Put a bead on the handle about ¾in, 20mm from the head, and place your thumb and index finger on the handle side of it. The head will be about 4¼in, 110mm long tapering from 3½in, 90mm to 3in, 75mm. The handle should be about 6in, 150mm long and about 1⅜in, 35mm thick. For extra life, less jarring and quieter use, you may wish to use a polyurethane headed mallet.

Arthritis sufferers often have difficulty holding onto a handle. If you have this problem and like carving wall panels or carving in the round, you will need to make a handle which fits in the palm of your hand. It should be made to a diameter which is easy to fit in your hand without the need for a firm grip, but still be round and tapered symmetrically, so you can pick it up from any angle.

The ideal mallet for those with arthritis will weigh 150–200gm, and depending on your hand size it will be about 4in, 100mm long with its widest diameter about 2⅜in, 60mm tapering to 1in, 25mm. For extra comfort, make a hollow for your little finger. You are

Top **The correct striking posture for a clean blow**
Bottom **Incorrect striking posture, which will cause a glancing blow**

Graham Bull is proprietor of the Whistlewood Studio and Whistlewood Craft Barn in Sydney, Australia. Self-taught, he has been a woodcarver for "about a third of a century" and teaches carving in all its forms to some 100 people each year, from school children to hobbyists and professional woodworkers.

CONTROLLING YOUR CHISELS

IN HIS SECOND ARTICLE ON HANDS AND TOOL HANDLES, GRAHAM BULL LOOKS AT CHISELS

In this article I will look at some of the more traditional or common designs of chisel, and show you how to design a handle which might help you do the job much better. For simplicity, I will avoid the issues of blade tangs (the part that fits into the handle) and how to fit internal and external ferrules. Instead I will stick to issues surrounding handle shape, weight and feel.

There are a number of issues which determine the best handle to use. For example, the design of the carving and the wood you are using may dictate the kind of mallet you need. The physical design characteristics of the chisel, the action you want to perform with the chisel and the kind of wood available for handles may also be deciding factors. And as if that's not enough, there is the nature of your hands themselves.

The best way to understand chisel handles is to take the major deciding factors just listed, and draft a basic list of handle parameters from which you can design your handle.

Let's say you are going to do an average size carving, about the size of a decoy duck, in a timber of average density. It may be something like Brazilian mahogany, (*Swietenia macrophylla*) weighing in at 550kg/m³. The majority of the shaping work will be done with a ¾in, 20mm straight sided gouge. Lets assume you also have average hand size and strength.

My first article recommended a mallet weighing 550–600 gms for this type of work. The duck in our example isn't particularly awkward to carve or highly demanding in terms of technical skill (unless you are going to decorate it with very fine feathering). So everything is about average.

The chisel we have chosen is what I would describe as a middle of the road workhorse. I expect most of you have a chisel like this in your kit, unless you always do very fine work. You aren't going to belt the hell out of it, but by the same token you want to be able to apply reasonable impact force.

WOOD CHOICE

First, you need a wooden handle that will take a reasonable amount of battering on the end of its grain, without splitting. The compression strength of the end grain of wood is quite different to that of it's long grain, and not all wood is suitable.

Two which are commonly used are European beech (*Fagus sylvatica*) and

A range of commonly used chisel handles, each fitted to a similar sized blade

Australian silver ash (*Flindersia bourjotiana*). Grainy softwoods such as Douglas fir (*Pseudotsuga menziesii*), Radiata pine (*Pinus radiata*) and Brazilian mahogany are unsuitable.

So with an average carving, using an average density wood, with a basic workhorse chisel, average sized mallet and average strength hands, it seems logical that you need the average chisel handle. So what is it?

I have photographed some of the world's most common woodcarving chisel handle shapes, each one fitted to blades ranging from ⅝ to ¾in, 17 to 20mm. Note the different lengths, thicknesses, and the mixture of round and 'square edged'. Each one is made from wood of about the same density and weighs between 30 and 60 gms. So which is the average, and why are some hexagonal and some round?

The hex handle was designed not for better grip, but so the chisel was less likely to roll off the workbench. It may also have evolved from early times when the craftsman made his own handles by trimming the corners off a square cross-section offcut from the workshop floor.

However, by virtue of its softness and flexibility, the human hand responds better to a curved shape than a square-edged shape. Try it! I won't open the debate on why handles are made with square edges, but in my opinion, they are inappropriate.

BALANCE

Next, look at the balance of the tool. For better control of a mallet, the balance should be skewed towards your hand and not the mallet head. It is even more important that the chisel conforms to this observation, as it is in your hand all the time.

You want your hand in control, and

The see-saw test shows whether your chisel is handle-heavy or blade-heavy

not the blade of the chisel, so the weight of the chisel should be more in the hand than top heavy and in the blade.

Now check your chisel. Chances are that if you put the end of the handle across your finger like a see-saw, the chisel will be blade-heavy. The picture showing the see-saw test compares a similar blade in different handles. The blade-heavy handle is European ash (*Fraxinus excelsior*) of about 700 kg/m³ and the handle-heavy handle is Australian gidgee (*Acacia cambegei*) of about 1330 kg/m³. This wood is an island desert wattle, used for about 40,000 years by the Australian Aboriginal for boomerangs and other tools and weapons.

If after trying a hexagonal handle and a round handle you prefer the round one, it is not surprising. What is even less surprising is you will probably prefer a handle which is significantly heavier than your current one. This is not to say the out-of-balance one is no good, but the handle-heavy one is better.

You need to decide whether a handle which feels better and offers more control, but might roll on to the floor, is more important than a less comfortable and less controllable chisel that might not fall on the floor. (It shouldn't happen at all if you are careful and your bench is not too cluttered up).

I will guarantee a round handle made from a wood like gidgee will feel so superior to a light-weight, blade-heavy, hexagonal handle, you will want to change all your chisel handles over!

HOLD IT

A common way of holding a chisel when using a mallet is to hold the hand low on the blade to give maximum control over the cutting edge. The thumb is pressing against the side of the handle, effectively clamping the chisel between the fingers and thumb.

Look at the picture showing the same action without the mallet. The right hand is on the handle to both steer the chisel and add power to the push. Note the palm of the left hand (in this case the chisel is being used right-handed) is not resting on the work surface. The weight of the hands and arms is being supported by the cutting edge of the chisel on the wood.

This is a common practice, but significantly reduces the control you will achieve over the movement of the chisel. If the hand holding the blade is 'locked on' to the work, that is resting on it, control is increased dramatically. It is also more comfortable.

TOTAL CONTROL

Now, I'd like to show you a refinement to your handle that will put you completely in charge!

If you hold the chisel firmly in your left hand, you will find that the mechanics of the hand, together with the pressure you are applying, tends to push the left thumb up the handle away from the blade. This reduces the efficiency of the thumb because it not only wants to slide up the handle, but it is pushing in the wrong direction. This can be counter-productive, depending on how

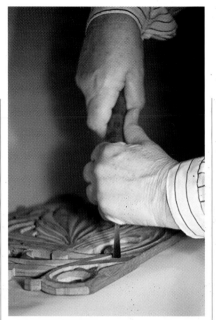

Top left **The chisel is held low down on the blade for extra control**
Top right **The right hand on the handle is used for steerage and power**
Above left **Rest your palm and wrist on the work for maximum control and comfort**
Above right **A thumb knurl gives total control**

much pressure you are applying.

The muscle structure of the thumb, particularly the pad of muscle at the base of it, makes it the strongest finger in your hand. So you should have it

working for, rather than against you.

Instead of it pushing up the handle and therefore expending its force in the wrong direction, you can re-direct the pressure downwards along the blade, and make it work for you. To achieve this add a ledge, knob or knurl to your handle, which the thumb can push down against.

Now, you have everything working for you. Your handle has the right shape and balance. You are resting your wrist on the work so your chisel is only cutting and not supporting unnecessary weight, and the strongest part of your hand is on

the knurl giving you every bit of control you could ever need.

Use your thumb to assist the pushing of the tool, by sliding the chisel through the fingers – not unlike the way a wood block cutting chisel is used (although it is the other way around and the fingers slide the chisel along the thumb).

DIFFERENT DESIGNS

You will not want every handle in your kit to have this configuration. At the beginning of this article I said one of the design parameters was the task you wanted the chisel to perform. The absolute control afforded by a chisel designed for fine detailing and finishing is not the sort of configuration you would want on a 1⅜in, 35mm gouge for shaping a rocking horse. For a rocking horse or large sculpture, a light weight blade-heavy handle is best, because the balance is skewed towards the action end of the tool and not your hand, giving you punch where you need it most.

You will get greatest satisfaction from the knurled handle by fitting it on smaller 'V' tools, fishtails, and any other favourite finishing chisels you have. ●

Graham Bull is proprietor of the Whistlewood Studio and Whistlewood Craft Barn in Sydney, Australia. Self-taught, he has been a woodcarver for "about a third of a century" and teaches carving in all its forms to some 100 people each year, from school children to hobbyists and professional woodworkers.

T he methods and techniques used in this project are applicable to most kinds of relief carving. Having followed them, you should be able to continue with further work of your own design.

Wood choice

Choose a piece of wood with straight and close grain. Avoid exotics with interlocked grain, visible as stripes on the surface. It needs to be ½-1in, 12-25mm thick: less won't give enough depth, but more may look heavy. For the owl, I used a piece about 8 x 6 x ¾in, 200 x 150 x 20mm, which fitted my tracing of an owl taken from a book illustration.

Suitable woods are sycamore, lime, certain types of mahogany, cherry and walnut. Be sure that the wood is free from cracks, flaws or knots which may detract from your carving. When buying, inspect wood carefully. Make sure it has no flaws or splits, particularly if buying a short length cut from the end of a longer board. The paint on the end of a board may penetrate the wood fairly deeply, and this will have to be discarded.

The design

Inspiration for relief carvings is to be found in book illustrations, greeting cards, calendars, embroidery patterns, children's colouring books, 'How to Draw' books and so on. The outline should be bold and clear without too much fine and fussy detail. Some contrast in texture adds interest. Illustrations are traced and enlarged either by marking squares over the drawing and then transferring the contents of each square on to a larger grid, or photocopying, or a pantograph could also be used.

Look carefully at the grain pattern on your wood to ensure that your design fits and is enhanced by it. If the grain is pronounced it may detract from the design, with marks appearing in odd places. It may be possible to adapt the design to the pattern by simply moving it on the wood

INTRODUCTION TO RELIEF

ZOË GERTNER EXPLAINS TECHNIQUES OF RELIEF CARVING IN AN EASY PROJECT

Zoë Gertner is a qualified teacher and studied anatomy as part of her degree. A professional carver since 1980, she works by commission and teaches woodcarving to people of all ages from eight years upwards, and from all walks of life. Zoë lives and works in Somerset and her work can be found in local churches and in private collections all over the world

or turning it round. Remember to check both sides of the wood.

Having decided which part of the plank to use, it will need to be sawn to size, and the edges planed straight and smooth.

If the wood is grimy and pencil marks don't show up clearly, the face may need planing. Before transferring the design on to the wood, draw an even border round it – ½in, 13mm wide in this case. If you use a marking gauge be

careful not to score into the border or you will have to plane out the scratches later.

I use carbon paper to transfer the design on to the wood. Tape one edge of the tracing to the wood, get it in place correctly, slide the carbon beneath it then secure the other edges of both papers. Redraw the outline on the wood if the transfer is faint. Keep the tracing safely as it will be needed to refer to levels.

Holding work

There are several ways to hold the work during carving. If the wood is the right size a vice will do, but place packing pieces underneath it so that it cannot slip down as you carve. Wrap a cloth round the edges to protect them.

If it is too large for the vice I rest it on a thick towel or duster, put it in the well of my bench against one of the walls, and fasten it down tightly with a G-cramp. Ensure that the cramp screw is below the bench and put a piece of wood between the cramp and the work, to avoid pressure marks.

A bench holdfast could also be used. If the wood is warped and won't lie flat on the bench, it must be packed from underneath with wooden wedges or it may bounce when using the mallet.

Cutting borders

The cross-grain borders are cut first, to prevent splitting. Using a mallet and a 1in, 25mm carpenters chisel, start at the corner of one of the cross-grain borders. With the flat face of the chisel to the outside, and absolutely upright, give a couple of taps with the mallet. Slide the chisel along the line about half its width, overlapping the original cut. Repeat the mallet blows with the same intensity and work across the wood to make a continuous cut.

Return to the original starting place, and with the chisel bevel downwards cut in at a fairly steep angle from inside the border, making a v-channel.

Don't lever the chisel at the end of each cut, the downcuts may not be deep enough, and you could splinter the border. If the chip does not come out cleanly, leave it – it will come out with successive cuts. With the line of meeting cuts don't hit so hard that you cut beyond the downcuts, so entering the border face.

Repeat the downcuts, pressing the chisel firmly against the previously cut surface, so they are in line. Widen and deepen the v-cut each time, starting a little way in from the corners, away from the long grain edge, so the wood does not split. Continue with the channel until it is approximately ⅜in, 10mm wide, and ¼in, 6mm deep.

Repeat the v-cut on the other cross-grain border line. However, where the tree trunk meets the border put a light cut across initially, then treat the sides as at the corners. Start each successive row of downcuts a little further away, so the trunk can be rounded over later without losing any width.

Cutting the border, the first line of vertical cuts is met with a line of angled cuts to create a shallow v-cut, enlarged by repeating the operation

Long-grain borders

With the chisel upright, as before, make a downward cut in one continuous line along the border. Too heavy a mallet blow will split the wood, so take care. Before the meeting cuts are made to produce a v-cut, put in light 'firebreak' cuts at 90° to the border, at intervals a little less than the chisel width. The meeting cuts towards the border can then be made without splits running too far. As the v-cut is widened and deepened repeat the 'firebreak' cuts.

In each corner pare away the sloping wood which remains where the borders meet, to make a neat right-angle.

Sorting levels

On the tracing, mark the background areas as level one.

These are the deepest areas, th first to be removed. Think of th design as if it were a topograph contour map, and mark th successive levels two, three, fo and so on, until the foreground reached. For a deep, complicate design there may be many level

The levels are relative to eac other and not equal in the depths, for example the grad ation between levels one and tw is not necessarily the same a that between levels four and fiv Do not forget that a rounde object has its highest level alor its midway line, both vertical and horizontally. In places, ha numbers may be needed. Kee the marked tracing in front of yc for reference as you work.

The outline

Before the background, level on can be removed the outline of th owl should be marked out with 60° v-tool and mallet. Cut alor the line direction so that an tearing occurs on the waste si of the line – watch the gra direction as you go round th owl. Tap steadily, witho hurrying, so an evenly sized ch emerges from the tool. Make th cut as continuous as the sha will allow. If the emerging ch obstructs your view, don't remo the tool from the groove, ju brush the chip away. Neatly jo up cuts so that there's no break the v-channel. If there are ti projections in the design, cut generous sweep around them, f the time being.

The v-tool gives a startin outline channel, which is the deepened using gouges of appr priate sweeps. In this projec gouges best suited to the curv are various widths of No. sweep.

Using a ⅞in, 22mm or ½i 13mm No. 3 gouge, turn it so matches the curve of the outlin and place it in the v-cut, pressir it firmly against the side slopin away from the outline. Give it couple of blows with the mall and move on round the lin making a continuous sloping cu Change to a narrower gouge cut round tighter curves. Be su that any gouge you use is not to curved or it will cut a series

callops, its corners digging into
he slope of the outline.

Meeting cuts are then made,
om the background side of the
, to deepen and widen the
hannel. Use the wider No. 3
ouge where possible, with bevel
ownwards. Cut at a fairly steep
ngle, to meet up with the outline
lope. Take care not to overcut
nto the outline and, as before, if
he chip does not come out
leanly leave it until the next time,
on't lever it out.

Widen the outline channel to
bout the same as the borders.
Vhere the channel is along the
rain put in firebreak cuts to
revent splitting. Work until a
mooth and unragged slope has
een cut all round the outline,
aring downwards to tidy it up if
eed be. Keep a constant slope
vith your downcuts, and do not
ndercut by holding the gouge
oo vertically.

Level one

Vhen clearing the background,
lways cut into a channel so that
he wood cannot rip or tear. This
s the reason for cutting round the
order and the outline.

Divide the background area,
etween opposite channels, and
nark the midway line. Using a ⅛in,
3mm No. 9, or ⅜in, 10mm No. 5
ouge, with bevel downwards,
nake rows of short steep cuts into
he channels. Towards the end of
ach cut avoid overshooting by
lropping the gouge hand to scoop
he chip out cleanly.

Begin a second row a little
ehind the first, but not quite as
leep, finishing within the first
ow. Proceed with this overlapping
equence until the midway line is
eached. Don't make a row of cuts
leeper than the preceding ones, or
he wood will tear.

At the midway line there will
emain a slight rise. Remove with
areful shallow cuts. If the
ackground needs further
leepening, use the same system
f cutting; it may also be
ecessary to recut the border and
utline more deeply to do this.

The background is smoothed
by using the same system of
verlapping cutting with No. 3
ouges. Remove ridges left by the
eeper gouge, taking care not to

dig the gouge corners into the
surface. Feel for high spots with
your fingertips, mark them with
chalk or pencil so you can see
them. Hold the gouge bevel
downwards, press the cutting edge
down on to the surface with the
first and second fingers of the left
hand and push the gouge forward
in a slicing movement with the
right hand. Take fine shavings with
the grain, overlapping your
strokes.

A few irregularities in the
background surface are acceptable,
as long as there are no tears or
raggedness. The final depth of the
background depends upon the
thickness of the wood used and the
design. As a general rule, it is
better not to cut deeper than half
the thickness of the board.
However, the deeper the

background, the more contrast is
possible between the levels.

Level two

To make the bird stand out, the
tree level must be reduced to
below that of the bird. Using the
¼in, 6mm No. 3 gouge, cut a
channel round the bird and its feet,
keeping about ⅛in, 3mm away
from the actual line. Make the cuts
which slope away from the feet
first, since these need to be
retained. Make sure that these cuts
slope quite steeply, and the gouge
is turned to match the curves.
Don't use a v-tool because it will
tear the grain as it cuts across it.

Make the channel with the
gouge bevel downwards, to
produce a clean cut. Repeat the

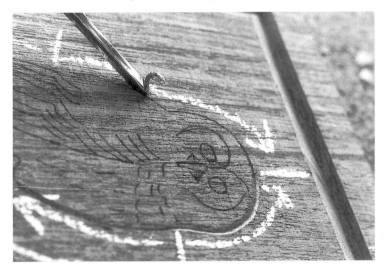

**Outlining the owl with
a v-tool. Arrows
indicate the direction
of cut so that any
splitting is on the
waste side**

**The owl outlined to
the depth of the
border, note
'firebreak' stop cuts
where cutting along
the grain**

series of cuts, until there is a clear outlining channel, but don't cut in too deeply.

Round over the branch and sides of the tree trunk. The highest level is along the centre, the surfaces are rounded down to join the background. The rounding cuts are made towards the outside of the tree. Start back from the edge and lift the gouge hand as you reach the edge, so the blade rounds over in one stroke. Control the gouge so the background is not stabbed, and pare back with shallow overlapping cuts, until you've worked back to the centreline.

Continue until the whole tree is nicely rounded, below the level of the bird. As the tree level is lowered, you may have to recut its outline channel and adjust the background level. Undulations and gnarling of the branches can be carried out at this stage but don't attempt any texturing or under-cutting as the surfaces may need to be lowered again. The outline edges should be tidy, and slope outwards.

The body

The legs and feet project from the lower part of the breast, which slopes below them. So a channel is cut where the legs meet the body, about ⅛in, 3mm from the line. With a ¼in, 6mm No. 3 gouge, turned to match the curve, cut the slope away from the top of the legs first, as these are retained. These are met from the body side to make a curved channel. Slide the gouge sideways at the end of each meeting cut to make a clean curve.

The wider No. 3 gouge is used to cut along the side of the wing. The gouge is sloped away from the curve of the wing. Begin these cuts from the top of the wing; if the

wood splits as you cut it will run into the body side of the line, which is to be removed anyway. Meet these cuts from the breast side, again starting from the top, to form the channel down the side of the wing.

The breast and lower part of the body can now be rounded over with overlapping cuts.

A wide shallow channel is made underneath the head and beak, with a ¼in, 6mm No. 3 gouge. Then, paring carefully, round over from each side of the channel, on to the head and breast. Then round off the top of the head, starting at the centre top, and work with overlapping cuts down each side, to meet up with the previously rounded lower half. The point where the upper rounding meets the lower is where a change of cutting direction will be needed. Make tiny cuts with the grain. While rounding, some of the shaping of the head may be lost. Reshape it by paring down the sides, re-cut in from the background, then round the edges again, to obtain a clear shape.

Lowering the background, cut down into the 'trenches' forming ridges that are then removed

Trenching around the eye; be careful not to lift out the eye

The face

With the ¼in, 6mm No. 3 gouge, bevel uppermost, match the curve of the beak to produce a channel round each side of it. Further carving of the beak is left until later.

The eyes are marked out next. It is important to use the sweep of

gouge which fits the eye circle; this case a ⅛in, 3mm No. 3 goug was correct. Start with cuts acros the grain, top and bottom of th eye. Then work along the grain, avoid splitting along the grain in the eye. Make sure the gouç slopes well away from the eye, if is too upright the eye will b reduced when it is rounded. For a channel round the eye beginning the meeting cuts acros the grain.

Wing feathers

To make rows of feathers overlap like the tiles on a roof, th uppermost row is marked out firs The surface beneath, and that the neighbouring feather, lowered, and then carved. This repeated, feather by feather, acros the wing.

Start with the first feather on th left, use the mallet and ¼in, 6m No. 3 gouge bevel uppermost an make a sloping cut round th lower edge. Then, by hand, c towards it to make a channel. Hol the gouge fairly steeply and tak care not to lift the feather tip at th end of the cut. Pare away th surface on the right to the depth the channel to make the surface the second feather. Then put in i sloping edge cut, follow this wi the meeting cuts and pare awa the surface on the right for th third feather. Continue feather b feather, across the wing. Par

way the surface beneath the ends of the feathers, so the next layer merges from beneath them. Then scrape each feather so it is smooth and rounded with no sharp edges.

Breast feathers

The breast feathers are cut in the same way as the wing feathers but using the ⅛in, 3mm No. 3 gouge. Between each feather it may be helpful to use the point of a skew chisel to make them meet neatly.

The lower breast feathers are shown by a few grooves marked with the ⅛in, 3mm v-tool – worked by hand or mallet. Place them so that they flow down and round the curve of the breast. Do not put in too many marks or they will look crowded. Start near the feet and cut towards them. Make a short shallow groove with the v-tool. At the end of each cut, drop the gouge hand to lift out the chip cleanly. If it remains attached, as it may on the upper surface, do not pull it away; cut it out using the point of the skew chisel. Work over the area, always cutting towards the feet. Keep each mark separate – don't allow them to run into each other.

The beak

With the point of the skew chisel, pare away a little from each side of the lower tip of the beak. Hold the chisel at an angle so that the slope on each side of the beak gradually forms a ridge along the midline. The ridge should be curved over and reduced at the beak tip, so it meets the face in a point. Round the top edge of the beak, using a ¼in, 6mm No. 3 gouge, cutting towards the top of the head. Scrape the whole surface with either the skew chisel, or the gouge end.

The feet

Start at the top of each toe with a ¼in, 6mm or ⅛in, 3mm No. 3 gouge, bevel uppermost. Cut across the grain, sloping away from the drawn line. Follow the curve round the edge of the toe to the tip of the claw, and continue round to join up at the starting

Feathers are indicated with a variety of cuts, the beak is carefully pared to shape

place. Turn the gouge and pare a channel round the toes.

At the sides of the toes, along the grain, slip the gouge edge sideways at the end of each cut to sever fibres cleanly. In the confined space between the toes, take tiny steep cuts. Shape the claws like the beak, but round over the midline. Delineate the claw by cutting a tiny channel across each toe. Carefully scrape the surfaces smooth.

Finishing

I decided that the tree trunk and branches did not need texturing; the owl is sufficiently interesting and further texturing would be too much. The tree was left showing the tool marks.

The owl, being fairly rounded, did not need undercutting. To see if it is needed, prop the carving up and look at it from a distance. If it appears flat, shadows can be produced by undercutting to suggest greater depth. The most probable places will be at the lower edge of the breast near the feet, the inside edges of the wing,

The finished piece

TOOL LIST
Numbers refer to Sheffield list

Firmer chisel	1in, 25mm
Skew chisel	¼in, 6mm
Gouges	½in, 13mm No.9
	⅛in, 3mm No.3
	¼in, 6mm No.3
	½in, 13mm No.3
V-tool	⅛in, 3mm 60°
Mallet	

along the sides of the toes, and in the hollows of the branches.

To undercut an edge, first shade with pencil the area to be cut to give some idea how it will appear. Use a No. 3 gouge to put in a series of cuts level with the background. Hold the gouge bevel against the edge to be undercut, not quite upright, and pare down to meet the first cuts, without sinking the tool beyond them. Don't lever the gouge against the edge, you may damage it. Repeat the cuts level with the background a little deeper under the edge, then pare down towards them, increasing the angle of undercut. The undercut edge is not supported underneath, so don't go too far under and weaken it.

After undercutting, clean up the background with the firmer chisel. Scrape the surface smooth then check for any stray splinters in the outline edges. Pare the edges of the borders smooth; a skew chisel can be used to tidy up in the corners.

Apply a colourless wax polish and use an old toothbrush on the textured areas, rubbing it in well. Irregularities on the carving will become visible, as will any raggedness. Pare these away, then scrape the pared surfaces. The faces of the borders may be sanded if you wish. Don't sand the carving or the crispness of your edges will be lost.

Another coating of wax is applied, left overnight to be absorbed, and polished. Repeat the waxing frequently to build up a good surface. ∎

This article is taken from one of Zoë Gertner's tutorial booklets, used in her carving courses. For full details contact her at: Deans Cottage, Bagley, Wedmore, Somerset BS28 4TD. Tel: 01934 712679.

PILOT PROJECTS

In creating his relief carvings and caricatures, Don Hunter draws on his experience of the aircraft industry

When I joined the De Havilland Aircraft Company as a boy in 1935 they were making wooden aircraft, and they carried on doing so right through World War II with the Mosquito and others. Looking back, I believe it was a short spell working in the carpenter's shop and wood mill that gave me a feel for wood. The beautifully made main wing spars and longerons machined from high quality ash, the wing ribs and other structural members of silky sitka spruce, filled the workshop with their woody smell. I still recall it with nostalgia today.

I have always been a golfer but on retirement found that I needed something extra to do indoors during the cold wet winters. That extra proved to be woodcarving, for no other reason than it was clean! So I bought myself a basic set of good quality knives, gouges and chisels and got going.

Craftsman checking the balance on wooden propellors

Combining interests in golf, aircraft and carving, this relief shows a Tiger Moth flying over the 18th hole on St Andrews golf course

Historic scenes

Inevitably my first efforts were relief carvings of vintage De Havilland aircraft, and my first three-dimensional figure was a golfer. I knew from my aircraft experience that I needed good clean-cutting wood and soon settled in the main for lime, jelutong and on occasion ripple grain sycamore. This I find makes an extremely realistic sea background for a flying boat.

When selecting the wood for a relief carving of an aircraft I try to ensure the grain runs along the line and length of the fuselage and across the wings, to give a good aerofoil flow and shape. This also adds to the correct aerodynamic look of the aircraft and gives a good stream-lined finish for polishing.

In carving vintage aircraft, with their profusion of wing struts and undercarriage struts and stays, first-hand knowledge of the aircraft is a great help. However, providing one has a detailed drawing or a good photograph of the subject, the detail can be checked as you proceed.

Flying colours

I rarely paint my work, preferring to use a touch of dark stain to add dominance where necessary on exhaust pipes, tyres and so on. For a carving of a Sunderland flying boat, which is usually painted white, I finally settled on white shoe cream, which when applied and polished gave the correct whiteness against the sycamore background.

After staining where necessary, and final sanding, I apply one coat of boiled linseed oil, allow it to dry and then polish with wax polish. The whole is then framed.

Local hero

In carving three-dimensional figures, my favourite is the caricature Pilot Officer Prune. To all in the Air Force, and many people outside it, Pilot Officer Prune is notorious. He is the legendary fool of the RAF, the clot whose every action serves as an example to be avoided.

Having roughly cut the outline to shape with a jigsaw or handsaw, I always start with the feet. Flying boots have a look and character of their own. Once they are almost complete, I then go to the top and carve the face. Again, if this is not right, it's not Prune. The work in between head and feet can then proceed and the final figure is sanded, oiled, wax

Pilot Officer Prune, a well loved caricature, with his dog Binder and a member of the Women's Auxiliary Air Force. (P.O. Prune reproduced by permission of the artist, Bill Hooper)

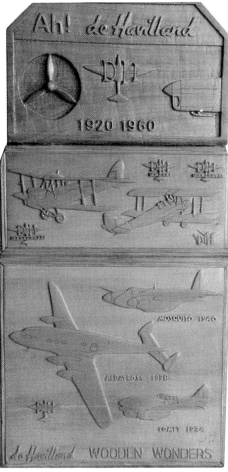

Tribute to De Havilland, exhibited at the Guild of Aviation Artists show in 1993

polished and mounted on the appropriate stand.

Although from time to time I have added chisels and gouges to my kit as fancy dictated, I find the half-dozen tools I originally bought, plus the two carving knives, more than adequate. However, I do use a number of small round, half-round and square engineers' files, with riffler files for the more intricate work.

Artistic honours

For many years I have admired the work of the painters in the Guild of Aviation Artists. In 1990 I plucked up courage to submit a relief carving of an aircraft for their open exhibition. To my great surprise it was accepted and I have had an acceptance every year since; in 1992 I was appointed an Associate Member of the Guild.

Having spent nearly 50 years in the aviation business, I still get enormous pleasure out of carving aeroplanes and allied subjects. If the people who see them get half as much pleasure as I do in making them, then I am content. ●

FLORAL FIREPLACE

ALAN TURNER EXPLAINS HOW HE BEGAN CARVING FLORAL FIRE SURROUNDS

As a manufacturer of Adam-style fire surrounds for the last five years, I realise the main selling point of any surround is its carved mouldings. These mouldings are usually purchased from one of a couple of manufacturers. They mass produce them using a cold pouring plastic, formed in silicon rubber moulds taken from original carvings.

These companies also supply mouldings for architectural use and furniture embellishment. The originals were obviously carved by craftsmen, and the mouldings produced from them are of excellent quality.

They are capable of absorbing stain and are applied to the surround prior to being sprayed. The majority of surrounds I produce are in veneered MDF, and the mouldings on the finished product match the colour of the surrounding veneer.

Having had no experience, and realising I could not match the quality of the mouldings I could buy, I still thought it would be interesting to try my hand at woodcarving.

Carving for the centre of the fascia (lime)

GETTING STARTED

My wife bought me *Decorative Woodcarving* by Jeremy Williams (GMC Publications), and I would recommend it to any beginner. There are sections on choosing the right wood, selecting chisels, sharpening, basic cuts, finishing, and several projects. It takes you step-by-step from the original design through to the finished carving.

Before reading *Decorative Woodcarving*, I had looked at a set of gouges in a local discount store. I must admit I was tempted by the low price. The only reason I didn't buy them was because they were not sharpened. The book steered me in the right direction and I now realise just how poor in quality they were.

After reading the book, I decided to go to a specialist supplier and purchase gouges from a reputable manufacturer.

A visit to Craft Supplies at Millers Dale found me the proud owner of several Pfeil gouges, a veiner, oilstone, slipstone, and four 6 x 2in, 150 x 50mm lime (*Tilia vulgaris*) carving blocks.

I had read the book, got the hardware and still hadn't made a single cut. I couldn't wait.

FIRST PROJECT

Deciding to follow one of the projects in the book, I chose to do a flower in low relief. The step-by-step guide was most helpful and soon I had completed my first carving. Although it was a very simple design and quite easy to produce, it was very encouraging to complete something which actually looked like a woodcarving.

My confidence increased as I carved some of the other examples in the book, along with some of my own design. Now it was time to attempt my first carving specifically for use on a fire surround.

The first carving was to be a patrae

Centre carving in lime

Above **Capital carved in lime**
Below **Corbel carved in ash (Fraxinus spp)**

(a small moulding which sits at the top of each leg, either side of the fascia). This was oval in shape, loosely based on a flower with a seed pod in the centre and petals radiating outwards.

I drew this freehand onto the lime block and began carving. What had looked quite effective as a pencil drawing, soon looked out of shape as I carved the outline.

The third dimension I created with the gouges exaggerated the lack of symmetry, and this was my first failure. But a valuable lesson was learned. I now draw my designs onto art paper, using compasses and ruler to ensure symmetry.

DEVELOPING TECHNIQUE

The floral mouldings on fire surrounds tend to be rather abstract. Flowers appear from nowhere in the middle of leaves, scrolls unwind and become leaves, and yet the whole comes together with believable effect. This allows me to use a little artistic licence, as no hard and fast rules apply.

I keep a sketch book of rough ideas from which I develop a full-size drawing. Once I am happy with this, I use tracing paper to copy the outline.

Reversing the paper over the carving block, I follow the outline with the pencil, imprinting the original lines onto the block. This only works with designs which are symmetrical, as it reverses the orginal. If I don't want this reversal, I use carbon paper and keep the tracing paper the same way up.

Initially, I spent a lot of time removing waste wood with a gouge, but as some of the carvings were up to 1in, 25mm deep I found it much quicker to use a jig-saw.

Cutting to within ¼in, 6mm of the final outline and finishing with gouges saves a lot of time. The real pleasure is in the actual carving of the piece and the sooner I reach that stage, the greater the enjoyment.

MORE MOULDINGS

My workshop, where I produce surrounds, seems the obvious place to do my carving, but I prefer to sit at the kitchen table. I mount the blocks on to a slightly larger baseboard and find I can do most of the carving this way, very rarely needing to use the workshop.

For a complete range of carvings for fire surrounds, I needed to produce patrae, columns, capitals, corbels, and several designs for the centre of the facia.

Most of these are based on a floral theme and, although urns and shells can be used, the floral motifs are more popular. Urns tend to look funereal and shells don't seem to be in demand.

Patrae in lime

A patrae usually matches the centre carving, as a flower found on it may be a smaller version of one on the larger carving.

The capitals I use are usually ½ capitals. They are semicircular so they sit flush onto the leg of the fire surround. These sit on top of a ½ column and, as they are made separately, can be used on various column types or perhaps on a ½ barley twist turning.

The corbels sit either under the mantle and appear to support it, or slightly lower down the leg below a boxed section which itself supports the mantle. This box section is decorated with a patrae.

A surround might be decorated with two columns, two capitals, two patrae and a centre carving. As you can imagine, the cost of producing a hand-carved surround is prohibitive and it is easy to see why the mass-produced mouldings are very popular, reducing the cost by 75% or more.

The carvings I have produced so far are quite simplistic. I hope in the future to attempt more detailed and intricate work, as my confidence and experience increase. ●

Alan Turner only started carving at the beginning of this year. He finds it a rewarding hobby for winter evenings. During the summer he concentrates on his other hobbies, walking in the Peak District and keeping Koi Carp. When the nights draw in, it's time to dust off the gouges again.

Born in Luton, after leaving school and technical college, Deborah Swaine worked in succession for British Aerospace and the City broking department of a large shipping company.

Since her marriage in 1976 she has lived in a beautiful part of Sussex near Lewes, and has worked at the local Agricultural College.

Besides her interest in woodcarving, Deborah enjoys gardening, painting and sailing.

When I was asked to contribute an article to *Woodcarving* my first reaction was, 'Why me?'. This was swiftly replaced by, 'Why not?', and the thought that if I could encourage other people to take up carving, then it would be worthwhile.

For many years now I have tried to acquire a new skill each year at the excellent adult education classes available in Sussex, and no doubt elsewhere. In turn I attended classes in pottery, upholstery, antique furniture restoration, navigation and cookery. I enjoyed all of them and learned a great deal.

Then in 1986 I joined the Monday evening woodcarving class at Oakmeeds School, Burgess Hill, Sussex and was privileged to have been taught for the next five years by a master carver — George Swaysland. He has recently retired from a lifetime of carving and is widely acknowledged as a consummate craftsman. His work is to be found throughout Great Britain and is in the great tradition of the medieval carvers, with influences from great exponents of the craft, such as Riemenschneider and Gibbons.

start something more complex. But no, the was yet more undercutting and finishing do to reach the acceptable standard.

George encouraged complete beginne to start on a low, two dimensional carvin thereby learning the fundamentals

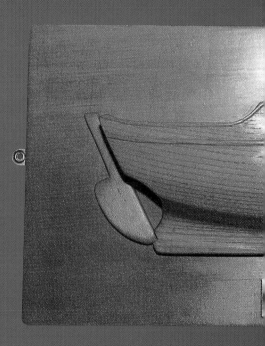

ACCIDENTAL CARVEF

DEBORAH SWAINE

A quest for learning led eventually to carving and the long apprenticeship of wood.

First leaf

That autumn evening when I started I was hooked. Without knowing a thing about the differing characteristics of various woods, the different tools used or the techniques, I was set to work carving a leaf in low relief out of a piece of chestnut. This still hangs proudly on my kitchen wall; as I look at it I remember turning up for class each week certain I had finished my leaf and hoping to

working with the grain, wood preparatio and finishing, proper undercutting, and tl absolute necessity of using the sharpe possible tools. Thus were the basic concep learned, including tool sharpening method

For roughing out the intended carvin some people choose to use a bandsaw reduce the amount of carving. I prefer to u hand techniques at every stage. Not only d I find this work therapeutic, the thoug does cross my mind that wood is a livir substance, and as such there is an affini that is increased by not using machines possible.

Most of my carvings so far have been birds and animals, particularly cats f which I have a passion. One or other of m cat carvings can usually be seen at the Fel Gallery in Lewes, East Sussex: a fascinatir shop full of cats of all shapes, sizes ar mediums.

Frog on lily pad, frog in elm lily pad in ash

oods

he variety and source of available wood is ndless and some are a little more difficult to arve than others. An example of difficult vood is the keruing from which I carved my rst human figure. The wood was an old

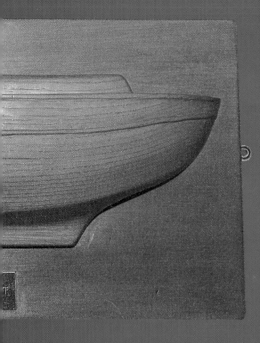

Half model, 1/31 scale of a Golden Hind yacht, in chestnut on pine

ate post, and at first I thought it was oak. owever, as the carving progressed, I found he wood to be extremely hard and laced ith a sticky sap.

'Abstracts are as much a challenge as life carvings.'

The finished piece is a female nude and, hatever its artistic merits, I am very leased with the finished appearance of this ttractive wood. The finish was achieved by sing metal polish as a burnish, then

itroen 2CV in ne. As well as aving a passion r cats I am also ad about 2CV's

polishing with Briwax. When carving this lady, the male class members suggested I bring in a large mirror and work from life. I continued to work from memory!

Apart from animals, I have carved a mahogany back for an old spinning chair and, staying with mahogany, I also carved the crest of the Honourable Company of Master Mariners (to which my husband belongs) and several house names as presents. Lettering is an art on its own and should appeal to those of a precise nature; no matter what script is chosen, the spacing and depth-to-width ratio of the cut is always very important.

Sculpture

Having spent time in carving a detailed half scale model of a yacht hull in chestnut on pine, I have lately branched out into larger scale sculpture. This takes the form of what I call my 'Skeltonian' carving. I work for John Skelton the sculptor on most Mondays. (For someone without any art training or background, I certainly seem to have acquired some superior mentors.) John Skelton asked me to help him finish a large stone carving which he was submitting to the Royal Academy Summer Exhibition.

Cat in oak

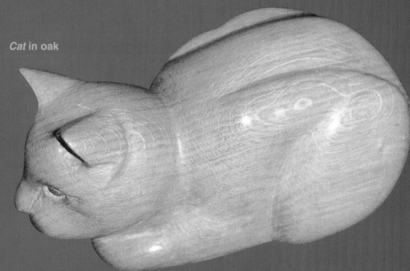

I think I prefer woodcarving — I ended up covered from head to foot in thick stone dust — most unpleasant. My 'Skeltonian' sculpture is an abstract design in a large piece of acacia wood. I initially scooped into the wood with an adze, finishing with a large gouge. When carved, acacia reveals a most marvellous pale lemon colour, edged in white. My tentative title is Inwood vision. Abstracts are as much a challenge as life carvings and I hope to continue in this area.

Woodcarving in all its forms is undoubtedly a source of pleasure and contentment — desirable attributes in these days of increasing stress. I would recommend it to anyone! ∎

GET A HANDLE ON IT

BERTIE SOMME TELLS HOW TO MAKE A BEAN KNIFE HANDLE

The bean knife handle is a common utensil in any household, yet it creates a sense of horror in many people. I find this strange because a screwdriver, for instance, can be a lethal weapon and yet, unlike the bean knife, very few are considered beautiful.

In countries like Norway everyone owns a sheath knife and wears them when going for a walk. They are not weapons, they are tools. A great deal of pride is attached to the ownership of a good knife and it is an important part of the national costume.

(*Buxus sempervirens*) is hard and, when finished well, marble smooth. The finished shape emphasised this.

Although this wood was very hard, the boxwood I chose carved beautifully and it was possible to obtain a very good result with surprising ease.

The method used for making this knife handle was arbitrary to some extent. The purpose of the exercise was to fix the blade in a handle, and any method would do, provided the blade was held firmly and well. Obviously the neater the method, the better the finished result.

For this knife I chose to make a slot, insert the blade (the slot had to be wider than the blade), and embed it with the shaped fillet in epoxy resin. The wood measured 3½ x 1½ x 1in, 90 x 38 x 25mm.

WOOD PREPARATION

The bandsaw is a useful tool which can cut deeper than any ripsaw or crosscut saw. I removed a section of boxwood from a log ready for converting. The boxwood came from an old priory and was reputed to be over 400 years old. This log had quite a pronounced twist, and had been in storage for over 20 years.

To obtain a square section, I cut one face off the trunk and then used the flat face to rest the log on the bench. I could have made up a carriage but that is a lot of effort for little reward. I used a push stick to guide and push the wood through the saw, while keeping my hands clear of the blade.

To make a knife handle straight away from a log like this is not really feasible. Even though this log had been in storage for over 20 years, it would not have quite the right moisture level. Also, when wood is removed from a large section it needs to relax. There is often some movement unassociated with moisture. Kiln dried timber, however, can be used right away.

When I had prepared the blank, I filled the slot with a shaped tongue and the gaps with epoxy resin. It was now ready for shaping.

The blade I decided to use for this project was from Norway, and made by Brusletto. It was a hunting knife blade and its main traditional purpose was to prepare meat by gutting or skinning.

I found the thickness of the blade useful for the type of hand-held work I do. I designed the handle to fit into the right hand, making it ideal for carving. An even better reason for picking this shape was that it shows off the wood so well. Boxwood

Above **Bandsawing the log using a push stick**
Below **The first knife is complete. The one behind it is ready for shaping**

SHAPING

I drew the outline on the blank and used the bandsaw to remove most of the waste. A sharp blade was essential as a blunt one could lead to accidents. Remember to always think ahead of your cuts and use a pushstick as much as possible.

The next step was to use the drum sander. You could also use a sander running from an electric drill or a washing machine motor fitted with a chuck. The knife handle blank shape

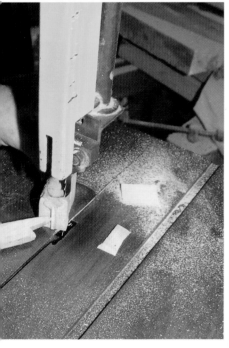

Above left **Starting to cut out the handle shape on the bandsaw**
Left **Using a push stick to complete roughing out the handle**
Above **Using a drum sander to further shape the handle**
Below **The blade is wrapped in a cloth while I cut the handle with a Swedish carving knife**

The movement is from the fingers and the knife is held so the knife handle hits the thumb of the right hand before the blade can cut the fingers.

This method must be used with care and relies on the handle meeting your thumb first. Since the handle of this knife did not project beyond the blade, only a shallow cut was possible.

was ideally suited to the drum and the coarse (60 grit) belt removed waste in no time. The knife blank was now roughed out and ready for further shaping.

First, I held the knife blade wrapped in a cloth and used a Swedish carving knife from Axminster Power Tools. This tool came with a sheath so it could be worn on a belt. It is a very useful tool and retained its edge well.

It is possible to cut the wood towards yourself safely, using what I call a paring cut. As I described in my article on spoon carving (see pages 14-17), the thumbs should be locked against each other so the hands don't move in relation to each other.

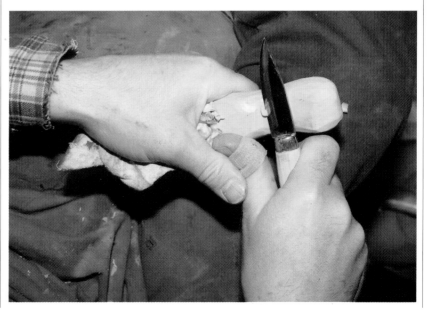

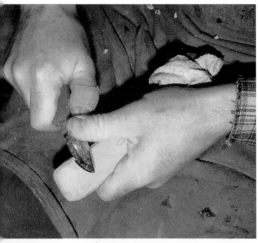

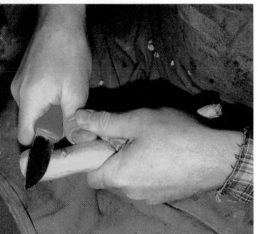

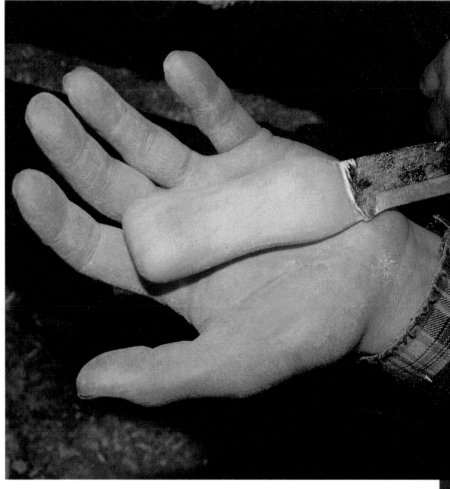

Top **The safest cutting technique used with a Finnish carving knife**
Above **The handle hits the thumb, stopping the motion of the blade, when carving towards myself**
Above right **The knife is shaped and ready for finishing**

TOOL CHANGE

Next, I changed my Swedish knife for a Finnish one, made by Marttini, on which the handle projects beyond the blade. Unfortunately, Marttini knives are difficult to come by. The blade is good and of the right thickness, making it the best knife I have come across for this purpose.

For these cuts, I was able to use the safest of all techniques, which is a continous push on the back of the blade by the left hand thumb. The thumb should not leave the back of the blade. I was also able to carve towards myself, as with this knife the handle hits the thumb and stops the motion of the blade.

FINISHING

The first abrasive I used was a silicon carbide 80 grit. It removed the bumps and to some extent even shaped the wood. After this I used 150 grit which removed the heavy score marks left by the 80 grit.

The grain appeared after this grade of sanding. After using 240 grit then the 400 or finer, no sanding marks should be visible.

I gave a heavy burnish with a cloth and then a liberal coating of Danish oil. The Danish oil was left for about half an hour, then vigorously rubbed with a lint free cloth to leave a beautiful dull sheen. These knife handles are fun and easy to make, with infinite variations possible.

ALTERNATIVE MODEL

I also made a knife handle from a sandwich of walnut (*Juglans spp*) with a thin layer of acacia (*Umbellularia*

The finished knife

Knife made from walnut and acacia

californica) on the outside. I laid the blade on a strip of walnut 5 x 1¼ x ½in, 125mm x 32mm x 12mm thick. Then I drew a pencil line around the outside and routed out the shape within about ⅟₁₆in, 2mm deep. I performed a similar operation on the other side although one side would have been sufficient.

I then embedded the blade in epoxy resin (I find Loctite brand marginally better than Araldite) and spread it over one face of the wood. I clamped the two sides together. When dry I treated the final outside layer in a similar manner to the first handle. I made two knife handles at the same time, end on end, as I didn't have to use so many clamps.

Once I removed the waste, fine acacia slivers were left which contrasted nicely with the walnut. I used polyurethane as a finish, for practical purposes more than anything else. I feel wood is less susceptible to the stresses and strains of moisture changing movement when coated with this much maligned substance, and it often brings the colour out. ●

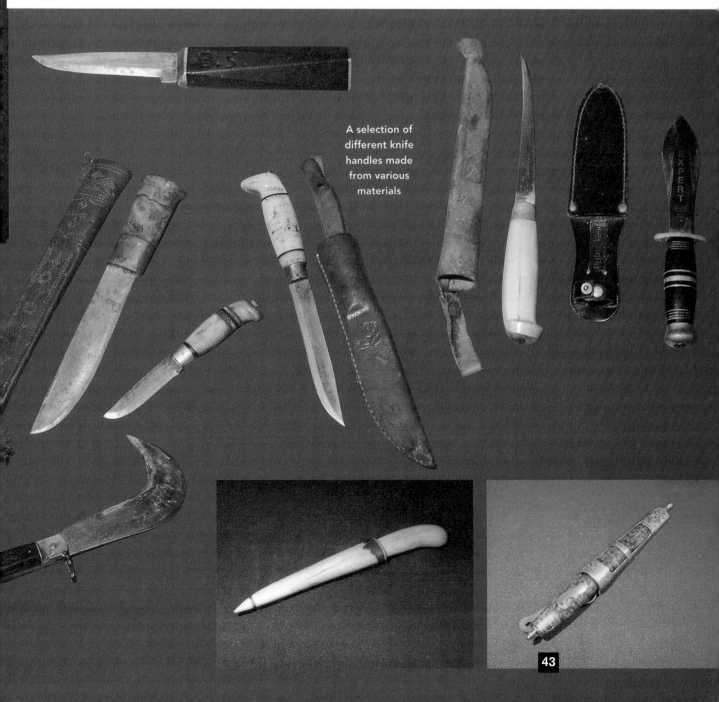

A selection of different knife handles made from various materials

BEGINNER'S DUCK

A few years ago, Albert Holding was a complete beginner: now his decoy duck carvings are both exhibited and sold. Here he describes his progress

When I first started carving ducks, I thought there were only two types – those you ate and those that swam. Now I know differently. I trained as a joiner, and spent all my working life in building and shopfitting, so I had a good background in woodworking. However it wasn't until I was near retirement that I had time to take a practical interest in woodcarving.

Group activity

I joined a small woodcarving group at Ladybarn Evening Centre in Fallowfield, Manchester. It included several very experienced carvers who could not have been more helpful, offering constructive advice when asked. I spent two winter sessions with the group, mainly using my existing woodworking tools and adding the odd knife and chisel.

During this time the local paper ran a small article about my work. This was just before my wife and I moved up to Cumbria. A major requirement for our new home was enough space for a decent-sized carving workshop, and we found a house with an extra large garage, which is ideal.

My first decoy duck was taken from a pattern in Patrick Spielman's book *How to Carve a Decoy Duck*. This led to several more, all smooth ones, sanded and waxed and using various woods, including yew from the village churchyard and chestnut and lime from trees felled by the local Highways Department. I was still using my basic tools, but had added a couple of surform rasps.

Hard sell

By now I had accumulated a fair number of birds so decided to try selling them. I booked a stall at a local craft fair. My wife Shirley and I sat there all day, and although my ducks got several admiring glances and comments, not one was sold. After a couple more of

Above **Early duck by Albert Holding, carved in a primitive style and sanded smooth**

Left **Albert's first entry to the BDWCA competition at Slimbridge, in the novice class**

When I first started carving ducks, I thought there were only two types –
those you ate and those that swam

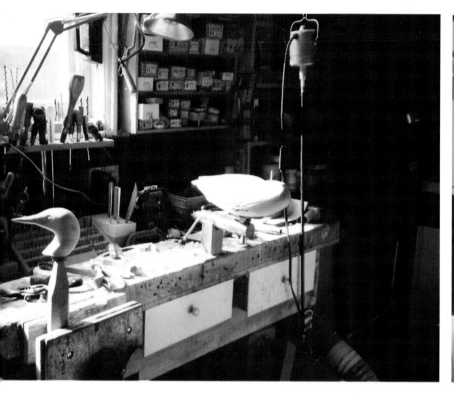

these local craft fairs we decided it was the wrong market for us and went back to the drawing board.

At about this time, *Woodcarving* magazine was launched and in one of the first issues there was an article on the British Decoy and Wildfowl Carvers Association (BDWCA). When I joined I received notice of the AGM and annual competition, which that year was to be held at Slimbridge Wildfowl Trust in Gloucestershire.

Turning point

This was to be a watershed in my carving career. My wife and I travelled down to Slimbridge, and joined the queue to enter my pieces in competition. My ducks were of the smooth primitive type I had been attempting to sell at home.

After a few minutes a woman competitor joined the queue behind us; she was holding the most beautifully worked flying mallard drake I had ever seen. (I now know that she was Judith Nicoll.) Having seen her entry I was all for running out of the door and jumping into one of the duck ponds, but my wife made me carry on and enter.

Such was the design of my ducks that the competition officials were not quite sure which category they belonged to. But one thing was certain: I was a novice.

Afterwards we looked around the marquee at the various woodcarving suppliers' stalls. Until then I had still been using my basic tools and rasps, and a newly acquired set of woodcarving chisels. I was quite staggered by the additional equipment available for carving and painting wildfowl.

Above left **Starting with just basic woodworking tools, Albert now has a fully equipped workshop**

Above right
Demonstrating his skills has been a good way to meet potential customers and others interested in bird carving

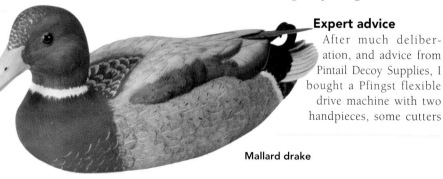

Mallard drake

Expert advice
After much deliberation, and advice from Pintail Decoy Supplies, I bought a Pfingst flexible drive machine with two handpieces, some cutters

Competition officials were not quite sure which category my ducks belonged to. But one thing was certain: I was a novice

Red-breasted meganser hen, Albert's second attempt in competition, which was highly commended at the BDWCA show

and stones, and several books on decoy carving. I also spent some time talking to bird carver David Tippey. The end result was that I arranged a two-day course with David to learn the basics of carving, texturing and painting decoys. This was extremely helpful, though I did come away each evening with a spinning head from trying to absorb too much useful information. I am most grateful to David for pointing me in the right directions.

Having completed the course I spent most of my spare time in my workshop. I soon developed some basic skills in realistic carving, but then found I needed to improve my painting. David had covered basic painting techniques, but this had been limited because the carving had taken precedence. I therefore contacted another carver I had met at Slimbridge, Pauline McGowan of Old Hall Decoys in Norfolk, and spent two days with her learning about painting. In that time I painted a mallard drake and a great northern diver, and returned home really thrilled with the results.

Art market

So I turned again to thoughts of selling my work. We discovered there was an annual art exhibition in the nearby village of Milnthorpe which accepted both paintings and sculpture. My wife entered some of her paintings and I put in several carvings. She sold one work, and I sold a couple of birds.

Encouraged by this early success, I answered an advert in the local paper for craftsmen and women to demonstrate and show their work at a craft centre near the village of Cartmel. In return for demonstrating decoy carving on two days a week, I arranged that the centre would have a permanent display of my carvings and sell them on my behalf for a percentage.

Show and tell

Initially I was nervous about demonstrating a skill at which I was fairly new, but again my wife encouraged and supported me. Soon I felt quite at home and really enjoyed talking to the visitors. We now know of several art exhibitions in the area which also accept carvings, and I have had reasonable success in selling my work through them. People actually come especially to look at my ducks, and this can generate further sales and even commissions.

Two more local newspapers have featured my work, which of course is good publicity for me locally. One highlighted a great northern diver I had done as a special commission for a Canadian couple; another did a story

when I was co-tutoring a carving workshop as part of the local summer school in Milnthorpe.

Award winner

I feel I have made good progress with my carving and have developed a new interest in both decoy carving and live wildfowl. David Tippey and I run the Northern Group of the BDWCA, which meets every three months and holds demonstrations and competitions. On my second visit to the national

Painted and textured hen shoveler

BDWCA show in 1992 I won a Highly Commended award for a red-breasted merganser in the novice class. This has moved me up to the intermediate class where the standard is higher, but this has not deterred me from entering.

There are still many ducks I want to carve, and I am also developing an interest in shorebirds and birds of prey, and have ambitions to visit Chesapeake Bay in America, the home of decoy carving. ●

Contacts
- Pintail Decoy Supplies: 01270 780056
- David Tippey: 01729 830547
- BDWCA, Membership Secretary: Alan Emmett, 6 Pendred Road, Reading RG2 8QL

BLADE RUNNER

IN THE FIRST OF THREE ARTICLES ON SHARPENING, ZOE GERTNER SHOWS HOW TO RECOGNISE A BLUNT TOOL AND RESTORE IT TO RAZOR SHARPNESS

The sharper your tools, the less likely you are to cut yourself. This apparent contradiction is as true for the woodcarver as the chef.

During my woodcarving courses my morning workshop routine is to sharpen the tools we are about to use before starting the day's carving. I like to have students who are complete beginners, because I can stress this good habit before they start carving on their own.

As most of my students do not have access to motorised sharpening methods, and you should not rely on power sharpening anyway, I teach the traditional method using a sharpening stone, slipstone, and strop. This does not take long and makes all the difference to how you use your tools, the finished carving and the pleasure of carving it.

If you use motorised sharpening you may be wondering why your tools no longer cut as they used to when you first got the system. When you rely exclusively on these machines the edges of your tools become feathered and ragged, and close examination will show tiny breaks along the cutting edges, resulting in your work becoming covered with tiny scratches as you carve.

To avoid this, if you occasionally return to the traditional method you will remove the feathering and give a keen edge to your tools again. Although motorised systems are quick and easy to use, it is still essential to know how to sharpen your tools by hand.

If carving is to be enjoyable and safe, your tools must be razor sharp.

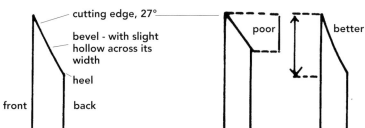

a correctly ground gouge has a slight hollow behind its cutting edge, across the width

if the bevel length (the distance from heel to the cutting edge) is too short, the tool will not cut because the heel obstructs its passage

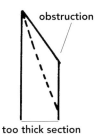

a tool which is too thick in section requires a longer bevel if it is to cut properly and efficiently

every time the tool is sharpened its edge loses a tiny amount, and the length of its bevel decreases. the tool no longer cuts easily, and the back looks short, stubby and rounded

this obstructs and needs to be removed by re-grinding the tool on a grindstone to restore it

scored surface in the same place within each cut

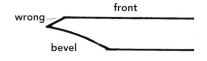

if there is a bevel along the top of the cutting edge your tool will be difficult to use because this wrong bevel acts in opposition

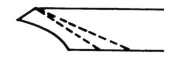

you will need to re-grind the edge back beyond this, and then re-grind the bevel again underneath

You should be most particular about this, since it is impossible to carve properly with blunt or ragged-edged tools. Sharpen frequently, and do not regard the time as wasted because it will be time well spent. Pushing dull tools through wood is hard work and unnecessary effort.

If you find your carving becoming tiresome, stop and re-sharpen. How often you need to do this depends on your wood (some woods dull tools quickly), the quality of your tools, and how well they hold their edges.

All kinds of woodcarving tools are brought into my workshop, many of which need attention to restore their edges so they will cut properly again. There is no mystique about this, but a great deal of pleasure when a battered or neglected tool can be put to good use. These articles will show you how to maintain and restore your carving tools so they will be a joy to use.

RECOGNISING A BLUNT TOOL

It is possible to work on and on, and not realise the tool has become blunt. The first sign is weariness.

As you carve, carefully observe the cuts being made. If you notice a series of small ridges, scratches or lines always in the same place within each cut (even if you have recently sharpened the tool), it is probably because the burr has not been removed completely or the cutting edge is nicked and the wood fibres at that point are being ripped out, not cut cleanly.

Below **A blunt tool will score the surface of the wood in the same place within each cut**
Above right **Hold the tool edge to the light, look along it, and you can see the damaged place.**
Right **Wood fibres will often remain clinging to a blunt cutting edge**

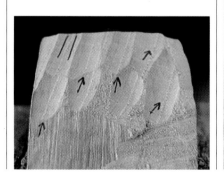

If you have been sharpening the tool by machine for a while, the edge will have become feathered and finely broken in places due to abrasion. If you hold the tool edge to the light and look along it you should be able to see the damaged place.

Softer woods show up the marks of a blunt tool clearly, and often the wood fibres will remain clinging to the cutting edge. You may be able to feel a burr along the edge when you run your fingernail across and outwards. Your tool needs sharpening by honing on a sharpening stone, then the slipstone and strop.

A tool with a deep nick or a broken corner will need grinding on an electric grindstone to remove the

blemish. (How to do this is covered later in the series). It is not possible to do this properly using an ordinary sharpening stone. When the blemish has been removed, the tool bevel can be replaced and the edge sharpened.

REGRINDING A BEVEL

Every time a tool is sharpened the bevel angle is imperceptibly altered, and in time the bevel length becomes shortened, thicker and rounded. Its angle becomes incorrect for the tool to cut properly. The tool will cut only when held at an inconveniently steep angle, and it becomes difficult to use. Re-sharpening makes no difference, and in fact aggravates it. Your tool now needs its bevel angle re-ground and lengthened.

A gouge which has been manufactured very thick in section will also need its bevel ground back longer and shallower if it is to cut properly and not only when held at a steep angle.

If you find your tool still refuses to cut easily and smoothly, even though the edge is sharp and you think the underneath bevel angle is quite long,

Below **Every time a tool is sharpened the bevel angle is imperceptibly altered. In time it becomes shortened, thicker and rounded.**
Bottom **A gouge too thick in section (left) will need its bevel ground back longer and shallower if it is to cut properly. The tool on the right has a finer section, is more efficient and easier to use.**

look at the inside curve of the cutting edge. Due to mis-handling with a slipstone, there may be a slight bevel or slope outwards across the cutting edge which will have the effect of increasing the cutting angle along the edge.

Some carvers advocate this and deliberately put an inner slope along the edge, but if you compare the ease of action of a tool with and without this inner bevel you will find a considerable difference. This is because the action of a gouge is to gouge out a chip in an upwards direction when you drop your hand in the correct cutting manner. If a bevel is put along the inside of its cutting edge it will try to oppose the gouging out action, the tool will attempt to sink into the surface and be difficult to control, as well as very hard work to use.

Also, if there is an inside bevel you will have difficulty establishing the correct angle at which to hone the tool edge on the sharpening stone to obtain the desired burr, which will then have to be removed with a slipstone held at a random and undefined angle, thus altering the cutting angle and ease of use of the tool drastically each time it is sharpened.

Such a tool can be remedied only by grinding back the width of the cutting edge to completely remove the internal slope, and then by re-grinding the outer bevel correctly, a tedious task.

Check all newly-acquired gouges for this and avoid them, unless you are confident about using a grindstone and have hours to spare.

If your newly-bought gouges are not sharpened and ready for use, they will need their bevels ground to the correct length and angle on an electric grindstone before they can be sharpened to cut properly. This is most inconvenient when you want to make a start with your new tools.

Should your tools be old, worn ones their bevels will also probably need to be re-ground to the correct length and angle before you can use them.

EQUIPMENT

For sharpening carving tools, you need a sharpening stone, a slipstone of the same grade as the stone, a piece of leather as a strop, and a cloth to wipe the stones clean after use.

Throw away your dirty old oilstone and treat yourself to a 1200 grit Japanese waterstone and slipstone of the same grade. These are clean, fairly inexpensive, quick and efficient to use. Oilstones are messy, smelly and expensive to maintain, and your carving quickly becomes grubby, especially if you are using a light coloured wood.

If you are a serious woodcarver, the combination 1000/6000 grit waterstone is the best buy, as the 6000 grit face is used for polishing the cutting edge after honing on the 1000 face. Polishing the cutting edge will give a superior edge because it reduces friction.

You will also need a 6000 grit slipstone. If you cannot get one of these the alternative is 8000 grit. An even better polishing stone is the 8000 grit waterstone which needs to be used with an 8000 grit slipstone.

GOUGES

A gouge is a tool with a curved cross section cutting edge. It may be straight-bladed (London Pattern) or have its blade bent forwards or backwards so its cutting edge is offset from the handle.

Gouges are sharpened differently from chisels, which always have a straight cutting edge. If you sharpen one as the other you will spoil the tool, so check by looking end on to the cutting edge. If there is the slightest curve it is a gouge. If you are still unsure press the edge into a piece of paper or soft wood which will show the shape clearly.

Assuming your gouge has the correct bevel length and angle, the stages of sharpening it are:
1. Hone on the sharpening stone to produce a burr along the edge.
2. Use the slipstone on the inside of the blade to remove the burr.
3. Wipe the tool edge firmly along the strop to remove any remaining metal particles on the tool edge.

These three steps will suffice for quite a long time, but as the tool is used it will wear, so the bevel angle and length will alter imperceptibly until one day it will not seem to cut properly, no matter how much you sharpen it. Carving with it becomes harder and harder work. Your tool bevel will need to be restored by re-grinding back to its original condition with an electric grindstone.

HONING

Place the stone parallel to the edge of the bench or table, making sure it cannot move. If it does, place it on a damp cloth.

If you have a Japanese waterstone soak it well in water, and when it has stopped fizzing it will be ready for use. Rub your slipstone over its surface to make a paste. For some reason the stone works better.

Apply plenty of lubricant, stand directly in front of the stone and place the right-hand edge of the gouge bevel on the stone at the top left corner. Hold the gouge at 27° to horizontal, with the handle in your right hand, and steady the blade with the index and middle fingers of your other hand.

Keeping both elbows into your sides, use your wrists in a rolling action, and draw the right-hand edge of the gouge diagonally across and down to the lower right-hand corner of the stone. Roll the gouge while moving it diagonally, so almost the whole width of the cutting edge is in contact with the stone, and you should end up with the left-hand edge of the bevel here.

Now slide the gouge round and up to the top right corner of the stone, keeping the left-hand edge of the bevel in contact as it moves up so the complete width of the blade has been in touch with the surface. If it has not, turn your wrists a little more, but take care not to dig in the corners of the tool or you will score the surface. Do not let the handle of the gouge wander round in a circle as you turn your wrists.

Next, moving the tool diagonally across to the lower left corner of the stone, twist the left-hand edge of the bevel, turning the length of the gouge to the right at the same time so the width of the blade is in contact again for its diagonal journey.

Here, slide the gouge edge in contact, which should now be the right-hand one, round and up to end in the original starting position, the top left-hand corner of the stone.

You should have described a complete figure of 8, and the cutting edge should have been abraded across its width and back again.

sharpening a gouge

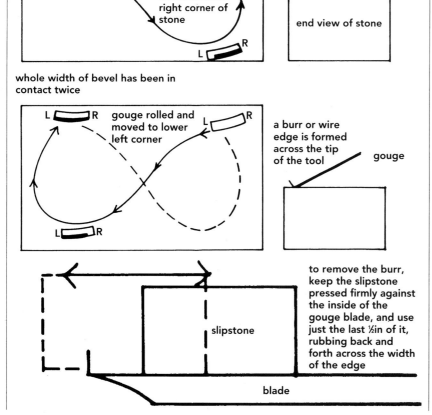

whole width of the bevel has been in contact with the stone, once

L⬜R L⬜R

gouge rolled and moved down to lower right corner of stone

L⬜R

a worn gouge will need a steeper angle a correct ground gouge is held at 27°

27°

end view of stone

whole width of bevel has been in contact twice

L⬜R gouge rolled and moved to lower left corner L⬜R

L⬜R

a burr or wire edge is formed across the tip of the tool gouge

to remove the burr, keep the slipstone pressed firmly against the inside of the gouge blade, and use just the last ½in of it, rubbing back and forth across the width of the edge

slipstone

blade

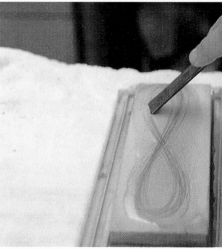

Top **A 1200 grit Japanese waterstone with slipstones of the same grade and a leather strop.**

Centre **Apply plenty of lubricant and stand directly in front of the stone. Hold the gouge at 27° to horizontal with the handle in your right hand, and steady the blade with the index and middle fingers of your other hand**

Above **Describe a figure of 8, and the cutting edge will be abraded across its width and back again**

When honing use light pressure on the stone, and do not hurry. Keep the figure of 8 as large as the stone will allow or it will wear, but be careful not to fall off the ends! Be generous with your lubricant or you will find the metal is rubbed into the surface and the stone becomes glazed and spoils.

The amount of wrist turning will depend on the sweep of the gouge, a deeper sweep requiring more turn. Do not turn too much or you may dig in the corner of the tool and round it, but if you do not turn enough the tool edge will develop a dip in the middle.

Uneven pressure to either left or right gives a lop sided cutting edge (mine always go like this) but this can be compensated for the next time you sharpen by pressing more firmly towards the less worn side to straighten the edge again.

Continue the figure of 8 action until a burr has formed along the cutting edge. A burr, sometimes called a wire edge, is the honed metal making a lip across the inner edge of the gouge. During the figure of 8 action, stop and test whether one has developed by stroking outwards and across the cutting edge with a fingernail. If you feel it catch there is a burr, and you have finished honing. This does not take long if you are using a waterstone.

If a burr will not form, it is probably because you are holding the tool too flat to the surface and the edge is not touching. Raise the handle a little higher, greater than 27° and repeat the figure of 8 action again. This happens when the bevel of the gouge wears and shortens, and you will need to compensate for this until you get it re-ground correctly.

After honing wipe the stone absolutely clean so the slurry does not sink in and damage the surface.

SLIPSTONE

All traces of the burr must be removed or the tool will have a dull spot and not cut properly. This is done by using the slipstone, rubbing along inside the curve of the blade. Your slipstone must be of the same type and grade as the sharpening stone.

Rest the gouge blade so the ferrule is pressed firmly up against the bench or table edge, with the blade resting on it. Hold the tool handle in the left hand, and place the lubricated slipstone inside the curve, to overhang the cutting edge by about ½in, 12mm.

Use a slipstone which is short enough to fit within the blade length and press it firmly and flat against the blade

A tiny gouge will require a small slipstone, and vice versa.

Now rub the slipstone back and forth, about ½in in each direction, at the same time moving it across the width of the blade. Keep a steady pressure on the blade while rubbing and take care not to tip the stone over the edge. This should not happen if you press well down while rubbing.

Continue until the burr is completely removed, testing with your fingernail as before at intervals. When you are certain it has gone rub a little more to make absolutely sure, because if it has not there will be a dull spot along the edge.

You can see whether the burr has gone by holding the tool edge up to the light and looking along it. If there is a burr or dull spot the light will reflect and you will be able to see it. A blunt or damaged tool will show these patches clearly.

Carry on a little longer with your slipstone if you see this, and check again. When the edge is burr-less you should not see anything as there should not be anything to reflect the light.

This method of using a slipstone ensures you have your fingers safely behind the cutting edge at all times, and by keeping the pressure while rubbing along the blade you cannot go over the edge and inadvertently alter the cutting angle. Do not be tempted to hold the tool in one hand and rub from the cutting edge in towards the handle. Always rest the gouge so it is steady on the bench.

Make sure you wipe your slipstone clean when you have finished using it.

STROP

Wipe both sides of the tool edge along the rougher side of the leather several times to remove any metal particles which may still be adhering to it, then dry the tool carefully, especially if you have been using a waterstone. Some woodcarvers like to apply a special strop paste to the leather. Crocus powder or Autosol metal polishing paste is also suitable.

POLISHING

If you touch the edge of your gouge after using it for a while you will be surprised at how hot it becomes. This is due to friction, and energy conversion from your mallet blows. The more polished the cutting edge the less friction there will be created in cutting, so the more efficient the tool. Hence the easier it will be to carve.

When carving fine delicate detail, especially in softer woods such as lime (*Tilia vulgaris*), a polished edge is essential.

To obtain this really sharp edge, after you have honed, slipstoned and stropped your tool on the normal 1200 grit waterstone, repeat steps 1 and 2 using a Japanese polishing stone (either the 8000 or the 6000 grit type) together with its corresponding slipstone. This will put a fine polish on the bevel and your tool will cut beautifully.

As these polishing stones are expensive, and you may feel you do not want to afford one as well as its slipstone. A good low cost alternative is to glue a piece of leather to a flat surface such as thick plywood, about 8 x 2in, 200 x 50mm.

Apply some Autosol metal polishing paste, then hone your tool in the paste. Make a slipstone-shaped piece of wood to fit inside the gouges, and cover with leather in the same way. Apply the paste to this, and polish the curved inside surface of your gouges. Autosol paste can be bought from car accessory shops. ●

Zoë Gertner is a qualified teacher and studied anatomy as part of her degree. A professional carver since 1980, she works by commission and teaches woodcarving to people of all ages from eight years upwards, and from all walks of life. Zoë lives and works in Somerset and her work can be found in local churches and in private collections all over the world.

THE CUTTING EDGE

IN THE SECOND OF THREE ARTICLES ON SHARPENING, ZOË GERTNER SHOWS HOW TO TACKLE BENT GOUGES, SKEWS AND SCRAPERS

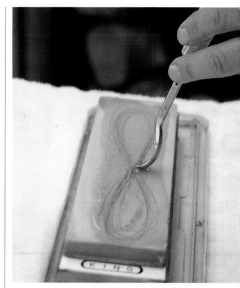

Sharpening front bent gouges: If you have gouges with bent blades, and their cutting edges offset and in front of the handle, you sharpen these in a figure of 8, because they are gouges, but you have to compensate for the bend of the blade by tipping the handle forward when honing on the stone.

For the basic method of sharpening a gouge, see the first article in this series on pages 47-51. If no burr is formed, increase the angle at which you are honing until one begins to form.

To remove the burr, prop the gouge against a wedge of scrap wood, so the cutting edge is accessible with the slipstone, and carefully rub into the curve from the cutting edge towards the handle, ensuring you do not rub across the edge, or you will alter the cutting edge of the tool. Then use the strop to wipe the tool edge free of any remaining metal particles.

Back bent gouges: These are

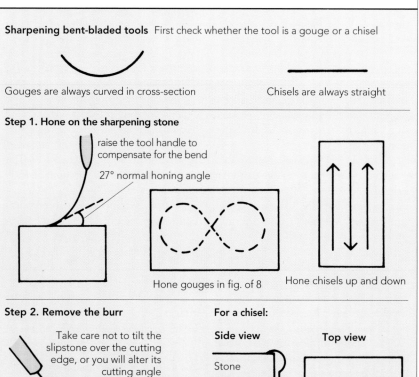

Sharpening bent-bladed tools First check whether the tool is a gouge or a chisel

Gouges are always curved in cross-section

Chisels are always straight

Step 1. Hone on the sharpening stone

raise the tool handle to compensate for the bend

27° normal honing angle

Hone gouges in fig. of 8

Hone chisels up and down

Step 2. Remove the burr

Take care not to tilt the slipstone over the cutting edge, or you will alter its cutting angle

Prop the gouge up and rub the slipstone back and forth, from the cutting edge towards the handle

For a chisel:

Side view

Stone

Bench

Top view

Rest the stone along the edge of the bench, with tool handle below

Rub the burr off from side to side, keeping the tool handle down

Step 3. Wipe the tool edge firmly along the strop

Top **When sharpening a bent bladed gouge, tip the toolhandle forwards to compensate for the bend of the blade, then hone in the figure of 8 action.**
Above **To remove the burr, prop the tool against a wedge so the cutting edge is accessible with the end of the slipstone, then rub this back and forth across its width.**

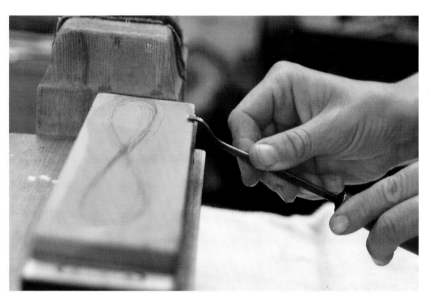

Above **Hold the back bent gouge so the handle is lower than the surface. Then hone the cutting edge in the figure of 8 action, keeping the toolhandle below the level of the stone.** Above right **To remove the burr, drop the toolhandle lower, so the cutting edge is resting horizontally on the bench, lay the slipstone inside the curve, and rub outwards, back and forth across its width.**

gouges which have the cutting edge offset behind the handle. Place the sharpening stone so it lies along the edge of the bench, and the handle of the tool can be manipulated from below the level of the stone. Then, using the figure of 8 action along the very edge of the stone, hone it to obtain a burr again. You will have to adjust the angle at which you do this according to the shape of the tool.

Remove the burr with the slipstone, resting the cutting edge so it is firmly on the bench, with the tool handle lower, and rub outwards and away from the handle as normal. Finish off by wiping firmly along the strop.

Note that in German tool catalogues, front bent tools are referred to as back bent ones, and vice-versa.

V Tools: I shall be covering V tools, including sharpening, more fully in a future article.

SKEWS

Carver's no.1 chisel: These are of little use in carving, despite their name. They usually have a bevel on each side of the cutting edge, so are sharpened in the same way as a skew chisel.

Skew chisel: If it has a bevel on each side of the cutting edge, put the sharpening stone end on to the bench, lubricate, stand directly in line with it,

and place one of the bevels so it is parallel and in line with the end of the stone nearer to you.

Hold the bevel flat against the stone, then gradually raise the tool handle until the bevel is angled at 13° to the surface of the stone. This is not easy to estimate, so if you think of it as being 'not quite flat', you will not be far wrong, and if you tip the tool until a

---

Sharpening back bent gouges

Side view

Stone

Bench

How much you drop the tool handle depends upon the bend of the blade

Rest tool on edge of bench and rub off the burr using the slipstone

Top view

Stone | Bench

Long narrow fig. of 8 along the edge of the bench

1) **Hone on sharpening stone**
2) **Remove resulting burr with slipstone**
3) **Wipe cutting edge on strop**

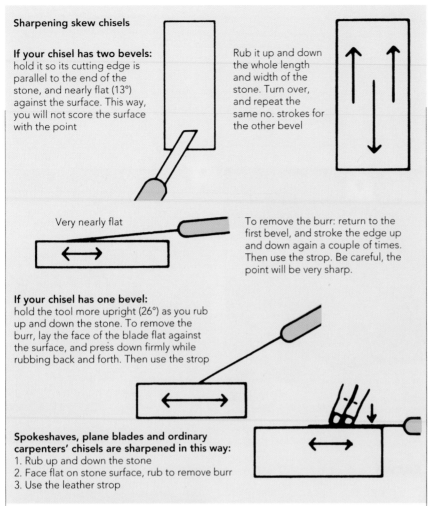

Sharpening skew chisels

If your chisel has two bevels:
hold it so its cutting edge is parallel to the end of the stone, and nearly flat (13°) against the surface. This way, you will not score the surface with the point

Rub it up and down the whole length and width of the stone. Turn over, and repeat the same no. strokes for the other bevel

Very nearly flat

To remove the burr: return to the first bevel, and stroke the edge up and down again a couple of times. Then use the strop. Be careful, the point will be very sharp.

If your chisel has one bevel:
hold the tool more upright (26°) as you rub up and down the stone. To remove the burr, lay the face of the blade flat against the surface, and press down firmly while rubbing back and forth. Then use the strop

Spokeshaves, plane blades and ordinary carpenters' chisels are sharpened in this way:
1. Rub up and down the stone
2. Face flat on stone surface, rub to remove burr
3. Use the leather strop

poke the point of the tool into the surface. Rub up and down about a dozen times, then turn over the tool and repeat for the other bevel, with the same number of strokes.

The first action will put a burr along the edge, the second will remove it, and replace it on the first side. Now turn to the original side, and draw the bevel a couple of times along the stone, handle moving towards you. Finally, wipe both sides of the chisel on the strop.

If the skew has a bevel on one side only, arrange the stone as before, but hold the tool at 27° to the surface, as before, tipping it until a tiny bead of moisture appears along the edge, and rub up and down to make the burr along the edge. Then remove this by turning the tool flat side against the stone, with about two-thirds of its blade length firmly pressed on the surface.

Rub the face up and down to break off the burr, taking care not to lift the tool blade from the surface. Finish with the strop, as usual.

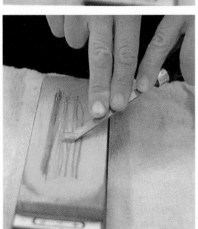

Left **With a skew chisel, place the cutting edge so it is parallel to the end of the stone, lift the tool handle until a bead of moisture appears along its edge, then hone up and down the stone at this angle.**
Below left **Repeat the same number of strokes for the other side, then turn to the first side and remove the burr with a couple of further strokes.**
Right **Tip front bent chisels forwards to compensate for the crank, then hone up and down the stone, keeping the cutting edge parallel with the end of the stone.**
Below right **With a back bent gouge, place the stone close to the edge of the bench, drop the toolhandle below, so the cutting edge is flat on the surface, and remove the burr by rubbing it**

bead of moisture just appears along the cutting edge, this will be the correct angle for your particular tool.

Using light pressure with your fingers, keep the cutting edge parallel to the end of the stone, and rub the bevel up and down, using the whole width of the stone. Take care not to

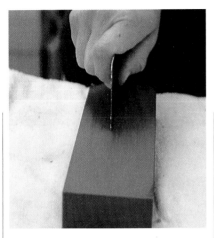

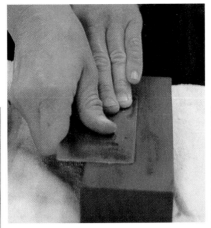

PLANES

Spokeshave, plane and bevel chisel: In carving, the spokeshave is used for fine shaping, the plane for levelling the base of a figure or the preliminary preparation and cleaning the surface of a relief panel, and the bevel chisel for lettering. These three tools are sharpened in the same way.

When new, they will probably need to have their bevels re-ground and lengthened using the grindstone, as the blades are rarely ready for use. Hollow grind the bevels to about ⅛in, 3mm in length, and 27° angle, before honing.

To sharpen, release the blade by unscrewing the holding plate, and then with the lubricated stone end on, hold the blade, bevel down, at 27° to the surface. Rub it up and down until a burr has formed.

Remove the burr by turning it over, so the bevel is now uppermost, and press it flat against the surface of the stone, rubbing it back and forth firmly. It should be possible to hear a change of note when it has gone. Test in the usual way with your fingernail to check. Then strop as usual, to remove any lingering particles.

Replace the blade in its holder, bevel downwards and lodged properly on its screwledges, tighten up the plate and adjust the screws until the cutting edge slightly projects from the mouth.

If you find it difficult to use a brand new spokeshave, polish its sole with the side of your slipstone, then metal polish, to remove the milling marks and reduce friction.

Front bent chisels: Among old tools, and also in certain sets of carving tools, you may come across a peculiar type of front bent chisel, one which has a straight cutting edge cranked forwards from the handle. They seem to be of little use, though once I used the end of one as a scraper in an inaccessible place.

Before sharpening, check that the tool is a chisel, not a very shallow gouge, by looking at the cross section of the cutting edge, because if you sharpen one as the other, you will spoil the tool.

Use the sharpening stone lengthwise, holding the tool bevel flat on its surface, and tip it slightly forwards. How much depends upon the crank of the blade. Rub the bevel back and forth until a burr is formed along its cutting edge.

To remove this, place the stone along the edge of the bench, and drop the tool handle below its surface, so the inner surface of the chisel edge is flat on the surface of the stone. Remove the burr by rubbing it sideways along the edge of the stone, back and forth, keeping firm pressure on the stone, then strop as usual.

MACHINES

Sharpening by machine: If you have a lot of gouges and chisels to sharpen, you will find it considerably quicker, though expensive, to use a mechanical method to sharpen and polish them. There are various makes and types on the market, based on a motor running at 1425 rpm, fitted with a felt wheel revolving away from you, to which a special abrasive paste is applied.

Press the tool firmly against the wheel, and the friction generated will activate the paste. The tool edge becomes well polished and sharpened without needing to use a slipstone on the inner surface of the cutting edge. Then thoroughly wipe the edge on the strop, for best results.

Be extremely careful not to overheat the edge and draw the temper of the tool.

Machine sharpening is particularly useful for sharpening narrow angled V tools and tiny U-shaped gouges where it is difficult to obtain a narrow enough

Above left **Hold the scraper at right-angles to the surface of the stone, and polish the longer edges by rubbing them up and down to make a slurry.** *Above centre* **To remove any burr, flatten the faces and then polish them. Keep firm pressure on the scraper, and rub it flat sideways up and down the stone.** *Above* **Tightly fix the scraper in the vice, with one of its longer edges parallel to the bench surface. Rest the back of a shiny gouge, (or, as shown, a ticketer) on the edge of the scraper. Raise the handle and drop its cutting edge down slightly, then push it outwards towards the bench, sliding it along the scraper, using the whole length of the gouge.**

slipstone to fit inside. It is also useful for touching up tools, but you will sometimes need to revert to the traditional water-stone honing, slipstoning and stropping method, especially when carving the softer woods, such as lime (*Tilia vulgaris*).

If you rely exclusively on sharpening by machine, the edges of your tools will become feathered or weakened. Tiny scratches will appear on your work, and the tool will not hold its edge. When this occurs, hone the tool in the conventional way to recover its edge.

SCRAPERS

Scrapers: A sharp scraper is a pleasure to use, and so frustrating if it is not sharp! It should bite, and produce tiny curled shavings as it cuts. Normally, both edges of the longer sides are sharpened, giving four useable cutting edges. A new scraper, unless it is made by Marples, usually needs to be sharpened before it can be used.

First, the surface of the metal across the two faces needs to be made square to the faces. Tightly fasten the scraper lengthwise in a vice so it cannot slip, and use a double cut file along the edge, until it is flat and shiny. Turn the scraper over, and repeat for the other length.

If you prefer the file can be fixed in the vice, and the scraper moved along it, but if you do it this way protect your hand from the sharp corners of the scraper by wrapping it in a cloth, and keep the scraper absolutely upright while filing. Alternatively, and quicker, run the edges across the grindstone wheel.

The filed edges need to be polished next. This is done by rubbing them along the lubricated sharpening stone. You may prefer to use the side of the stone, to avoid making a groove in it, but if you take care to use the whole width and length of the stone, this should not happen.

Continue until a slurry is made, and the edge is polished, then turn it over, and repeat for the other length. If you use too coarse a stone for this, you may find a burr is formed along each side.

These rough burrs are removed by flattening the faces, placing each firmly against the surface of the stone, in the same way as when removing the burr from a plane or spokeshave blade. Place the scraper flat on the stone for about one-third of its width, and holding the remaining two-thirds, firmly rub the face up and down and around, until a change of note is heard.

A scraper cuts by means of a little hook or burr, which is made by slightly bending over the metal along the very edge of each length.

Fasten the scraper in the vice, lengthwise, and so it is exactly parallel with the bench, and with about one-third of its width above the faceplate and the bench surface. It should be exactly horizontal, and the correct angle at which to make the hook can be made with reference to this. Be sure it cannot slip, as you will be putting some pressure on it.

Use a gouge with a shiny back to it, or as shown, a ticketer, and rest it

across the upper edge of the scraper, so it is horizontal, but at right-angles to the face of the scraper, and pointing towards the bench.

Hold the gouge in the right hand, steady it with the index, middle and third fingers of the other hand, and press the back of the gouge blade firmly against the scraper edge. Now tip its cutting edge down a little, so it is no longer horizontal, but as near to 85° as you can estimate. The handle should be higher than the cutting edge at this point.

Keep your fingers well back from the gouge cutting edge, and firmly push the tool along and outwards at the same time, holding it at this slightly dipped angle. Press hard while pushing along the whole length of the scraper, and you should be able to feel a tiny burr, if you test with your fingernail.

Turn the scraper round, still with this length uppermost, so the other face is now towards the bench, and repeat the action. Then turn the scraper about, and repeat along the opposite edges, and you should end with four sharp cutting edges along the tool.

A small hook should have formed along the four edges, each of which you should be able to feel with your fingernail. If you are standing in the right light, you can see these being formed as you press with the gouge. Your hands will be quite safe, as they are always behind the gouge cutting edge, and you will be pushing away from yourself. The scraper is safely held in the vice, and you can press firmly, accurately and in complete safety.

As the scraper is used, it will become blunt (some woods will do this more than others), and dust instead of shavings will be produced. To re-sharpen, go through the stages from polishing the edges on the stone, onwards. Only when the metal edges are badly worn and out of true will you need to file or grind them. If your scraper is too large to use easily, cut it in half with a hacksaw. ●

Zoë Gertner is a qualified teacher and studied anatomy as part of her degree. A professional carver since 1980, she works by commission and teaches woodcarving to people of all ages from eight years upwards, and from all walks of life. Zoë lives and works in Somerset and her work can be found in local churches and in private collections all over the world.

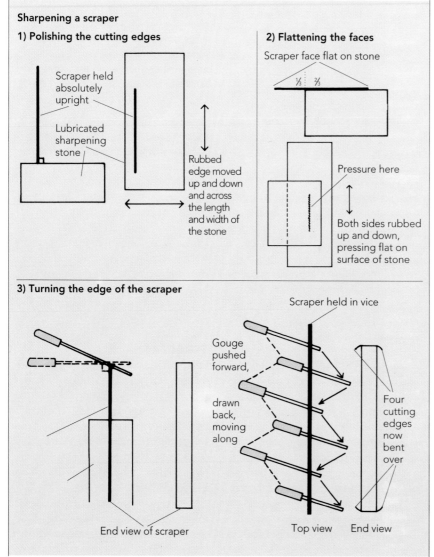

Sharpening a scraper

1) Polishing the cutting edges

Scraper held absolutely upright

Lubricated sharpening stone

Rubbed edge moved up and down and across the length and width of the stone

2) Flattening the faces

Scraper face flat on stone

⅓ ⅔

Pressure here

Both sides rubbed up and down, pressing flat on surface of stone

3) Turning the edge of the scraper

Scraper held in vice

Gouge pushed forward,

drawn back, moving along

Four cutting edges now bent over

End view of scraper

Top view   End view

STAY SHARP

IN THE FINAL ARTICLE OF HER SERIES ON SHARPENING, ZOË GERTNER SHOWS HOW TO RE-GRIND BADLY WORN OR DAMAGED TOOLS

Tools need re-grinding occasionally, either because they are worn, or because there is a nick in the cutting edge, and it is usually your favourite tool which needs it first.

As a tool is honed on a sharpening stone, its bevel is imperceptibly shortened, so it develops a heel, which impedes the cutting action. The tool resists being pushed through the wood, which is why suddenly your carving becomes hard work.

You think it is blunt, so you re-sharpen, but further honing actually exacerbates the condition. Re-grinding to remove the heel and replace it with a hollow is now essential.

A glance through tool catalogues will show several types of grindstone, at various prices and of various qualities.

One which revolves through water is ideal, as you cannot draw the temper of the steel by overheating it, but one without a water trough will do as long as you dip your tool edge in cool water after each stroke across the wheel.

Place a magnet in the water bath to collect the metal particles, so the water remains clean and they do not rust on the surface of the stone.

Grinding is a messy, unpleasant job, so wear protective clothing and plastic gloves if you object to ingrained metal in your skin. Proper eye goggles, not spectacles, are essential. The shields fitted to the machines are not adequate. Do not use the sides of the wheel to grind the tool edge as this can cause it to shatter, and keep all inflammable items well away, as impressive sparks can be produced.

If the wheel surface becomes glazed it must be re-dressed, either with a diamond dresser pencil or a dressing wheel, both of which can be bought from good tool shops or specialist suppliers.

When grinding use light pressure and do not force the tool against the wheel. Be sure the wheel is correctly balanced within its shield and always use the toolrest.

GOUGES

To re-grind the bevel on a gouge, lightly hold the tool edge at right angles to the revolving surface, and look to see if the cutting edge is actually on the stone. If it is, lower the handle a little more, until the gouge edge is clear, as the re-grinding must commence back from the cutting edge, at the heel.

At this point, for a gouge the tool is rolled across its width, at the same time moving it across the width of the wheel. This is done by turning the right hand and wrist, and steadily but lightly drawing the tool across the surface of the stone, using the toolrest to control the angle as you do so.

If you are not using a water-cooled grindstone, be sure that after each

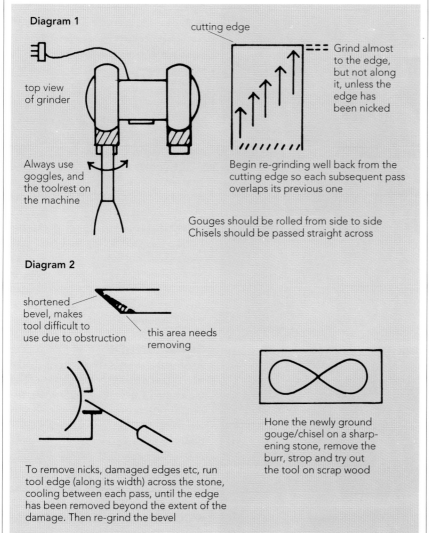

Diagram 1

top view of grinder

Always use goggles, and the toolrest on the machine

cutting edge

Grind almost to the edge, but not along it, unless the edge has been nicked

Begin re-grinding well back from the cutting edge so each subsequent pass overlaps its previous one

Gouges should be rolled from side to side
Chisels should be passed straight across

Diagram 2

shortened bevel, makes tool difficult to use due to obstruction

this area needs removing

To remove nicks, damaged edges etc, run tool edge (along its width) across the stone, cooling between each pass, until the edge has been removed beyond the extent of the damage. Then re-grind the bevel

Hone the newly ground gouge/chisel on a sharpening stone, remove the burr, strop and try out the tool on scrap wood

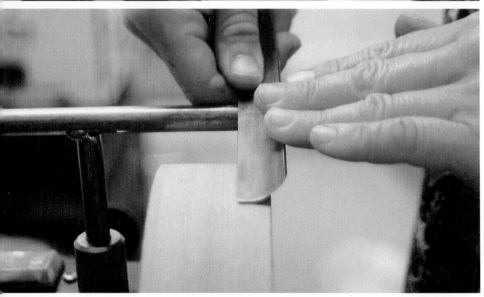

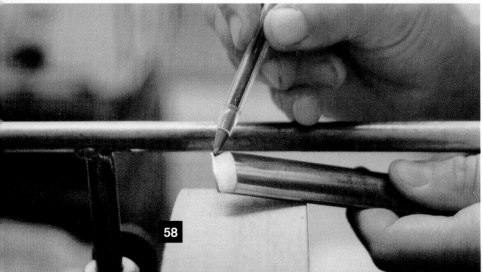

From top to bottom
● Where the bevel meets the under-neath surface of the blade, a worn gouge develops a heel, and looks fat, short and round when viewed from the side
● Starting at one side of the tool bevel, place the gouge so the heel touches the surface of the stone, and lightly steady the tool blade with the fingers of your other hand. Make sure the heel, not the cutting edge, is in contact with the wheel
● Gently turning your hand and wrist, roll the whole width of the gouge across the width of the stone, to finish on the opposite side of both tool and stone. Do not press down hard, but lightly rest the tool on the surface
● Repeat the process, moving the tool fractionally towards you, so metal is removed from the heel towards the cutting edge

journey across the width of the wheel, you dip the edge into cool water to prevent it overheating and subsequently losing its temper.

If too much pressure is used against the stone, or the edge is overlong in contact, it will become blued, a clear indication it has been overheated. Should this happen, the cutting edge will be softened. You have spoilt your tool, and it will have to be re-tempered before it will cut properly again. If you wish to know more about this aspect, you should consult metal working books.

BEVEL LENGTH

As a general rule, the length of the bevel should be approximately one half the width of the gouge, and this is the distance back from the cutting edge at which you should begin grinding. Obviously, if you have a very wide tool, say over an inch, you modify this.

Make successive journeys across the wheel, if necessary dipping after each, and gradually raise the handle while doing so, to work towards the cutting edge. Little by little, remove the metal, and stop just before the very tip of the cutting edge.

Remove a little more metal from the area just behind the edge to hollow the bevel slightly. This will prevent the thickness of metal here obstructing the passage of the tool through the wood as it cuts, and reduce the friction and force needed to work it. Experience shows that, viewed from the side, a shallow angle of about 27° is most efficient.

After grinding, the gouge should be honed on the sharpening stone, and the burr removed with the slipstone, as described in my previous articles.

If the gouge fails to cut properly after this, and you are sure you did not draw the temper (the edge will be blued if you did) it is probably because insufficient metal has been removed from behind the edge, and the bevel needs more hollowing, or, more likely, your tool has been made too thick in section and needs its bevel extended up the blade.

Straight chisels and V tools are ground in the same way, but are not rolled when passed over the wheel surface. Draw the tool across, keeping the bevel surface flat against the wheel. As in all tool grinding use the toolrest at all times so the tool is held steadily and accurately on the stone.

DAMAGED EDGES

Restoring damaged edges, gouges with inside bevels and badly angled V tools: If there is a deep nick in the cutting edge, or a corner has broken off, if the blade has broken through mis-use, or the edge becomes badly mis-shapen due to careless sharpening, the edge will need to be straightened up before the bevel can be re-ground.

Run the damaged tool edge across the wheel surface, dipping the edge in cool water between each stroke, until the edge becomes straightened and squared off. If you have a gouge with its bevel on the inside of the blade, or a badly shaped V tool remove it in the same way.

Then proceed as described before to make a new bevel, working forwards from the new heel to the cutting edge. This can take a long time, especially with a large tool.

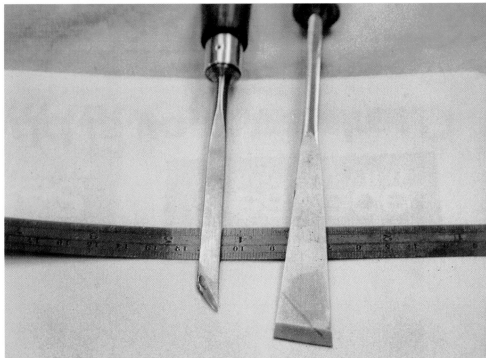

Top **When restoring damaged edges, gouges with inside bevels and badly angled V tool blades, grind the mis-shapen edge directly against the wheel to remove nicks and excess metal, and to straighten it. When the damage is removed, re-grind the bevel**

Above **Skew chisels. Right: too obliquely angled to be of much use. The angle will restrict its use in confined places. Left: An angle of about 45° is of more use**

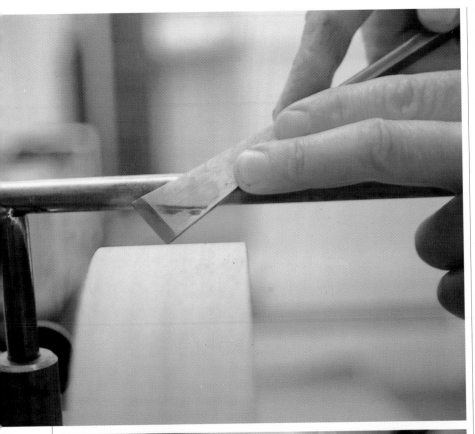

Left **Showing area needing to be removed. Re-grind straight across to remove the excess metal before attempting to replace the bevel on each side of the cutting edge**

SKEW CHISELS

For some unaccountable reason, almost all newly-bought skew chisels resemble lop-sided carver's no 1 chisels, and are too obliquely angled to be of any use. An angle of 30 to 45° is desirable so the tool will fit into confined areas. Anything greater than this will be too clumsy.

If your new skew chisel is of any make other than Swiss or Sorby, it will need re-grinding to a more acute angle to be of any use. You can also convert the rather useless carver's no 1 chisel into a more useful skew chisel in this way. It will also need the bevel on each side replacing with wider and shallower ones, to make it cut properly.

Draw a pencil line across the cutting edge at the desired angle, about 40°, to act as a guide, and remove the excess metal from the cutting edge, holding the chisel edge against the revolving stone as described above. Be careful not to blue the point of the tool. The metal here is very fine, and this can easily happen if you do not cool it in water between each pass across the wheel.

The bevels are then re-ground on each side of the altered edge. These should be at as near to 13° as possible and hollowed slightly, or the tool will not cut easily. Then sharpen as normal. If it does not cut easily, deepen the hollowing and lengthen the bevels behind the cutting edge on both sides, and re-sharpen.

I cover the grinding and sharpening of V tools in my articles on pages 102-109. ∎

Zoë Gertner is a qualified teacher and studied anatomy as part of her degree. A professional carver since 1980, she works by commission and teaches woodcarving to people of all ages from eight years upwards, and from all walks of life. Zoë lives and works in Somerset and her work can be found in local churches and in private collections all over the world.

Above **Place the cutting edge at right angles to the stone. Drawing the tool across the surface, re-grind each side equally, removing metal from the heel towards the cutting edge to create a shallow bevel**

Most second-hand tools will require this attention before they are useable, as will a gouge with an inside bevel from mis-handling with a slipstone, or carving tools which are not made sharpened and ready for use.

FASCINATING FOOTWEAR

DAVID THORNABY BROUGH

THE CARVING OF A SHOE IS AN EASY PROJECT FOR A BEGINNER AND COULD LEAD ON TO A COLLECTION OF HISTORICAL FOOTWEAR IN WOOD.

Footwear is as old as mankind itself. When first we climbed out of trees and began walking upright to hunt and kill for survival we covered our feet for protection. Little has changed. We still cover our feet and each year billions of pounds are spent on footwear.

Styles vary from country to country, region to region. They have been used as barter in place of money, carried armies to victory in mud splattered battle fields, and played their part in reaching the South Pole and the top of Mount Everest.

Countless books have been devoted to the history and development of boots and shoes, as evidenced, no doubt, in your own local library.

For my part I became fascinated by the subject as a woodcarving interest in the early 1980's and here, a decade later, I am still devoted (my wife says obsessed) by the challenge that each carved boot brings. The variety is endless. Just look around you. On the tube, the bus or train, in the supermarket, restaurants or merely walking down the street. You don't come across many folks without them. Each boot (substitute shoes if you wish) is as individual as the person wearing it. It is the one piece of apparel that moulds itself to you. Take off a shirt or jacket and it loses shape — take off a boot and note how it stands erect in the shape of your foot.

Part of the ever growing collection of carvings of historic footwear

Tools

⅛" V-tool
No 29 front bent spoon gouge
No 2 ¼" corner chisel
No 2 ⁷/₁₆" corner chisel
Straight gouges
No 3 ¾"
No 4 ¼"
No 5 ⁷/₁₆"
No 9 ³/₁₆"
No 10 ⁵/₁₆"

These are all the chisels you require to carve the boot in this exercise.

Obviously, if you wish to make a bigger boot you would use larger chisel sizes accordingly.

Wood

Choice of wood is a personal thing, but for me the best timber is kiln-dried lime. It carves easily, and is ideal for staining and polishing. A word of caution to those of you beginning wood carving for the first time — ensure that the grain in the wood is as straight as possible and dense. Remember that at all times during the carving you should be observing and thinking ahead. I consider that 60 per cent of the work is looking and 40 per cent actually carving.

A good size of boot to start with is approximately 4″ x 2″ x 1¾″

just above the sole and cut with long sweeping motions towards and around the toe. Turn the boot and do likewise on the same side toward and around the heel. Turn the boot over, and do the same on the other side. At this point you should round slightly more on one side of the toe than the other. This will create the effect of a right or left boot. Obviously you need to shape the sole on the selected side accordingly.

The boot-strap

Next place the boot toe down in the vice, to create the loop — the strap used for pulling on the boot. Take your ⁷/₁₆″ 11mm corner chisel and make a cut of about ⅛″ 3mm deep either side. Extra care should be taken on this cut, since you are going into the endgrain, and there is a danger of splitting down the grain if you are

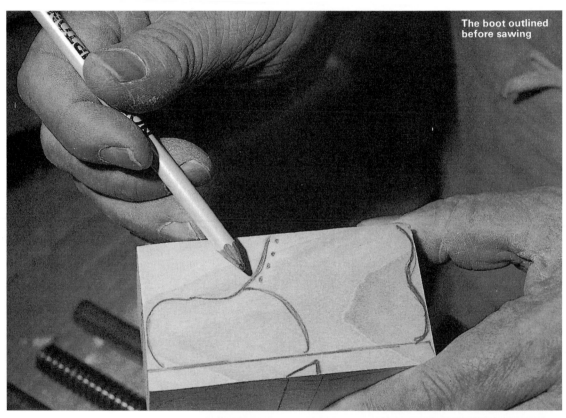

The boot outlined before sawing

100mm x 50mm x 45mm. You can use a template of a boot or, as I do, simply draw freehand direct on to the wood. By drawing freehand you ensure that each boot is unique. The first stage is to use a fretsaw, either hand or electric, and cut out unwanted wood, leaving you with the basic shape. Remember to cut out the 'V' on the underneath, that separates the heel from the ball.

There is no need to use sophisticated machinery to secure the boot in place. I use a bench vice and find it effective. Place the boot in the vice on its side. Using the ⅛″ 3mm V-tool cut a ¼″ 6mm deep groove right round the boot to separate the sole from the upper.

Next shape the rounded toe using the ⅜″ 9.5mm corner chisel. Begin at the middle of the boot

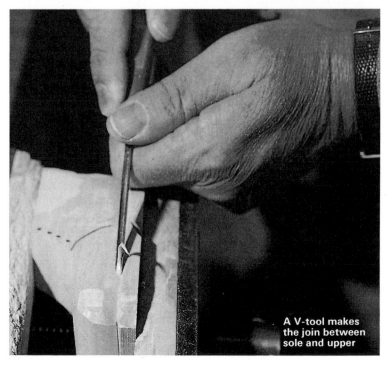

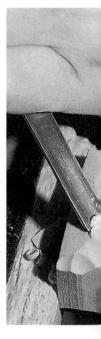

A V-tool makes the join between sole and upper

too heavy. With the same chisel come into the loop from the side to form a small V. If the top cut is not deep enough for your liking, then you can cut down and take in from the side to give a bigger loop. Replace the boot in the vice on its side, and with the same chisel remove the high spot left by the cuts, to create a rounded effect on the top where it joins the loop. Repeat this procedure on the other side.

Cutting in the bootstrap

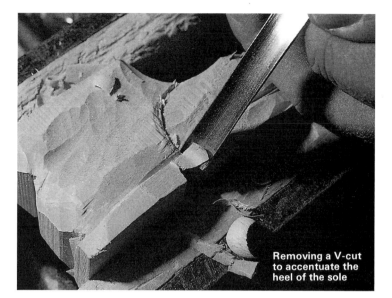

Removing a V-cut to accentuate the heel of the sole

Separating the flaps from the tongue

Place the boot in the vice toe uppermost and side on. Using a pencil, draw in two lines ½" 13mm apart to create the flaps on either side of the tongue; where the shoe lace' eyelets are positioned. Using a No 3 x ¾" 19mm straight gouge cut into each line to about ⅛" 3mm deep. For these cuts you must take the same care as you did on the loop, as you are going into the endgrain.

This next cut is very important since it will give you the shape of the tongue. Position your chisel in about the middle of the tongue and angle down into the cut that you made on the pencil line. In other words you are cutting a V-shape similar to the loop. Repeat this on both sides of the tongue. When you have angled out the flaps you will be left with a high spot in the centre of the tongue. Make use of this and with a No 9 x ³/₁₆" 5mm gouge make three grooves cutting down gently from the top, either left or right

Hollowing creates the flare at the top of the boot

depending on whether it is a left or right boot. This will give the effect of folds in the leather.

Reposition the boot in the vice side on, to shape out the side 'leg' of the boot. Take the base of the loop as the level to which you will cut down from the top of the leg. This will create the slight bulbous effect you see on a well worn boot. Use a No 5 x ⁷/₁₆" 11mm gouge and, beginning at the flap end, scoop downward and continue along to the side of the loop. Turn the boot round and repeat on the other side.

Leaving the boot in that position and using the same chisel, mark down the pencil line that runs from the bottom of the flap to the V-cut on the sole. This cut should be about ¹/₁₆" 1.6mm deep. Angle

the chisel and cut out the mark from the front — in other words pointing toward the back of the boot. Then finish off by cutting out the 'V' from front to back on the sole.

Hollowing out

We are now nearing completion and about to hollow out the top and determine the thickness of the tongue. Draw a pencil mark linking the back ends of the flaps then continue the line all the way around the top, about ¼" 6mm in from the sides. Keeping within the pencil line, and a No 4 x ¼" 6mm gouge and working from the back of the boot make a series of cuts around the top of the boot. Having

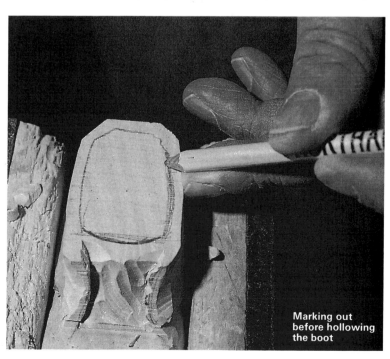

Marking out before hollowing the boot

Start off hollowing with a straight gouge, changing to more bent tools as the hollow deepens.

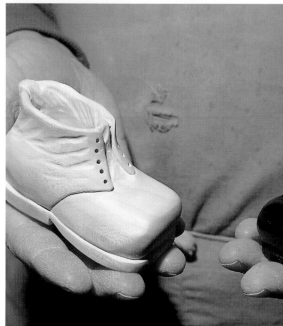

The tongue and flaps are carefully refined after hollowing the boot

gone all the way round repeat the process, this time cutting slightly deeper. Remember to remove the waste as you proceed.

Change over to a No 10 x ⁵/₁₆" 8mm and continue scooping. Be careful not to weaken the side walls by cutting too heavily. From personal choice I normally stop when I am level with the bottom of the tongue, however, you determine your own inside depth. To add a touch of authenticity, undercut to form the indentation where the heel of the foot would bed itself against the back of the boot. Do the same under the back of the tongue, using a No 29 front bent spoon gouge.

You will notice that the top of the tongue is still joined to the sides of the boot. This is to ensure that when you are hollowing out you do not break off the tongue. Separate it from the side flaps using a No 2 x ⁷/₁₆" 11mm; make a shallow V-cut on either side at the top of the tongue.

That completes the cutting stages, but before sanding drill out the eyelets. Simply mark out pencil dots where you wish the eyelets to be on each flap and then drill through accordingly.

I use a medium grade abrasive paper, as it allows me to continue the shaping of the boot — particularly on the hollow just below the rim, around the loop,

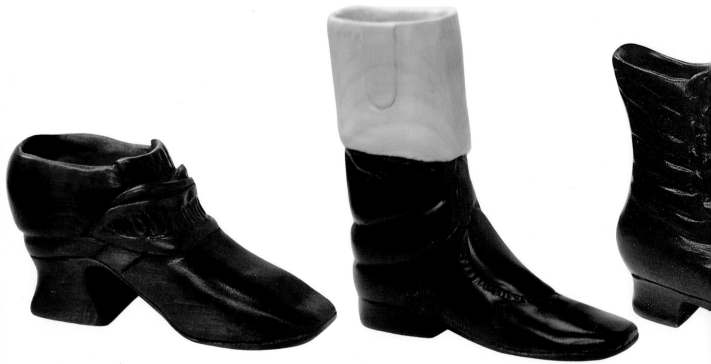

and on the toe, heel and sole areas, not forgetting the inside and the flaps.

Finishing

There are several options for finishes: two or three coats of boiled linseed oil which will protect the wood and leave it in its natural colour; two or three coats of clear varnish, but my preference is to stain the boot either brown or black with Liberon spirit based dye. I follow this with two or three coats of Ronseal spray satin finish varnish, leaving about 30 minutes between coats. It is left overnight before applying three or four coats of wax furniture polish. This not only enhances the appearance, but produces an authentic smell to the boot. Please avoid beeswax, since you will find it retains finger marks.

I hope my fellow woodcarvers will forgive me if I have over simplified the instructions, but I have endeavoured not to baffle with technical detail. The more experienced of you will, I hope, adapt my methods to suit your own experience.∎

The eyes are drilled and the boot sanded smooth, the boot on the right has been stained and polished

Barry Black's wooden boot collection has grown to 500 items

BARRY'S BOOT COLLECTION

Barry Black collects timber, and to display his collection of woods he carves a boot in each sample. To show off his collection, now standing at some 500 specimens, Barry has built a display case, with a compartment for each boot.

The boots are carved using a Dremel power tool, and Barry has become sought after to demonstrate his boot making skills. Barry is a carpenter and joiner and his contacts in the trade have enabled him to increase his collection. Barry also carves other subjects for sale at crafts shows, turns wood, and restores and makes furniture for a few lucky clients.

An Australian cedar boot (*Toona australis*)

A boot in snake wood (*Piratinera guianensis*)

RELIEF PAT

I used to spend almost as much time agonising over and perfecting my relief carving patterns as I did on the actual carving. Now, although the artistic and creative parts of the process still take up considerable time, they are much more enjoyable. I have managed to simplify the mechanical aspects, and partly compensate for my moderate drawing skills, by using references and some basic techniques.

Rich sources

First it is important to find just the right subject. Photographs taken on foreign holidays or in local beauty spots, reference books, magazines, newspapers – all can be excellent sources of ideas.

If you want to copy printed materials exactly, you should get permission from the publishers first, particularly if the carving will be entered in competition or offered for sale, otherwise you will be infringing their copyright.

However, it is often better to adapt images, or use combinations of different elements. In this way you can create an interesting and original pattern.

Essential details

Whatever the source of ideas, when it comes to adding accurate detail, good reference books – readily available from your local library – are indispensable.

You don't need every detail on your pattern. Although they may be important to the finished carving, they can often be added later. Use reference books, your original photograph or a simple notation on your pattern to remind you what to do when you get to that part. For example, if you are carving a roof, it is a waste of time to draw in every shingle on the pattern or wood blank; a simple representation to show the size and shape will do fine.

The details that *are* necessary for the pattern will outline the main elements and provide guidance for taking out the bulk of waste wood. Details that show where to leave extra thickness for intricate work, or on which level each part is, are also important.

Reproduction techniques

I use three basic techniques for reproducing patterns: a pantograph, tracing paper and a photocopier. They are straightforward and don't require advanced drawing skills. Which one you choose will depend on your source.

Pantograph

The pantograph allows you to trace an outline or details from your photograph or other source onto another piece of paper without damaging the original. You can automatically scale the image up or down as required.

Another advantage when using the pantograph is that you can still see the original clearly. In a complicated scene or one that does not have clean outlines, you can reproduce the subject more readily than with tracing paper. You do have to work with a steady hand though, and may have to smooth out some lines on your copy afterwards.

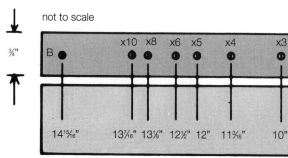

not to scale

¾"

B x10 x8 x6 x5 x4 x3

14¹⁵⁄₁₆"   13⁷⁄₁₆" 13⅛" 12½" 12" 11¾₆"   10"

'ERNS

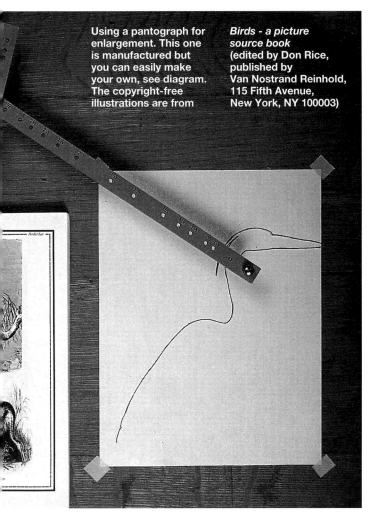

Using a pantograph for enlargement. This one is manufactured but you can easily make your own, see diagram. The copyright-free illustrations are from *Birds - a picture source book* (edited by Don Rice, published by Van Nostrand Reinhold, 115 Fifth Avenue, New York, NY 100003)

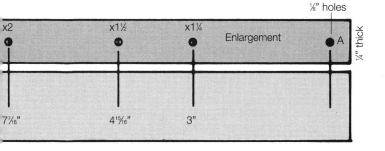

Making a pantograph

This simple device consists of four identical sticks with holes drilled to act as pivots and to set the desired enlargement.

Using the pattern, make the sticks 16in long, ¾in wide and ¼in thick, carefully drilling the holes at the correct distances from the first hole. Mark the ends A and B, and mark the enlargements by each hole as shown.

Use short ⅛in bolts to hold the sticks together at the pivots, leaving them snug but loose enough to move. For the follower (pointer), use a longer bolt and sharpen the last ⅛in to a round point and polish it. Thread a nut onto the bolt before sharpening, then remove the nut when you are done to clean up the thread on the bolt.

For the hole where the pencil will go, drill the hole to fit your pencil snugly, or drill a looser fit and wrap tape around the pencil to make it snug.

Assemble the pantograph as shown in the diagram, making sure the correct ends are joined together as marked.

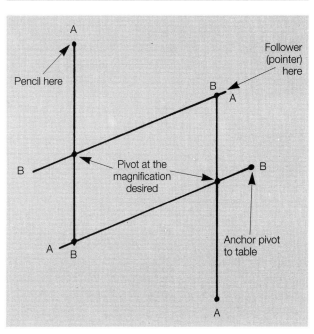

Tracing paper

This is my favourite and most frequently used method. Where the outline on the original is clear, it can be more exact than the pantograph and less finicky.

Buy good quality tracing paper that you can see through easily. Tape down your picture so it won't move, and tape the tracing paper over it along one edge only. This allows you to lift it up to inspect the picture when you get to areas that aren't well enough defined, without ruining the alignment. Use a sharp soft pencil and don't press so hard that you leave an imprint on the picture.

While you are tracing, you can make changes to your subject more easily than drawing it freehand, since you have a reference to go by. However, you can't change the size using this method, so it has to be combined with photocopying.

Photocopier

The best use of the photocopier is to enlarge or shrink the redrawn image to fit your final pattern. (You can photocopy pictures directly, but most either lose important detail because there isn't enough contrast, or the copy is too cluttered.)

To scale an image, measure the part that is most important for the fit you want. For instance, with a building the height from the top

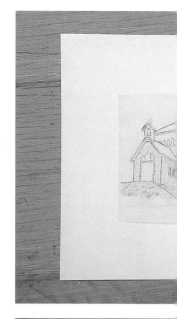

If you tape tracing paper along one edge only, you can lift it to check details without ruining the alignment

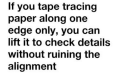

of the roof to the ground may be the deciding measurement; while for a deer the length from the tip of the nose to the tail may be important.

Then use the following formula:

$$\frac{\text{required size}}{\text{original size}} \times 100$$

This gives you the percentage enlargement or reduction for the copier.

If this is too much for the machine to do in one step, make your first copy at the maximum, then calculate the new percentage required to bring it to

Original photograph, by Michel Theriault, and tracing. Note that some details such as the tree have been omitted

Enlarged twice on the photocopier to get the required size

Right **Perspective**

the size you want. If your original s so large that it won't fit on the copier, fold it in half and make the same enlargements or reductions to each side, then cut and tape the final copies together.

A sense of perspective

You may need to combine several images, which will take a bit of planning. First select the different elements and rough out how you want them to come together. Then you need to take some time getting the perspective right.

In any painting, drawing or relief carving there is a natural

horizon and a vanishing point. If you stand at the edge of a field and look as far as you can, you will notice that the field at the far end will fill approximately the bottom two-thirds of your vision, and the sky about one-third. Where they meet is the natural horizon. If it is a long field, the fences appear to converge at the far end, at the vanishing point.

With relief carving, you have a very limited depth, so the size and position of the images are the only real indications of perspective. Large objects and those at the bottom of the frame will appear to be in the foreground, while small objects and those higher up the frame, nearer the vanishing point and the natural horizon, appear to be in the background. Bear this in mind when deciding the relative size and position of the different elements.

Use the diagram as a reference point when making a pattern; it may even help to pencil in the horizon and vanishing point.

Assembling the scene

Now you have chosen, drawn and correctly sized all the elements, cut them out and put them on a large sheet of paper the same size as your blank. Adjust them as needed, sketching in the connecting details so that the whole does not look disjointed. When you are happy with the overall effect, tape each image down, cover the entire scene with tracing paper and copy the whole thing, creating one complete pattern.

Copying on to the blank

The best way to transfer your pattern to the blank is with carbon paper. You can transfer just the defining lines necessary for the first stages of carving, and keep the pattern as a reference for the detailing or another project.

If you are working on a very large piece, tape your pattern to the blank first so it doesn't shift, then you can move a smaller piece of carbon paper around and trace each section.

Using the pattern

Once you have copied the lines to your blank, you can begin work. Keep your pattern handy to give an indication of how deep to go, or where you still need more detail. It's also useful to keep the original pictures for reference. ■

Michel Theriault lives in Ottawa, Canada. His interest in carving started with a hobby knife and a stick. He is self-taught, largely from woodworking magazines and books, and now carves in relief and in the round, specialising in pierced relief mirror frames. Carving, turning, general woodworking and writing all compete for his time, along with a full-time job and a wife and two young children

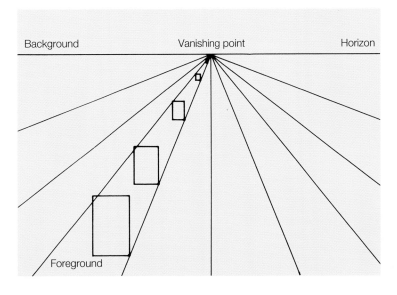

TALKING TIMBER

IN THE FIRST OF TWO ARTICLES ABOUT CHOOSING SUITABLE WOOD, DICK ONIANS EXPLAINS THE NATURAL PROPERTIES OF TIMBER

Some carvers begin their carving career with any old piece of wood. Not knowing any better, they struggle with a completely unsuitable piece and, having no notion of how long an easier wood would take, finish triumphantly.

Other carvers have heard of limewood (*Tilia vulgaris*) and embark on that. They also have a great sense of achievement, but the first group probably learnt more about tool and wood behaviour.

There is nothing like a piece of deal (technically, a particular size of plank of pine, fir (*Abies alba*) or spruce (*Picea abies*)) for teaching the direction of the grain and the importance of sharp tools.

A wood like iroko (*Chlorophora excelsa*) or a knotty piece of yew (*Taxus baccata*) will develop strength in the hand and arm, and awareness of sudden changes in the grain. Lime is too easy for the determined carver but does give confidence to the less committed, who might be put off by a more demanding wood.

Before considering the choice of wood, I will look at the way timber is made and its particular strengths and weaknesses. In the next article, on pages 75-9, I consider in more detail the properties that make specific timbers suitable for the carver.

No two pieces of wood, even from the same tree, let alone from the same species,

Above **The edge of a board of lime. The darker porous outside layer is the bark. The white is true wood or xylem. The pale brown between bark and wood is the bast**
Right **A section of an oak stem. X = transverse or end sections. Y = radial section. Z = tangential section. The brown stripe is a shake caused by felling**

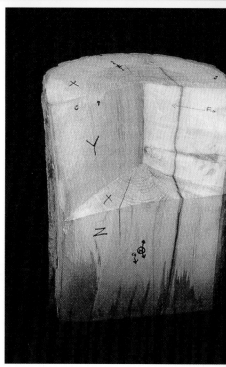

will be identical. So remarks about wood appearance and behaviour are inevitably general.

A tree grows upwards to the light, bearing an enormous weight of branches, and has to endure wind stress. Therefore the main direction of its constituent elements follows the line of the stem or branch. This is known as the grain.

These elements, severally or together, provide a means for sap movement up the tree, storage of food in the form of starch, and provide strength. The sap moves down the tree

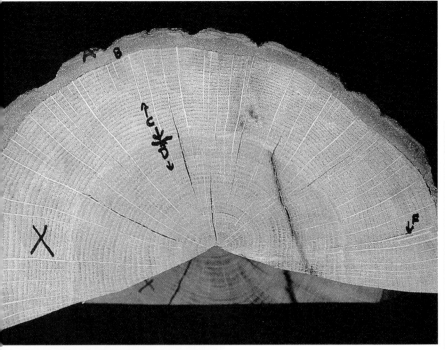

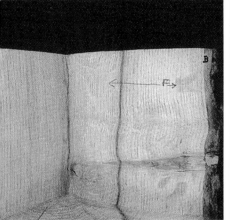

Above **A transverse section of an oak stem. A = Bark. B = Bast or Phloem. C = Sapwood. D = Heartwood. F = A Ray**
Left **Radial sections of the oak. A = Bark. B = Bast or Phloem. C = Sapwood. D = Heartwood. F = A Ray. The horizontal brown line on the right is a knot**
Below left **Tangential section of the oak. G shows typical early wood with thin walled cells in a ring-porous hardwood. H is latewood**
Below **The brown stain on the surface of the wood (E) is the remains of the cambium layer. F shows the end of a ray**

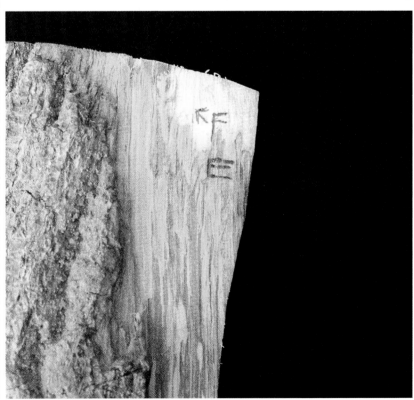

in the layer between the wood and the bark, known as phloem or bast (hence the name basswood for the American lime (*Tilia americana*)).

SUGAR STORAGE

Wood sends sap up the tree to carry minerals from the ground, take up food material from store cells for the creation of new twigs, leaves, flowers and fruit, and to provide some of the ingredients for the creation of sugars in the leaf by photosynthesis.

These sugars are deposited as food stores in the growing area of the stem. This is the cambium layer, which in the growing tree is the sticky layer between the phloem and the wood. The sugars are then used to create new wood, bast or bark cells and some are stored in special cells called rays, or in the vertical storage cells which we sometimes see as light coloured dots or clusters on cut end grain.

ANNUAL RINGS

At the beginning of the growing season the tree sends larger quantities of sap up the tree. This means the conducting cells have thinner walls and larger cavities. Later in the year the cells are denser as more strength and less sap is needed.

The result is the annual ring which is formed changes colour from the early to the late wood and, in some woods, conifers particularly, there is a marked difference in cutting. The early wood of pine for instance is very soft and easily torn, whereas the late wood is dense and cuts crisply.

This problem is not so marked where there is a gentle transition, as in slower grown timber and the so-called diffuse-porous woods like lime, which have the thin-walled conducting cells widely distributed throughout the growing season. In tropical timbers the periods of growth are influenced by rainy seasons which may not even be annual. In some species growth is so even that rings are hard to detect.

Very often the pith, or medulla, is visible in the centre of a stem or branch. Most branches and twigs grow out from this. Some start as an invisible line of cells but most can be traced back. The tree grows around the branch, which also goes on increasing in size.

FIGURE FEATURES

The grain of the enclosed branch grows in a different direction to the trunk and there is considerable disturbance of the grain where the two grains meet. This may produce a beautiful pattern, but is usually very hard wood and means the chisel entering the wood has to change direction constantly to cut cleanly.

The pattern of the grain known as the figure, can, if strong, be very attractive on simple shapes but can also be distracting in finely detailed carving.

Other factors which affect the figure are the way the tree has grown. If you see the bark of the tree twisting, you can be sure that the grain twists too. This means if a plank or thick slab is cut out of the tree, the angle of the wood fibres to the surface will change from side to side. This is known as spiral grain.

An even more awkward feature, commonly found in tropical hardwoods, is interlocked grain. This

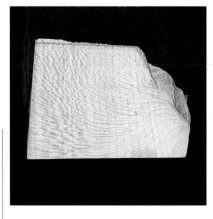

Above **Radially cut plane tree wood is known as lacewood because of the ray pattern**

Above right **A riven section of an oak stem. The pith is in the dark fissure running down the right side. The grain around the knot is typically disturbed. This branch was cut off some years before the tree was felled and the wood has grown around it. The outside of the log shows no sign of a dead knot within**

Right **Stripy figure in a mahogany-type wood showing light and dark stripes**

is caused by the wood spiralling in one direction for a year or two, then spiralling in the opposite direction, and so on alternately.

When a piece is planed it looks like stripes of mown grass. When you look into the ends of the fibres sloping up towards you they appear dark, but when you look at the fibres sloping away they appear light. This is called stripy figure. In most timbers this makes clean cutting very difficult as one side of the chisel may be cutting well while the other will be tearing the grain.

Cutting across the grain is the only safe method. For this reason you should be wary of the American mahoganies (*Swietenia macrophylla*), iroko (*Chlorophora excelsa*), afrormosia (*Pericopsis elata*), satinwood (*Chloroxylon swietenia*), obeche (*Triplochiton scleroxylon*), utile (*Entandrophragma utile*), khaya (*Uhaya ixorensis*), African walnut (*Lovoa trichilioides*) and many other tropical woods. I have met it in elm (*Ulmus spp*), oak (*Quercus robur*) and even in lime. It is best to use this figure for simple broad forms where a sanded finish could be acceptable.

SOFT AND HARDWOODS

The terms softwoods and hardwoods can cause confusion, particularly if you contrast yew, which is a softwood, with balsa (*Ochroma pyramidale*) which is a

hardwood. With the introduction of pine, fir and spruce woods for construction and carving after 1660, the importers of these timbers were selling woods which were soft by comparison with oak and the other common native timbers. They became known as softwood importers and the name has stuck.

It was only later the taxonomists classified the plants according to their ways of producing flowers and fruit. The needle- and scale-leaved trees were found to belong to one group, the gymnosperms, which means having literally naked seeds. The broad-leaved trees belong to the angiosperms which have seeds in vessels.

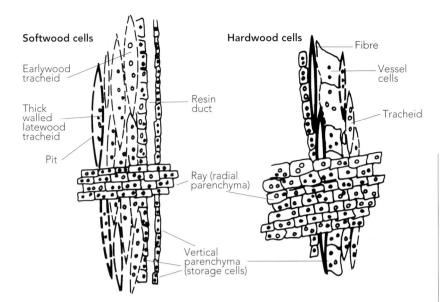

Softwood cells
- Earlywood tracheid
- Thick walled latewood tracheid
- Pit
- Resin duct
- Ray (radial parenchyma)
- Vertical parenchyma (storage cells)

Hardwood cells
- Fibre
- Vessel cells
- Tracheid

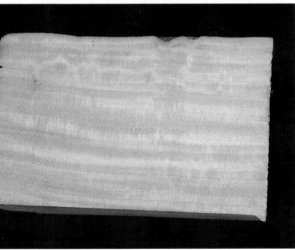

Left **The effect of splitting a piece of satinwood with an interlocked grain**
Below left **The satinwood when planed and sanded smooth has a lustre in its cell walls which enhances its beauty but it is very difficult to carve**

Softwoods come from a more primitive life form than the hardwoods. The softwoods have a less sophisticated cell structure, being composed mainly of cigar-shaped cells called tracheids which conduct the sap in a zigzag fashion through connecting holes or 'pits' in their walls and also provide strength.

Softwoods contain very small rays and often have resin canals. The hardwoods are made up principally of vessels (short hollow cells stacked one above the other), 'fibres' which are dense elongated cells and are more abundant in the late wood, and tracheids.

Both types of tree have some vertical storage cells. Yew and balsa by these criteria are respectively a hard softwood and a soft hardwood. Ginkgo (*Ginkgo bioloba*) is an exception to the broad-leaved rule having a fan-shaped leaf but being a primitive life form with the same physiology as softwoods.

HEARTWOOD

To use wood effectively you must understand the role of water in the life of the tree. A cross section of a well grown tree trunk usually shows a band of lighter coloured wood next to the bast. This is the sapwood and it is through this the water moves from the ground to the leaves.

As the tree grows in diameter, however, not all the wood is needed for conducting sap and the core becomes inert. As this would leave it without means of combatting disease or repairing itself, the tree deposits waste products into the wood next to the sap, to provide a natural preservative.

The trees which produce the darkest heartwood are generally the most resistant to decay and woodworm. Timbers with light coloured heartwood such as sycamore (*Acer pseudoplatanus*), lime, holly (*Ilex spp*) and birch (*Betula spp*) rot very quickly if not cared for. Any sapwood, being light, also rots fast. Sapwood also contains sugars and nitrogen which are readily consumed by moulds and other fungi, bacteria and woodworm.

Because of the so-called extractives which give wood its colour and natural preservatives, many woods are regarded as poisonous, especially in dust form, causing allergic response and in some cases are carcinogenic. It is wise to avoid breathing the dust of all woods.

MOISTURE CONTENT

The main constituents of wood material are principally forms of cellulose and lignin. It is the cellulose element which gives wood its main strengths. Lignin confers stiffness.

Cellulose is closely related to the glucose that is created in the leaves. Its chemical formula is the same but has one less water molecule. Because of this, wood and water have a strong affinity. Wood is rather like a sponge. If you soak a sponge in a bucket and take it out, the free water drains out of it. If you squeeze a piece of freshly felled wood in a vice, water will drip or even stream from it.

Once all the loose water has drained from the sponge, even if it is squeezed very hard, the sponge will still feel damp. In the same way wood, once the free water has gone, still has water bound in the cell walls. It is when this water starts to be given up that problems of splitting arise.

The trouble with wood is, water is lost from the end and side grain at different rates and, in most woods, more rapidly than it moves from the core. The outside surfaces of the wood therefore shrink at a different rate from the inside.

Splits or shakes (called checks in America) form on the ends and sides. As end grain loses water 10 to 15 times

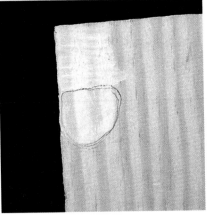

softwoods 1in, 25mm stickers are used.

Air dried timber is kept out of the rain and sun, and is dry when it has fully attained the moisture content the surrounding air will allow.

Kiln drying involves an accelerated process in a chamber where the atmosphere around the wood is artificially controlled. It starts with cool steam and moves at a varying pace set out in schedules for different timbers, to warm, dry air. This can take a matter of weeks. Air drying, however, takes about one year for every 25mm of thickness. Some woods take much longer, especially if kept in the log.

SEASONED CHOICE

The process of drying the wood is called seasoning. Seasoned wood does not mean much unless you know what it is seasoned for. If you buy expensively dried timber with a moisture content appropriate for a centrally heated house, and use it for outdoor sculpture you are wasting money. Conversely, if you buy damp wood and put it into a dry workshop you are inviting disaster.

The moisture content (MC) of wood gives the weight of the water in the wood as a percentage of the weight of the wood material. A small sample is weighed, then dried in an oven for about 18 hours at a few degrees above the temperature of boiling water. When it has stopped losing weight, the dry weight is subtracted from the wet weight, divided by the dry weight and multiplied by 100. The fibre saturation point (FSP) where all free water is lost and the bound water starts to be released is around 30%MC.

In a British summer, air-dried timber will be seasoned to about 14%. A centrally heated house will require a MC of around 10%. This is useful information when you bear in mind moulds and fungi, except dry rot, require at least 22%MC to survive and woodbeetles cannot breed in wood at less than 10% or 11%MC.

Many carvers acquire wood in log form rather than seasoned block and wish to keep it in a large piece. The usual advice is to remove the bark, paint the ends and lay it horizontally on blocks where the outside air can circulate freely, but the rain and sun cannot reach it. Keeping it in a shed or garage may ruin it if the place becomes an oven when the sun shines.

Some timbers do not season well. If they are first split or sawn lengthways into halves or quarters they will dry faster, with less splitting. They will probably distort, so if they are planed and glued into their original position when dried, the pattern of the grain may not fit perfectly. This, however, is preferable to any other form of building up, if the figure is important to the carving.

I usually keep one or two pieces at least 18in, 450mm long in the log and cleave the rest. If the ends have been exposed for a day or two I paint them with disinfectant or fungicide on the exposed surfaces. This kills off fungus spores, which are omnipresent, before sealing the ends. ●

Dick Onians is head of the carving department of the City and Guilds of London Art School. Since 1968, as well as teaching, he has been working as a professional sculptor in wood and stone. He inaugurated the City and Guilds Institute Creative Studies course in Woodcarving.

faster than side grain, splitting is worse at the ends. This can happen even when the ends of wood are sealed with paint or wax. Typically 5–6ins, 125–150mm is affected at each end. This renders useless the pieces tree surgeons so thoughtfully cut into 9 or 12ins, 225–305mm lengths.

To reduce splitting, timber yards usually leave the logs for some months to lose most of the free moisture. They then convert them into boards 4in, 100mm thick or less. Next they are air or kiln dried.

DRYING

Air drying involves stacking the boards in horizontal layers with piling sticks or stickers at approximately 24in, 610mm intervals. Each sticker is placed immediately above the one below to avoid bending the boards. Hardwoods dry more slowly so are separated by ½in, 12.5mm stickers. For

PRIME CUTS

IN HIS SECOND ARTICLE ABOUT CHOOSING WOOD, DICK ONIANS EXPLAINS WHICH QUALITIES MAKE GOOD CARVING MATERIAL

In my previous article on wood (pages 70-74), I mentioned some of the problems with timber growth which make carving difficult. Here, I describe other problems you may encounter and what you should consider when acquiring wood.

Usually, interlocking and spiral grain can be detected on the outside of a log or a prepared piece of wood. But knots and inclusions of bark or even foreign objects such as stones, nails and arrowheads sometimes do not appear until the carving is well advanced.

Dead knots sometimes rot while the tree is growing around the stump of a branch so you may discover a cavity filled with crumbs and a stain spreading outwards. To meet such eventualities you should keep all off-cuts so you can patch the hole with matching grain.

ODDITIES

Burrs, or burls as they are known in North America, are knobs growing on the tree. These are caused by insect, microbe or virus activity, which stimulates the production of many leaf shoots or eddies in the grain.

The result is the grain grows in many different directions and is usually very beautiful. It is also unpredictable and has to be worked with the sharpest chisels or rasps, and sandpapers or rotary cutters. Some burrs are a bit like dense leather.

A fork in a tree or branch may produce flamelike or other strong patterns, but like knots they can be very hard and difficult to cut cleanly.

Another visually attractive feature which may pose difficulties is ripple figure. This is sometimes visible on the underside of a leaning tree and is commonest below a branch where it emerges from the tree.

When wood is cut cleanly it may look as though the surface undulates because the cells are holding the light differently as

Left **A knot cut off in oak with wood grown around it**
Above **A cut branch of beech almost grown over in 20 years**

Top left **Ripples visible on leaning beech**
Top right **Quebec yellow pine (left) and southern yellow pine (right)**
Centre left **Ripples in a split lump of sweet chestnut**
Above **Ripples as they appear after planing**
Right **A distorted beam of pine reaction wood**

they rise and fall over what were folds in the growing wood. In splintery wood such as yew (*Taxus baccata*), this is hard to cope with, but a more cheesy wood such as lime (*Tilia vulgaris*) can be worked easily and look good too.

GROWTH RATE

When acquiring wood it is not only the so-called defects you should notice. Texture may have a strong bearing on the carving qualities of a wood. Coarse textured wood such as teak (*Tectona grandis*) and slow grown oak (*Quercus spp*) may crumble on fine edges but is quite easy to cut, because there is little dense latewood.

Ash (*Fraxinus spp*), oak, elm (*Ulmus spp*) or any other ring-porous timber which has grown fast, has a small proportion of the thin-walled earlywood cells in relation to more dense, fibrous latewood. Fast grown ash with six to ten rings to 1in, 25mm is strong but is hard to carve when seasoned.

Likewise, slow grown softwoods are easier to work as the transitions from early to late wood are less abrupt. Québec yellow pine (*Pinus strobus*), for instance, is a delight, albeit an expensive one. But southern yellow pine (*Pinus plaustris*), the same species grown in more favourable conditions, is very difficult to carve.

Generally, apart from woods like Québec yellow pine, most available modern coniferous wood is grown too fast. Suitable pine, fir or spruce (*Abies spp* or *Picea spp*) will have about 20 annual rings to 1in, 25mm.

LEANING TREES

Timber merchants do not usually sell branch wood but they may sell wood from leaning trees, which can have the same characteristics. Yet another difference between softwoods and hardwoods is in the way they react to leaning.

Softwoods put on much more wood on the underside of a branch or leaning trunk. This 'reaction wood' is strong in compression and consequently called compression wood. Conversely, hardwoods develop more on the upper side. This wood is strong in tension and called tension wood. All reaction wood is liable to distort when stresses are released as it is worked on. Compression wood may be brittle and tension wood may be furry when rip sawn (sawn along the grain).

WET AND DRY

When buying timber ask for the moisture content or at least find out when it was felled and how it has been kept. If it is wet, the intended sculpture may be rough carved and left to dry. If the piece will be very thin in section when finished, carve it to completion while green.

This works very well with bowls. It reduces the risk of splitting and wet wood is much easier to carve. Sycamore (*Acer pseudoplatanus*), field maple (*Acer campestre*), holly (*Ilex spp*), ash and beech are difficult to work when dry as they are either hard or tough. Dried beech, for instance, is best avoided as the mallet-driven chisel almost bounces back out of it. This does not apply to the pinker, steamed variety.

DISFIGUREMENTS

Wood which has worm holes should be avoided although the small dark-lined tunnels of the pinhole borers are safe enough and some tropical woods may have had an infestation of a forest longhorn or termite which is not able to survive in the British climate. Blue or grey stains from mould on the wood may disfigure it, possibly making it crumbly or 'brash'.

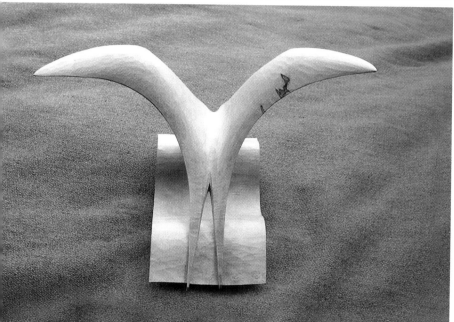

Any light patches in a dark heartwood like laburnum, oak, tuliptree (*Liriodendron tulipifera*, not to be confused with tulip wood which is a form of rosewood, (*Dalbergia frutescens*)) and walnut (*Juglans spp*), are likely to have shakes radiating around the heart. These probably arose when that part of the tree was still slender and subject to being whipped by the wind.

Sometimes the tree secretes extra waste products in and around these shakes which can act like cement, so what appears as a shake is no longer an open crack but behaves like sound wood. The heart of the tree is often subject to problems and is sometimes removed by sawmills. Lime is sometimes rather crumbly around the heart.

Another type of shake to beware of is the ring shake. This follows part or all of the length of an annual ring and is harder to deal with than other shakes. It is common in sweet chestnut (*Castenea sativa*).

CUTTING EDGE

Timber merchants sell softwood boards sawn square edged '(s/e)'. Hardwood boards are sold usually unedged '(u/e)' or waney edged, which means they still have the side of the tree showing, usually with the bark as well.

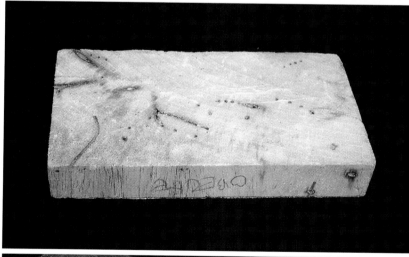

From top to bottom
● **Reaction wood. Compression wood of cedar (left), tension wood of ash (right). Note the off centre pith and the irregular colouring. The right hand side of the ash has been cut with a chisel to show the advantage over the dull sanded finish on the left**
● **A tern by Dick Onians (January 1990), carved in green field maple within one week of felling to eliminate splits. The black mark is a silica deposit which is almost uncarvable**
● **Obeche with pinhole borer damage**
● **Spalted beech**

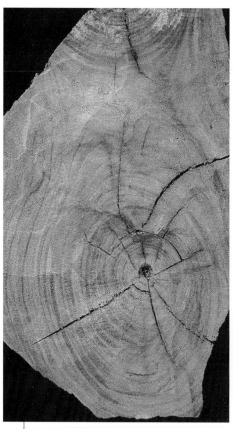

Far left **Transverse section of a fork in walnut. Note the disease in the top limb and the arrowed ring shakes on the bottom one. The many shakes around the typically large pith were almost certainly present in the growing tree** Above left **The brown lines on the near corner of this lime board are a shake which was repaired by the tree** Left **Padauk freshly cut on the end but with varying degrees of brown where it has been exposed for different periods**

As this waney edge is irregular, measurements are averaged by a rough and ready method. Serious defects are not charged for. Some yards sell short lengths from planks but most do not like to be left with unpopular lengths. Most will freely cross cut them for you to carry, but any machining costs extra.

Planing all round (PAR) usually adds 10% to the price. Most wood is sold in thicknesses of 4in, 100mm or less, as this is the thickest most customers require. It is also difficult and expensive to kiln-dry thicker stuff.

Apart from shakes arising from drying, the carver in the round does not mind if the wood distorts as moisture is lost. Carvers of panels, however, should be aware of how planks are cut from the tree.

Wood shrinks hardly at all along the grain but it shrinks tangentially or around the annual rings about twice as much as it does radially. This means the way in which it is cut out of the tree affects its stability.

A piece of truly quarter sawn wood, where the rays run virtually parallel with the surface of a board and the annual rings strike the broad surfaces at about 90°, is the most stable form of wood. The surfaces should stay flat with slightly more shrinkage at the sapwood end than at the heart.

This method of converting timber is wasteful, so the modern definition of quarter sawn-wood is the annual rings meet the surfaces at between 90° and 45°. Most boards, however, are sawn in the same direction one after the other. This way the only truly quarter sawn piece is the crown plank, which includes the heart.

SHRINKAGE

The remaining planks tend to cup, which means they shrink on the surface further from the heart. A squared block with the rays running diagonally will become diamond shaped. This movement should make little difference to a carving in the round unless it is laminated.

As I explained in my last article, it is water loss which causes shrinkage. It is important to remember this if a plank, however sawn, is left clamped to the bench for a long time.

If it does not reach equilibrium with the relative humidity of the air in the workshop before you fasten it, it will lose moisture from the top surface and cup, making holding difficult. When not working, it is sensible to turn the piece around or stack it against the bench so it can dry on both sides.

FINE BALANCE

In choosing the right timber for a carving you must consider colour, figure, ease of working, strength, durability and availability in the required size.

Fine detail will not show as well in a dark wood as in a light coloured one. Likewise a strong grain pattern will camouflage detail. We all like an easy wood to work with but sometimes this comes with loss of strength in the wood, too marked or not enough figure. Sometimes, however, availability may force you to use something difficult like yew, and you find the colour and muted figure amply repay the extra effort.

Yew coloured by linseed oil (sculpture by Dick Onians)

Woods like laburnum, mulberry (*Morus nigra*), padauk (*Pterocarpus spp*) and tulip tree change colour markedly on exposure to light and oxygen. Ultra violet light inhibitors only delay the change from bright colour to drabness.

Purpleheart (*Peltogyne pubescens*), on the other hand, is a boring pink on first cutting but quickly turns a rich purple. Usually light woods go dark and dark woods lighten on exposure to light.

PRESERVATION

Durability is a main consideration for outdoor work, particularly where water is likely to build up, as in ground contact. Modern preservatives if thoroughly applied can reduce the risk of rot but are expensive, except for creosote which has other disadvantages.

The colour of wood exposed to the weather gradually changes to a silvery grey. Varnishes are effective only briefly. As the wood moves, moisture gets trapped under the varnish and rot or mould staining occurs. Danish and Tung oils are best for keeping the colour but need re-coating every few years.

When selecting timber for particular work the strengths have to be taken into account, so slender forms have the grain running along them. It is not always possible to arrange this for all parts of a carving and you may have to take risks, but the design can often be adjusted.

Left **Mulberry sculpture by Dick Onians showing the original greenish yellow which has now changed to a rich deep brown**
Above **A carving consisting of four thicknesses of 100mm, 4in boards of jelutong, showing how the lamination is almost unnoticeable (Dick Onians, 1967)**

Sometimes it is necessary to join long weak limbs such as arms, not only for strength but also to make a sculpture larger than the available block. When this is done a wood with either no figure, like lime, or one with a wild figure such as some walnut, makes the join less obvious. Fudging the join with filler usually looks horrible.

EXPERIMENTAL REWARDS

Most timbers have been carved at some time. A wood like birch (*Betula spp*) is not used much in Britain but its availability means it is much used in Scandinavia. Horse chestnut (*Aesculus hippocastanum*) is a difficult wood, inclined to be brittle and have spiral or ripple in the grain. Sweet chestnut is generally lovely to carve, almost as easy as lime but with a figure similar to oak. It is durable and stable.

Lime and jelutong (*Dyera costulata*) are dull woods but easy to carve and lime especially takes fine detail. At least jelutong has a lustre. Their blandness does make lamination into larger blocks easier without clashing variations in figure.

Very soft woods such as balsa (*Ochroma pyramidale*) and obeche (*Triplochiton scleroxylon*) are almost impossibly difficult to carve except with the sharpest edge tools or with rotary burrs and abrasives. Obeche also has an interlocked grain.

Except for the softest woods, try out anything you can find. I have successfully carved mulberry, catalpa/ Indian bean tree (*Catalpa bignonioides*), cotoneaster (*cotoneaster waterei*), arbutus/strawberry tree (*Arbutus unedo*) which is very hard, and the heartwood of various cypress species (eg: *Cupressus*

macrocarpa, Chamaecyparis lawsoniana), rowan/mountain ash (*Sorbus aucuparia*).

Also worth trying are sumach (*Rhus typhina*), rhododendron (any species large enough to be carved), plane (*Platanus X acerifolia* or *X hispanica*), various magnolias including tulip tree, broom (any variety of Cytisus or Genista large enough to be carved), elder (*Sambucus nigra*), hornbeam (*Carpinus betulus*) and alder (*Alnus glutinosa*).

There are many more garden and wild trees which are not commercially available. There are innumerable exotic timbers, too, although those found in builders merchants' yards may be splintery or mushy.

Many of the exotics have interlocked grain. Some woods, teak (*Tectona grandis*) for instance, contain silica and quickly dull the chisels but are pleasant to carve. Some are hard, like African blackwood (*Dalbergia melanoxylon*), lignum vitae (*Guaiacum officinale*) and ebony (*Diospyros spp*). They need very thick edges to your chisels but have their reward in their colour or figure and their durability.

To discourage irresponsible felling of exotics, they are best avoided unless they are from ancient stock. There are quite enough excellent native trees which can be used instead, and regrettably go to waste. ●

Dick Onians is head of the carving department of the City and Guilds of London Art School. Since 1968, as well as teaching, he has been working as a professional sculptor in wood and stone. He inaugurated the City and Guilds Institute Creative Studies course in Woodcarving.

Jeremy Williams started carving at the age of 14, over 40 years ago. His family's connection with woodcarving can be traced back to the early part of the 19th century.

During the past 15 years he has practised professionally with work sold widely both in England and overseas.

Jeremy is a fully qualified instructor with extensive teaching experience in Adult Education Centres included Salisbury College of Technology.

Since 1982 he has run his own courses in woodcarving. These have proved to be popular with beginners, many of whom have been amazed with the results they have achieved.

PIERCED CARVING

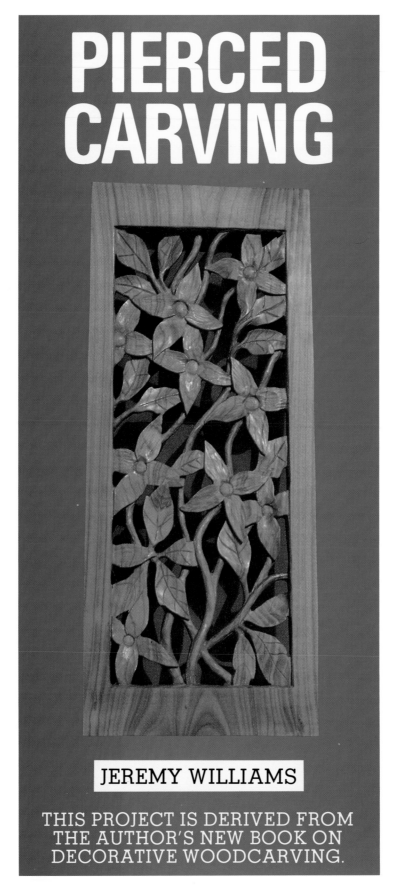

JEREMY WILLIAMS

THIS PROJECT IS DERIVED FROM THE AUTHOR'S NEW BOOK ON DECORATIVE WOODCARVING.

Pierced work is where the wood not forming part of the carved design is totally cut away. It is the type of treatment used to produce screens, such as you find in old churches. It can also be used to great effect for wall plaques, or for mirrors, with the wall colouring or the reflection from the mirror complementing the design.

The essence of pierced work is to produce tracery having a sense, or feeling, of spacial lightness that other forms of decorative carving are unlikely to achieve. To be successful, two important things need full understanding on the part of the carver. The design needs to have negative parts (which eventually become the cut-outs) sympathetic to the carved positive elements. The wood used should be selected with due regard to both how well it will accept fine detail, and how strong it will be when carved on short grain.

So, let's take these points in reverse order and look at the question of the wood first. One reason for doing this is that having chosen a length of board, it is much easier to fit the design to it, rather than doing the drawing first then having to hunt down the right size of timber.

Use wood that has good inter-cell strength, like lime, basswood, sycamore, wild cherry, walnut, or butternut. Certainly avoid any of the mahogany types, since they have little strength to hold together delicate parts of the carving when worked across the grain. Although oak has been used for centuries for architectural carving, it would not be one of my first choices. It is hard to work, and like the mahoganies does not take kindly to being carved delicately or short grain.

I find air-dried timber best for this work, as it lacks the extra hardness associated with kiln dried wood. The board needs to be around ¾" 20mm thick when planed and thicknessed. If you go beyond 1" 25mm thick the carving will look too heavy.

Pierced design

As regards the design, the subject matter is personal. I prefer to use a foliage pattern, as the inter twining stems and branches add to the spacial effect. The theme of this carving project is based on climbing clematis. It was produced as a single-sided panel in cherrywood.

I draw the design on thin layout grade paper, rather than thick drawing paper, as it allows you to superimpose successive sketches as you develop the design. You can buy layout paper in the usual pad sizes, and you will find it less costly than tracing paper. Start

w sheets into the pad by
drawing the size of the wood you
an to use. Work with a broad
t pen to give a bold outline.
en you can lay over fresh
eets of paper to complete the
sign, and each will locate
cely.

It is always better to draw thick
es than thin; you stand a better
ance of being able to carve
at has been drawn. Conte
ayons work well, as do charcoal
cks, and if the final sketch is
rayed with artist's fixative you
ll avoid too much smudging.
Pierced work needs in-built
rength, so keep the stem thick-
sses oversize initially; you can
rve the stems back later, when
the other cutting out has been
ne. Aim to tie cross-grained,
licate parts to neighbouring
eas of the design, as this will
ve them greater strength.
After drawing the design, shade
all the negative pierced parts.
is will give a good impression
how the final carving will look.
ake sure that none of the cut-
ts are too tiny, as these could
ove troublesome later. Equally,
member to check that the gaps
d shapes are compatible with
e sizes and sweeps of your
uges and tools.
Use carbon paper to transfer
e drawing on to the wood, then
er-draw with a felt-tip pen, on
e outside edges of the design
es. You will get a clearer

picture, and also a 'safety-net' of
spare wood, which will assist
when sawing out the spaces.
Hatch in all the negative or
pierced parts, and stand well
back to judge if the design is
really what you want.

Negative wood
The next stage is to roughly

remove all the negative wood.
This can be done with either a
jigsaw or a coping saw, by first
drilling entry holes. Now one
word of warning. Keep all the
drilling and cutting well in the
waste wood. If you cut into the
design at any time, you will have
a problem, and yes, it is easy to
make silly mistakes.

**Beware of cutting
into the design
when removing
waste with coping
or jig saw**

Ensure that sides are kept perpendicular, if tools are angled as shown the size of the design will vary with the depth of cut

After drilling and sawing, remove the remaining waste wood back to the lines of the design. This can be carried out using a wood rasp, or rifflers, but if you prefer, gouges and chisels can be used. With gouges and chisels it is best to work with the carving resting on a backing board of some sort, to protect the workbench top. As much as is possible, the sides of the design should remain perpendicular; it is far too early to undercut. Using the rasp at an angle is best avoided, keep the tool as close to a right-angle to the main surface as you can.

With the majority of the waste removed the contours of the carving can be developed, using gouges. Try to create as much variation as possible. The leaves, flowers and stems need to dip and twist to look realistic. This may well mean setting some parts of the design down to levels much lower than others. Use the depth of the wood to its fullest potential.

Shaping the stems will require using both gouges and a No 2 skew chisel. The stems will have better light reflection if they are carved with a slight middle ridge along their length, rather than being rounded over. Where one stem passes under another, there is no need to dip it to its full thickness. Half the thickness for each stem at the crossing point will be enough. Nor is there any need to continue rounding the

Left
Outline the upper features with a v-tool

Left
Set in the depths to give the appearance of overlapping

side shape of stems completely down to the back of the carving. It can be left looking more like an inverted letter **U**, since viewing is normally only from the front. The only exceptions to this is when the carving is double-sided, or when it is to be backed with a mirror.

Panel back

It is best to work the back of the panel before the front has progressed to its final contour shape. This way some latitude will be retained for last minute adjustments. If the panel has a border

frame, the rear of the design can be set-in slightly by using a router fitted with a flat-bottom cutter. The small gap this creates at the back when the carving is finally hung will again add to the feeling of spacial lightness.

Over-thick stems and leaves should be reduced with gouges again working from the back. It is a good idea to have the face of the carving cushioned by a clean cloth, or some sheets of paper, to prevent wood chips becoming embedded. Delicacy can be brought to the leaves and flowers by feathering their edges from behind.

Surface contrast

Now to a vital question: whether

not to sand. Like all relief
vings, pierced work generally
ks better when not subjected
ver-enthusiastic sanding. Tool
s act as small light reflectors,
ing a crisp look to the work. If
rub away with too much zeal
will deaden the look. The
ter your skilful use of gouges,
the sharper they are, the less
aning up there will be. It is by
means uncommon that some
icious use of a fine abrasive
er will still be required; if only
ake off some of the hardness
he cuts. You certainly should

Right
**The thickness of
the design can be
reduced from the
back with a router**

Below
**Shaping the stems
requires the use of
gouges, skew
chisels and fishtail
tools**

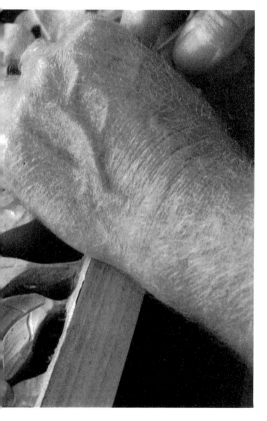

**Over-thick stems
and leaves are
reduced from the
back**

need to use anything coarser
240 grit abrasive paper and
u can clean up with 500 grit
he better.
ind that greater emphasis can
btained if there is an element
contrast of finish between
ective parts of a carving.
project admirably shows the
trast obtained through com-
ng differing surface treat-
ts. The leaves are smooth,
he flowers, and stems, retain
r tool cuts. The final finish
isted of two coats of danish
ollowed when totally dry and
, by clear wax polish.■
orative Woodcarving, by
my Williams, is published by
Publications Ltd.

Right
**To increase the
contrast the
surface of the
leaves are
smoothed, but tool
marks remain on
the flowers and
stems**

DRAWING F

Once when I was demonstrating woodcarving to a group of interested onlookers, the questions and comments came thick and fast, but one took me totally by surprise. 'You must be ever so artistic. I wish I could woodcarve, but I can't even draw.'

Surely the lady was not referring to me. Artistic! I have never considered myself to be artistic, and throughout my life everything has pointed to the fact that I am artistically inept.

At first flattered, I soon realised that this comment raised several important questions, two of which particularly concern woodcarving. First, is the ability to draw essential to woodcarving? Second, do we all have a latent artistic ability waiting to be realised?

When I first stumbled across woodcarving, and wood sculpture in particular, I never stopped to consider what skills were required. I just knew I wanted to have a go. If I had thought it was necessary to be artistic I would never have contemplated the idea. However, I soon realised that to carve in three dimensions I had to sketch at least two views to bandsaw out the timber. Only then, after purchasing my set of gouges, when it was too late to back out, did I realise I needed to be able to draw.

Snap solutions

My first sketches were appalling and improved little in proportion to the effort expended. It was with

First take as many photographs as possible from all angles. They will be useful reference material later. Key views are the front, back and both sides. Make sure the image is the same size in each

great relief that I discovered how to get outline drawings without sketching. Modern technology has come to the aid of the ancient art of woodcarving. I photograph the views I need to work from and enlarge them with a photocopier to the full working size.

I find it helps to photograph the subject from as many angles as possible, and often use an entire film on one subject. These photographs will be of immense value throughout the carving: there is no such thing as too much reference material.

The critical photographs are the front, back and both side views. Take them at exactly the same distance from and at the mid-height of the subject, to reduce distortion and ensure that the image will be the same size in each picture. Always use a tripod and make sure the subject is square on to the camera.

Copy right

Armed with the photographs, you can calculate the percentage enlargement for the photocopier. First, using the front and one side

OWER

...iew, check that the subject is ...e same size in both pictures. If ...ot, retake them if possible, or a ...eparate percentage will have to ...e calculated for each view. Then ...se the following formula:

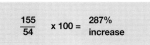

$$\frac{\text{Required size}}{\text{Image size}} \times 100 = \frac{\text{percentage}}{\text{increase}}$$

...or example, assuming that the ...mage is 54mm high and you ...ant the finished carving to be ...55mm high, this would give ...ou:

$$\frac{155}{54} \times 100 = \frac{287\%}{\text{increase}}$$

When the photographs are photo-copied with this percentage enlargement, the outline of the image can be transferred with carbon paper directly from the photocopy to the timber.

In perspective

Remember to take account of perspective: the further away part of the subject is from the camera, the smaller it appears. This can be overcome either by checking and adjusting the size of the limbs by using the photograph of the opposite view, or by leaving spare timber round these areas when bandsawing so that they can be carved accurately later.

This system works well when you can photograph your subject in detail. With a little ingenuity it can be often still be used where at first it seemed impractical.

Recently I was persuaded to carve a frog, and chose to do it sitting cross-legged reading a book – not a pose many frogs adopt. Bearing in mind that the skeletons of most creatures are surprisingly similar, I persuaded a friend to sit in the desired pose. Again, photographs were taken from all angles and when they were enlarged I drew over them to change the outline into a more frog-like figure. Using as much reference material of real frogs as I could find, the carving was completed with relatively few problems.

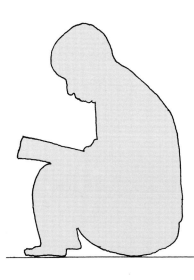

With a little imagination, photos can be used even for unlikely subjects. Here the outline of the human figure has been traced from the picture and a frog outline superimposed. This could then be enlarged on the photocopier

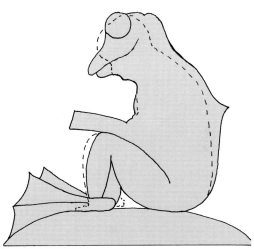

With the outline drawings, and pictures of real frogs, the carving was completed with few problems

Maquettes

The British Woodcarvers Association organised an exhibition on the theme of childhood. I wanted to challenge people's preconceptions so decided to carve a starving African child. My search for relevant photographs was disappointing. The only one that inspired me was a tiny picture showing only the head and shoulders, so I had to find a way to produce outline drawings for the body.

I constructed a simple skeleton of a child from copper wire, which was bent into the required pose and fixed to a baseboard. Using a modelling material I then built up a simple form of the body. Since I only wanted the outline shapes there was no need for detail.

The baseboard was fixed at 90° to a drawing board. The outline of the model was projected onto paper using a set square at 90° to the drawing board. The set square was held against the edge of the model, and the point marked on the paper. This was repeated at numerous points around the model. Eventually the marks on the paper were joined together to create an accurate outline drawing. This was then enlarged to full working size.

Enlarging with a grid

Once again I could have used a photocopier to enlarge the drawing, but in this instance I covered the outline drawing with a 1cm grid. I measured the timber and divided it by the number of squares in the grid. This gave me the grid size for the working outline.

You can use a calculator and measure out the squares for the larger grid, but it is much more accurate to use a pair of compasses. In the diagram, if AC is the width of the timber, draw a line AB at any convenient angle. Set your compasses at any reasonable width (AD) and use them to step off ten equal divisions along the line. The tenth mark, point E, is joined to point C. Use a set square to draw nine lines parallel to EC from each of the divisions along AB. Where these parallel lines intersect line AC, will be the points from which to construct the larger grid.

As reference for the body of a starving African child, a simple wire skeleton was built up with modelling material. As this was only to get the outline shape, no detail was needed

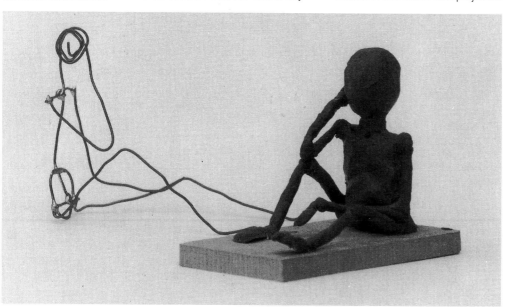

Next the maquette was fixed to a baseboard and a set square used to transfer the outline shape to a piece of paper

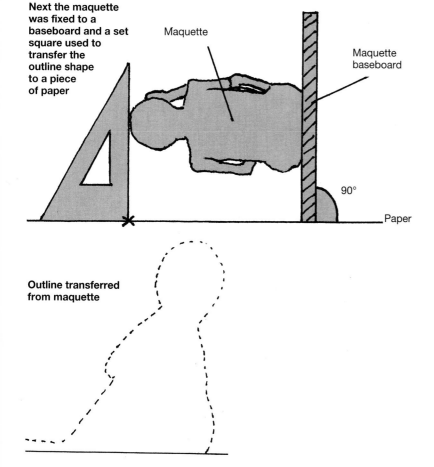

Maquette

Maquette baseboard

90°

Paper

Outline transferred from maquette

A grid can also be used to enlarge a drawing accurately

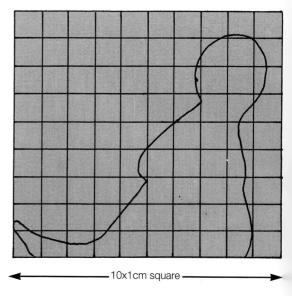

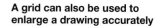
10x1cm square

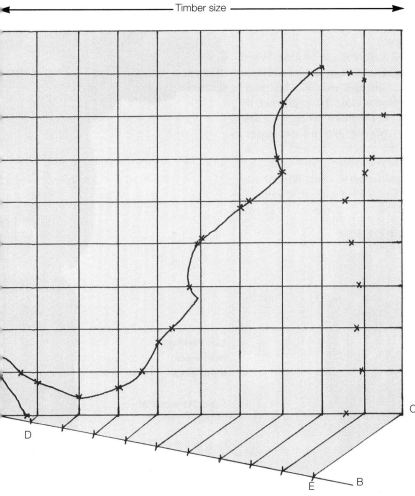

I took note of the points where the outline intersects the small grid and duplicated these on the larger grid. Then the points were connected with sweeping curves, ensuring that the line flowed easily. Again I had achieved an outline drawing without the need to sketch.

Art for all

The comment suggesting I was artistic began to tug at my conscience. Was I a fraud, not being able to draw? Eventually I invested in a sketch pad and pencils. Tentatively at first, I tried my hand at a few drawings. Totally amazed, I found I could draw acceptably well. What had brought about this change? I now believe we all have an ability to draw. We can all create mental images. Most people can hold a pencil. What is lacking is the determination to link the two.

Woodcarving had taught me to observe my subject very carefully. Working in three dimensions had given me a greater ability to understand form and shape. This led to a greater understanding of what was required in a drawing. I am sure that my new-found ability has in fact been latent within me, waiting to be awakened.

I hope that on a future demonstration day I shall again meet the lady whose comment started off this train of thought. I will be glad of the opportunity to explain that her lack of drawing ability need not deter her from woodcarving. Indeed her efforts at carving may well release her ability to draw, as it has done for me. ∎

THAT'S THE WAY

KEN FARRELL DESCRIBES HOW HE MADE A SPECIAL PUPPET

Two of the criteria for a traditionally made glove puppet are that the head should be lightweight and the wood should hold a good edge. Nearly all puppeteers therefore choose lime (*Tilia vulgaris*), and most of my puppets are also limewood. The only drawback is its unpleasant musty smell.

To add interest to this puppet I used alder (*Alnus glutinosa*), which grows wild along watercourses and was once used for clog soles. Cutting the green tree fills the air with a strong yet pleasant scent. Like lime it is lightweight and carves well, but the grain can be wild, not unlike common hawthorn.

Glove puppets usually have 4in, 100mm heads, with 5in, 125mm heads for the principal characters. As this one is a bit special I made him a bit larger than usual.

First stage was the drawing. When I decided to carve a caricature of Prince Charles, I thought that, like his great, great grandmother, he might not be amused, so I reduced his age by a few years. I played around on paper, moved the eyes in a bit and the nose out a bit, enlarged the ears and subtracted from the chin. When I was reasonably satisfied with the drawing, I made a plasticine model to check

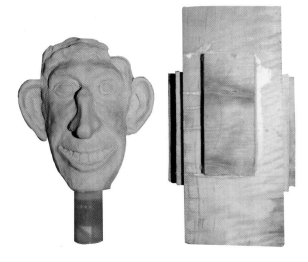

Left **Plasticine model and alder block**

Right **Here one is!**

ONE DOES IT

dimensions. Then I bonded two pieces of 5 x 2in, 125 x 50mm alder and stuck some extra bits on with Cascamite to accommodate the features, and left it overnight.

Step two was to drill a hole up the neck to fit my index finger, long enough to cover the second joint. After pencilling in some guidelines taken from the drawing and model, and fixing it firmly in a vice, it was ready to carve.

WASTE DISPOSAL

Woodcarvers always used to use whatever tools were available, bits of flint or broken bone or whatever. I do likewise but have a far greater range at my disposal. My objective is the finished carving, and I prefer to remove the bulk as quickly and simply as possible.

An Arbortech rotary cutter fitted to an angle grinder is ideal for removing initial waste. It can kick back like a chainsaw, so the newcomer should beware. However, held firmly and handled with confidence it is an excellent carving tool.

Above right
Drilling the neck

Right **Rotary disc cutter used to rough cut the front outline and the profile**

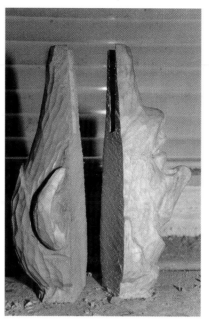

Far left top **Keep centre line and start by relieving the nose**

Far left bottom **Features are carved with chisels and a ⅝in gouge**

Left **At this point the head is sawn in two**

Opposite from left to right
● **Hollowed out head ready for gluing**
● **Fine detail is added to the eyes and teeth and the whole head is sanded smooth**
● **Hands are made in sycamore and shaped using a coping saw, axe, chisels and finally knives**
● **Painted prince helps the carver with stapling to the glove**

First I removed the front outline, then rotated the piece and roughly carved the profile, removing the corners to give it some form. To reach this stage didn't take long. The rotary cutter can be used for finer detail, but I am happy when most of the bulk has gone and prefer to use chisels from then on. The pleasure one derives from carving with a mallet and chisel is very satisfying and cannot be shared. You learn about the wood and get a feel for the carving.

For me the unique aspect of woodcarving is that the finished model remains untouched, you merely remove the shroud. The Buddhists say leave the uncarved block, to give it a name will spoil it. I think they mean that if you use a log as an ornament there is no limit to the variations you can imagine. Once given a name, such as Charles, you can hardly see another carving there.

I did a test and placed a 10in, 255mm high limewood log on the coffee table in the centre of our living room. I sat and looked at it until I saw a chap vaulting a fence. My ego overpowered me, I took the log to my workshop and let him out. I used no prompting marks at all. The Buddhists' sayings sound wise (do nothing) but I suspect they are crafty: what they really mean is they're no good at carving.

CARVING CHARACTERISTICS

Back to our developing block. The obvious place to begin is the nose, or rather either side of the nose. As the grain was wild I was careful never to venture too deep, taking a little off at a time. The head was completed using half a dozen tools: a v-tool, two firmer chisels, two knives and a ⅝in, 16mm gouge.

As I mentioned, one of the main priorities is that the puppet should be lightweight. Top quality puppet heads are hollow, so when the carving was almost complete the head was sawn in two. The half heads were gripped in a vice and 'the brain' removed with the rotary cutter and then a gouge. I rubbed down the matching faces on a flat surface of aluminium oxide sandpaper and glued them together with Cascamite.

Reliable adhesive is a must, pins or screws cannot be used. I have used a hot melt glue gun but you must work quickly and abort in seconds if the joint isn't satisfactory. The drawback is having to saw the stuff: it blocks the set on the saw every couple of strokes. It's safer to clamp and leave it overnight.

Once glued up, carving becomes difficult so I place the work on foam and work one-handed. If I did have to remove an appreciable amount I would use an electric file. When it's finished, I rub the carving down with aluminium oxide and finally with a fine grade sandpaper.

The hands were carved from sycamore (*Acer pseudoplatanus*), which is harder than alder and makes a nice sharp sound when the puppet's hands are clapped together. I bored holes to fit my third finger and thumb. Both my

Punch and Charlie

knuckles on these two digits are the same diameter, so all my puppets can be used on either hand. Most glove puppets are for the right or left hand. To remove the bulk waste I used a coping saw and an axe, then carved the hands and fingers with chisels, finishing with knives.

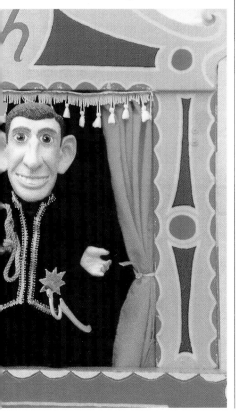

FINGERS AND THUMBS

Expert puppet masters across the Channel insist that four fingers and a thumb are too many, and that three fingers and a thumb look more realistic. If you believe that you'll believe anything. The Japanese say if there's a finger missing it looks like it's a Yakusa/the Japanese mafia. I have both three- and four-fingered puppets, but very few people have pointed out my mistake.

In the city centre in Durham there is a bronze horse and rider. I was taught at school that when someone pointed out to the sculptor that he had forgotten to give the horse a tongue, he committed suicide. I decided to give Charles a full hand to help keep me from the Tower. Put a good taper on the wrists so they don't clash together when the puppet claps its hands.

A unique feature of my puppets is that they all have legs; they perform standing with their feet on the stage. The leg and shoe were two pieces of sycamore 1in, 25mm square hot melt glued together, whittled and finished with an electric file. I painted the components using Humbrol acrylic colours. The glove is made from strong dark cotton which is stapled to the carved components. The final stage is to make the clothes, but this is perhaps more suited to a needlework magazine.

I steal a march on all other woodcarvers because their work stands on view for criticism, whereas my puppets are continually moving, even if only slightly, which is enough to deceive. I put a few appropriate words in his mouth, a few errs, ones, the odd Camilla and in a well worn Punch and Judy phrase, 'That's the way one does it'. ●

Ken Farrell spent forty years working in forestry and horticulture, and was a self-taught hobby carver.
Punch and Judy crossed his path a few times over the years so after some research he plucked up courage and became a puppeteer. He crafts the puppets in the traditional way, makes all the necessary props, and performs at fetes, fairs and private parties.

How does a complete beginner, who has only previously carved in low relief, manage when faced with the prospect of producing a sculpture in the round? I have been teaching carving for a good number of years, and many times at the start of a course, when the choice of subject comes up, I have heard beginners say: 'Oh, I couldn't do that, it's too difficult.'

What is seldom realised is that experienced carvers get just as many doubts at the beginning of a piece. When you look at a finished carving you never know how many tears were shed in its creation, what problems were encountered or how they were overcome.

Not so long ago I held a series of tutorials to help beginners progress to more complex subjects. The following is just one person's experience. Her name is Joy.

The design

Previously Joy had only carved in low relief and this was to be her first attempt at carving in the round. The subject, a curlew, was purposely chosen to tax her ability and was something Joy would probably not have undertaken without some guidance. In taking on this project she was able to progress rapidly to more complex work and to gain confidence.

These are some of her thoughts, hopes and tribulations when she was thrown in at the deep end.

Joy: 'At first I thought it all rather daunting. Actually to have to carve a bird in the round. My goodness, how would I manage to overcome the carving of the very thin beak and the slender legs? It would have to be a bird seen locally. Could I start with a curlew and see what happens – maybe change it into something else? If the beak broke off, could I splice in another bit of wood?'

Jeremy: 'Let's think through the design. It's going to be virtually impossible to carve the full length of the legs without the wood snapping. Why not have the bird wading – after all it is a wading bird. This would mean you would only see the top half of the legs. Also the beak can dip into the water, and for extra support let's

CARVING WITH JOY

JEREMY WILLIAMS TAKES ONE OF HIS PUPILS THROUGH HER FIRST CARVING IN THE ROUND

have some reeds by the tail.

'If you are going to splice in wood, you need to do it early on. After the head is shaped it would be too late to make changes – the spliced piece would look like a stick coming out of a ball.'

Joy: 'Have it feeding among stones?'

Jeremy: 'Do curlews spend much time near rocks? I see them as marshland or estuary birds messing about in mud, but put some stones in if you want. It is essential to carve what you have in mind, don't try to follow my thoughts.

'So let's start by choosing the wood and then do a side-on drawing.'

Joy: 'I was presented with a block of limewood and it was almost impossible to imagine a bird emerging from this shapeless object.'

During the first session, Joy ▮ to get to grips with the look c curlew and do some drawi There was quite a lot of hea searching about the drawing. lives near the sea and must h seen literally hundreds of bir Various bird books w consulted to find a curlew wadi

Joy: 'Did I know enough ab curlews to carve one? As I live a creek, with plenty of bird lif peered through binoculars, the birds were unobligingly fly off with irritated cries.

'I looked at lots of boo eagerly searching out wad birds. What did a curlew re look like? Jeremy had said I m be able to "see" the bird. Cou "see" the detail? What are the feathers really like?'

Using her drawing, the out was put on the block of lime. wood measured 300 x 16 110mm, 11¾ x 6¼ x 4¼in allow plenty of thickness for base to be developed la Shrinkage cracks were presen one end, but as they did not right through, it was possible use that end for the tail supporting reeds. The profile bandsawn to shape.

Joy: 'Jeremy suggested t between the neck and the ba and also between the legs and reeds, pilot holes should be dri then enlarged with gouges.'

Curlew profile on the wood, the raised area by the beak allows for detail on the base

The carving

Because of the width of the base, it was not possible to cut the plan view of the bird with the bandsaw. Body shaping had to be done by hand with carving tools. Deep fluted gouges (No 8 or 9) were used for rapid wood removal, but care was needed to ensure they did not groove any of the convex areas. For these, shallow-flute types (No 3 or 4) were used.

Jeremy: 'Use a 19mm, ¾in No 3 gouge for shaping the body. The trouble using one with too steep a sweep, like a No 9, is you could take off too much wood from the back and also you could create grooves.

'Go gently, use just light cuts. In the "dip" of the body, in front of the tail, use a No 5, or a more rounded gouge. With a shallow one the blade edges will keep catching.'

As the outline drawing was cut away it needed to be redrawn. Likewise the centre line was repeatedly redrawn to maintain body balance.

Joy did some of the roughing out work at home and discovered a problem I had not come across before.

Joy: 'I carried on at home, with the block clamped to the kitchen table, chipping and chiselling away with enthusiasm long into the early hours. At breakfast next morning I wished the lid had been on the muesli jar the night before. How do you sort wood chips from rolled oats?'

The problems

Back in the studio Joy carved on, reducing the tail area to position the reeds on one side. The reeds, tail and the wing tip were structurally linked together.

Joy: 'The beak, legs and body seemed to be shaping well. Then to my dismay I suddenly found the legs appearing too far forward. Something seemed to be going wrong. If I took off too much wood my elegant wading bird would end up looking like a sparrow.'

Jeremy: 'Don't worry, at this stage the bird is a real heavy-weight — you've got plenty of wood to spare. You still have room to manoeuvre things about. Having wood to spare is like having money in the bank; you don't have to pinch and save all the time. Just slim the body and the legs should look all right.'

Joy: 'Why is the wood starting to tear? It's not cutting at all well now.'

Jeremy: 'Try stropping your gouge. Torn wood is usually a sign that tools are blunting.'

After slimming the body and

A bandsaw couldn't be used to cut the plan outline because it would have cut into the base

Trimming the body successfully corrected problems with the leg and thigh

Holes under neck and tail are enlarged, reeds and legs support the body, a temporary prop helps with the head

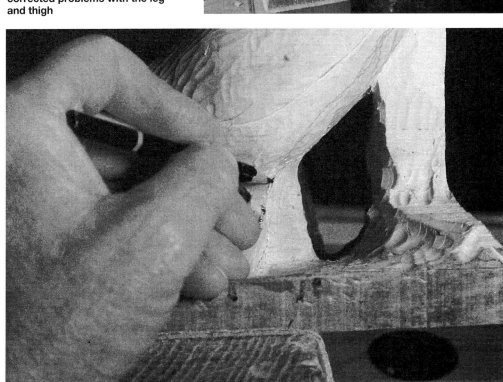

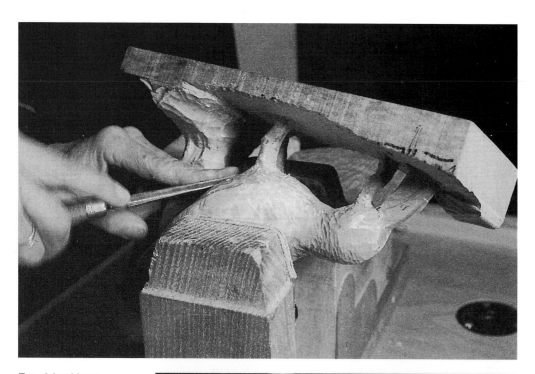

Top A backbent gouge was useful under the body of the curlew

Right The beak remains thick while the body and legs are scraped, some work has started on the base

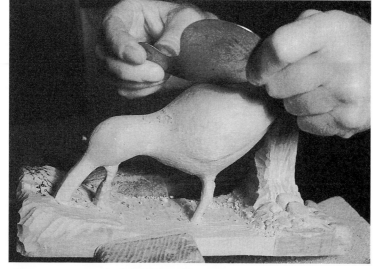

Left Carving completed ready to be cleaned up and finished

the legs Joy developed another problem. Too much wood had been taken off the left thigh, and Joy was getting depressed.

Jeremy: 'With every carving there is usually a low point when things don't seem to be working out well. The only way to gain more wood for the thigh is to reduce the surrounding body. Fortunately there is wood to spare. The body is still too fat; trim it and you should be okay. Reducing the body will tend to fatten up the thigh, but it only works when there is wood to spare around the mistake. Had you cut all the body right down to the final line early on, you wouldn't now be able to make any changes.

'Always try and keep your options open as long as you can by gradually reducing the wood. Avoid getting locked into the final shape too early on.'

Back-bent gouges proved useful for all the difficult areas that straight and front bent gouges could not easily reach.

The finish

The beak was left thick and the block supporting the head and neck were retained through to the end of the structural carving. Prior to sanding, the bird was scraped using a goose-neck scraper.

Jeremy: 'I think Joy did very well indeed. It is only right she should have the last word.'

Joy: 'I had problems making the foreshore (the base) look realistic; particularly the seaweed effect I wanted. It proved too difficult. Stones, I thought, that's what I'll do, they'll be easier to carve. Perhaps I got carried away; one stone, then another, and another – they just kept growing out of the wood.

'I never did achieve my seaweed effect, but it was all great fun. I can't wait to start the next project. Maybe all the sea birds in the creek.' ∎

Jeremy Williams started carving at the age of 14, over 40 years ago. He has had extensive experience as a teacher, and since 1982 has run his own courses in woodcarving, which are particularly popular with beginners. He contributes to several woodworking magazines and has also written a book, *Woodcarving Step by Step*, published by the Crowood Press

Right The finished curlew, Joy's first carving in the round

SIGNS OF LIFE

STEPHEN EGGLETON MOVED TO EAST ANGLIA, AND STARTED CARVING SIGNS FOR LOCAL VILLAGES BY DEFAULT

The Banham village sign. Carved in oak in 1978, stands 8ft, 2.4m high

When I moved to Banham in Norfolk from the south of England almost twenty years ago, my attention was drawn to the decorative carved wood signs, which are a feature of the towns and villages of East Anglia. I was surprised to learn that they are a relatively recent addition to the local landscape.

The village of Banham was without a sign of its own, and as the Queen's Silver Jubilee was approaching, it was decided to erect one as part of the celebrations. Since I was teaching art and pottery in a local school, I was invited to put some ideas together.

VILLAGE HISTORY
Generally speaking, when it comes to designing a village sign, you aim to collect any interesting bits of village history and blend them to make a picture that is both interesting and pleasant to look at. Bearing in mind the sensitive nature of village life, one must also steer clear of any material that might be controversial or any design that might offend a conservative rural eye.

Banham is famous for its cider-making and also has a long history of brick and tile manufacture. These were the two elements which I brought together on the sign.

Trained largely in ceramics, and having dabbled a bit in small-scale sculpture, I was ill-equipped for carving on this scale and even less well prepared for the jungle of diplomacy and bureaucracy which had to be negotiated.

Having got the 'all clear' from sundry bodies, including the village sign committee and the lord of the manor (yes, we still have such things in East Anglia), planning permission had to be sought in the normal way from parish and district councils. It was some time before work on the carving could commence.

I borrowed three gouges from a local furniture maker and began work. I had a few ordinary chisels of my own, and with a craft knife and a spoke-shave, I considered myself to be pretty well equipped!

I had chosen to use English oak (*Quercus robur*), thinking that this would be a durable and robust timber.

Top **The carving of the relief section of the Old Buckenham sign**

Above **Detail of the finished Old Buckenham sign**

Right **Old Buckenham sign in place with its coats of arms**

As the carving was to be double-sided, I used a 3in, 75mm board for the relief section, fixing it to the name board with heavy dowels - bits of broom-handle to be precise.

PRIME CHOICE

When the carving was complete, it had to be painted, so I took advice from all the rural chaps, and used a lead-based primer. This being the old method, and also highly poisonous, was of course unquestionably the best! On top of the primer I used ordinary household undercoat and then put the colours on with Humbrol modelling enamels.

There was a bit of an unveiling ceremony, with the press in attendance, and local dignitaries to pull down the flag. I clapped with the rest, but as the Union Jack snagged on the carving and was tugged free, I began to have uneasy feelings about those broom-handle dowels.

I was soon receiving requests from other villages in the locality, and so began an ongoing process of learning. There was so much to discover, not only about materials and techniques, but also about the handling of

truculent committee members, green right owners, planners and the like.

SOUND ADVICE

I soon discovered that oak does not take kindly to being painted, and I had to resort to a friendly paint chemist for advice. His suggestion was to use an acrylic primer, and avoid the use of oak which, because of its high tannic acid content, reacts against most paint. This was sound advice, and I found that even oak could not shrug off acrylic primer, especially when the first coat is thinned with water to soak the surface of the wood.

Humbrol enamels failed to stand up to the constant exposure to weather, and faded quickly. I had to seek alternatives, and by the time I had made a few more signs and repaired others, I had developed a system of materials as follows:

● **Step 1** Carve relief section in Brazilian mahogany (*Swietenia macrophylla*)
● **Step 2** Add two coats of acrylic primer – first coat thinned
● **Step 3** Next add two coats of household undercoat
● **Step 4** Coat fully with household gloss to give weather protection
● **Step 5** Decorate with Keeps sign-writing colours

This system has proved successful, and I have signs standing untouched since they were erected in 1986 and still looking good. The environmentally aware among you however, will have noticed the flaw in

....

North Pickenham village sign, 1990. 8ft, 2.4m high

my foolproof system, which was acceptable in the 1980's, but isn't now. I am actively seeking alternatives to the mahogany, which carves well, takes paint, and also stands up to the vagaries of the English climate. I have trials under way using cedar of Lebanon (*Cedrus libani*), which look promising. If anyone has any other bright ideas, I should be glad to hear them. I have also recently changed my colours from Keeps old fashioned oil-based colours to their sign-writing enamels, which keep their colours and lustre better.

I have to admit that I am jolly glad to have my first sign with its mistakes, standing in the village here, where I can keep an eye on it and tidy it up when necessary. One New Year's Day a few years ago, I received a call from a rather agitated villager. The carved section of the sign had been pulled off by revellers the night before, and had been found standing in the middle of the village street. I thought of my broom-handle dowels and sighed with relief that here was the opportunity to replace them with strong oak ones. I joined in the tutting for the irrespon-sible youth of today, and sent up a little prayer of thanks for their unwitting act of public service. ●

Steve Eggleton trained as an art teacher at Portsmouth College of Education, and moved to Norfolk in 1975, where he has taught and worked as a woodcarver and sculptor ever since. More recently his work in wood has extended to the making of musical instruments. Specialising in double-basses, he carves a face on each instrument instead of a scroll.

Left
Frame inspired by sun-faded Cretan windows

Below
Starting point, a block of wood roughly bandsawn into a cone shape

Bottom
Features are constantly pencilled in as the work progresses

LOCAL COLOUR

VICKI OTTÉ DESCRIBES
HOW THE SCENES AND
CHARACTERS OF CRETE
INSPIRED HER RECENT WORK

During a recent holiday in Crete, I was struck by the tiny windows framed, often smothered, in bougainvillea and salmon-pink geraniums. Some windows and arched doorways were remarkably carved, bleached and peeling from the sun, but with a wonderful patina of age and faded beauty.

Because of the nature of my work, the roughness of it, crude in design and always with a human element, my eyes were drawn not only to the dark little windows but to the scenes being framed. Often they were old women, dressed in the catholic black seen all around the Mediterranean; scuttling in headscarves to buy baklaves, the strange rings of stale-looking bread, carrying memories of war and poverty; watering crowded flower pots and whitewashing the step.

Basic shapes

So having decided or been compelled to set down these contrasts – the startling blues and yellows of the house paint, the mahogany coloured faces – I started with a block of wood about 12in, 300mm high. Cézanne said that all natural forms are based on the cone, sphere and cylinder. So the first stage was to bandsaw the block into a cone shape, then I roughed in the position of arms leaning out of the window.

Small details such as the tilt of the head can completely change an expression

Body language

was immediately struck by how a small detail can decide an impression. A person leaning [ch]in in hand can depict boredom, [co]ntentment, misery or antici[p]ation simply by altering the hand [p]osition or giving a slight tilt to [th]e head. Will she be a dreaming [m]aiden hankering for a different [li]fe, or a weather-beaten octoge[n]arian as faded and charming as [th]e window frame?

As I work I am constantly [p]encilling in features to avoid [co]nfusion, and roughly estab[li]shing a centreline, like a centre [p]arting through the head and [b]ody. I never actually measure but [it]'s a good idea to see the figure

Vicki Otté trained at art school in Norfolk, England, where local seaside scenes were an ideal source for her fascination with colour, the bizarre and the human form. Her wooden figures are odd, different, endearing, ugly – in fact just like ordinary people. She enjoys the challenge of special commissions and exhibits regularly around the country

Above and right
Some figures had pinned arms, with dowelling on home-made wooden pins

Below
Framed figures became a recurrent theme

in two halves, keeping in mind that the two sides must be a reasonable match.

Using only a knife, I begin to whittle and as usual the 'Thing' takes over. It's a relief not to bother with feet for a change so the hands become quite a focus, capable, oversized and chunky. I also make a feature of the hair, gouging out the tresses in thick gorgon style.

The obsession with windows is satisfied by a small picture frame shape, painted a faded hue reminiscent of those old Cretan windows, with a small inner shelf so that the figure can rest snugly.

Pinned and painted

More figures follow, and this time I find it interesting to pin the arms. This is easily done with dowelling on home-made wooden pins. It gives an old-fashioned puppet

look and means the stubby substantial arms and hands have more emphasis.

The carving of three figures, like something out of Hansel and Gretel, was cut from an old beech log. They were not really wearing red socks, but I couldn't resist some artistic licence.

I used a light oak stain for the Mediterranean skin tone and matt acrylics for the rest. These newish acrylics work on wood and fabric, drying quickly. Although used with water, if thickly layered they look like oil paint or, alternatively, can be thinned to give an almost translucent watercolour effect for colour changes on cheeks and lips. I find these paints are also a lot kinder to my expensive sable brushes.

Lost tradition

I didn't see much evidence of a local craft tradition. With the wealth of sculptures and friezes from classical Greece, I expected a abundance of talent. Yet the fe wood carvings I saw were all fo the tourist trade. All were of oliv wood, which apparently has tendency to split, and either ver simple walking-stick heads o peasant pipes and spoons.

Nowhere did I see the Gree shepherd of my imaginings whittlin away outside his hut. Perhaps I wa in the wrong place, though there wa certainly an abundance of sheep goats, huts and olive trees.

Below
Scuttling to the shops

Below right
Sketch for the group of black-clad women

Bottom
Carving of Cretan women, from a beech log. Red socks were the result of artistic licence

Unique objects

Although many woodcarvers follow patterns and traditional designs, the important characteristic of the artist-craftsman is that every object is a one-off.

The Jolly Steamer was made with this in mind: I could not repeat it nor would I want to. Each figure is less than 5in, 125mm high, and they are all interchangeable. Some have pinned arms, some pinned feet. The steamer itself is roughly made of tulip wood and about 18in, 450mm long, 12in, 300mm high. Every figure is whittled in the round, and artistic licence abounds.

These tiny people are very satisfying to make because you soon get to the interesting, delicate work. On a large piece it can be exhausting just getting rid of the waste wood before you start.

Apart from a bandsaw to rough the boat into shape, and plenty of sandpaper, the only tool used was a knife. I made very light cuts, turning the figure around frequently in the vice or, as often in my case, dangerously in one hand, with the wrist of the restraining hand resting against the workbench.

The Jolly Steamer was displayed in the Letchworth Museum in Hertfordshire, an example of an ancient craft simplified for the enjoyment of all in a contemporary way. ∎

The Jolly Steamer. Figures are no more than 5in, 125mm high, and are all interchangeable

VICTORY OVER THE V

IN THE FIRST OF TWO ARTICLES ON V TOOLS, ZOE GERTNER LOOKS AT USES FOR THE TOOL, CHOOSING A GOOD ONE, AND SHARPENING

Take a look at the V tool among your carving tools. Does it look worn with ragged cutting edges? How long ago did you sharpen it, or has it never worked properly? Do you actually know whether it is of any use to you?

The V tool is one of those tools which frequently baffles the aspiring woodcarver. It is usually first met in the factory-selected set of tools you get as a present. During the year, many such tools are brought into my workshop with the comment "It won't cut properly", and "I don't know how to sharpen this", and "What's it for, anyway?"

The V tool is immensely useful for all kinds of jobs in carving, so these two articles should clear up any problems you may be experiencing with yours.

USES OF V TOOLS

A V tool can be used for marking out a relief design before reducing the background, cutting channels in end grain or along the grain, and for texturing in all sorts of ways. One can be used for incising veins on leaves, or showing distant detail such as hills or buildings in relief landscapes, as well as marking out detail on carvings in the round, which is actually just relief carving on a rounded surface.

A good one is tremendously useful, and like any sharp, efficient tool is a pleasure to use.

V tools are available with various angles in various sizes, and with straight and bent blades, which are rather confusingly numbered according to their make and style. As its name implies, this tool cuts a V channel by means of its two straight blades, each of which is bevelled on its outer surface.

Obtainable with angles of 45°, 55° (Swiss), 60° and 90°, the straight bladed 60° tool is the most versatile, with the ¼in, 6mm width being the most useful size. The width is measured across from the tips of each blade.

Anything much larger is likely to be unwieldy unless you carve tree-trunk sized work, but smaller ones can be useful for texturing. I have found little need for the 45° and 90° tools, though this will depend on the type of carving you do.

Only very infrequently do I use V tools with a bent blade which, if used with a mallet, are not only difficult to steer but also easily broken, as well as awkward to sharpen.

I particularly favour the 60° V tool because to mark out the outline of a relief carving, this angle enables you to lean against and away from the outline as you deepen this initial V with gouges. Premature under-cutting occurs with a 45° V tool, and a 90° V tool will encourage a too vertical cut.

V tools are sometimes referred to as parting tools, which is a little confusing to a woodturner, for whom a parting tool is completely different both in use and appearance.

A V tool usually has a number denoting its angle stamped on its blade, as in this table:

BUYING A V TOOL

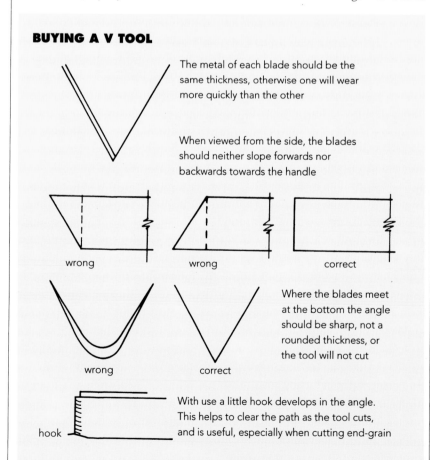

The metal of each blade should be the same thickness, otherwise one will wear more quickly than the other

When viewed from the side, the blades should neither slope forwards nor backwards towards the handle

wrong   wrong   correct

wrong   correct

Where the blades meet at the bottom the angle should be sharp, not a rounded thickness, or the tool will not cut

hook

With use a little hook develops in the angle. This helps to clear the path as the tool cuts, and is useful, especially when cutting end-grain

Straight V tools		
London pattern		Swiss make
39	60° angle	12
45	90° angle	13
-	55° angle	14
41	45° angle	15

Note that a London Pattern no 45 V tool has an angle of 90°. When ordering it is best to specify the required angle together with its width, rather than the number. V tools with forward bent blades are numbered differently from those with straight blades.

CHOOSING A V TOOL

When selecting a V tool, look at it end on from the cutting edge. The thickness of the metal of both blades should be the same otherwise one will wear faster than the other, and they should be at equal angles to an imaginary centreline passing through the point where the blades meet at the bottom of the V.

The thickness of the manufactured blades is critical. If too thick the tool will only cut when held at a steep, uncomfortable angle unless you regrind and extend the bevel lengths considerably with an electric grindstone. The tool will then need to be resharpened on the sharpening stone.

Turn the tool so its bevels are uppermost, and check that the two blades meet each other at a sharp angle, and not in a rounded thickness. If the join is rounded the meeting point will need to be extended into a long

Below from left to right
● **The tip of a well worn and damaged V tool**
● **V tools to avoid. In the one on the left the metal is too thick, and with the right hand one, the blades are of uneven thickness**
● **When viewed from the side, the cutting edges should be at 90° to the length of the tool, not sloping like this one**

bevel before the tool will cut, because the sheer thickness of the metal at this point will obstruct.

Next, when viewed from the side, the cutting edges of the blades should be at 90° to the length of the tool, neither sloping forwards, when the blades will obstruct, nor backwards towards the handle, when the nose will obstruct and the tool will not cut properly.

As with all woodcarving tools, check the blade is fitted centrally in the handle or it will be difficult to guide either by hand or mallet, which gives more control.

SHARPENING

Sharpening V tools seems to give problems, but it is easy if you have the correct equipment, which comprises a 1200 grit Japanese waterstone, a slipstone of the same or finer grade, and a leather strop. I recommend Japanese waterstones because they are reasonably priced, clean and efficient.

To obtain a superior edge, after

Above **To sharpen, hold the tool at 27°
to horizontal and rub each blade bevel
up and down the stone**

honing it on the 1200 grit stone the
tool should be polished on an 8000
grit polishing stone, together with its
corresponding slipstone, following the
same procedure.

Although the tool can be sharpened
by polishing on a rotating wheel if you
prefer, you should not rely exclusively
on this because after a while feathering
along both cutting edges develops. This
is visible as scratching and tearing in
soft wood, and the tool will not hold its
edge for long.

To correct this you need to revert
to the good traditional method of
sharpening as follows, which takes very
little time and should be part of a
woodcarver's repertoire of skills. For
sharpening purposes, the V tool is
treated as if it were two straight chisels,
joined together.

Place the sharpening stone end on
to the bench, and lubricate accordingly,
depending on the type of stone you are
using. Then holding the tool so the
cutting edge is just in contact with the
surface of the stone, with the cutting
edge of one blade in line with the
narrow end of the stone, rub the bevel
up and down the stone at such an angle
that a burr is formed along its edge.

To find this angle, tip the tool
handle up until a bead of moisture is
formed along the cutting edge. Having
honed up and down the stone, using
the whole width and length of it so it
wears evenly, run your thumb nail
along and outwards from the blade to

Left from top to bottom
● **Use a narrow or shaped slipstone to remove the burr from inside the V, taking care to keep it flat on the blade**
● **For a bent V tool you need to tip it forward to compensate for the bend**
● **To remove the burr, work inwards from the cutting edge with short strokes. Keep the back end of the slipstone high so you do not drop below the edge and alter the cutting angle**

tell whether the burr has formed or not. If so, it will catch slightly.

Using Japanese waterstones, this is very quickly formed, and need only be slight. If a burr is not forthcoming, raise the tool handle a little higher, and try again.

Repeat this for the other blade, as far as possible using the same pressure, angle and number of strokes, so each cutting edge is evenly honed, and one does not wear faster than the other. If you find your stone slips as you hone, place it on a damp towel.

SLIPSTONES

To remove the burr you need a special narrow slipstone called a knife edged slipstone, which is narrow enough to fit inside against the flat inner surface of the blades and fine enough to reach the bottom of the V.

Alternatively, the edge of a multiform Japanese waterstone slipstone might fit. As these are almost impossible to obtain, the edge of a normal Japanese slipstone can be filed narrower, or rubbed on the side of the sharpening stone, until it is slim enough to fit. These types of stone are soft enough to reshape to a more useful size.

When I buy a new slipstone I usually cut it with a hacksaw into two pieces, one third/two thirds, then re-shape the smaller piece with a file so it will fit inside my V tools.

When both blades have burrs along each cutting edge, rest the V tool on the bench with its ferrule against the edge of the bench. Lubricate the slipstone and press its flat side against the inner surface of one of the blades. Using the last ½in, 12mm of it, rub back and forth, keeping the pressure inside the blade of the V to rub away the burr.

Do not tip the slipstone to create an inner bevel or angle or you will alter the cutting angle of the tool, and it will not work properly. Test that the burr has been fully removed by running your thumb nail outwards and across the edge. If it still remains continue using the slipstone until no trace is left.

Repeat the process for the other blade, then strop by firmly drawing the tool edges along the leather to remove any metal still lurking along the edges.

If your V tool has a bent blade, sharpen it as above, but tip it forward to compensate for the bend, and slightly swing it sideways so the cutting edge is at right-angles to the length of the stone, and then hone each blade until a burr has formed along each cutting edge.

To remove the burr, prop the tool up against a wedge or block so you can approach removing the burr by rubbing in towards the tool from the cutting edge. Keep the back end of the slipstone high so it does not drop below the cutting edge as you rub away the burr, or you will alter the cutting angle.

You will only be able to use very short strokes before the slipstone is obstructed by the curve of the blade, so be patient.

An alternative method of removing this burr is to file an old worn slipstone into a fine edged 'wheel' to fit inside the curve of the tool, and rub outwards, rotating it while pressing against the blade as described for the straight bladed V tool.

When you have finished sharpening, clean your stones thoroughly by wiping with a cloth so the slurry does not sink in and damage the surface. For a really superior cutting edge, essential if the wood you are carving is soft, polish the cutting edges by repeating the procedure as described using a 6000 or 8000 grit polishing stone with its corresponding slipstone and strop.

THE HOOK

After some use you will see a little hook developing at the point where the two blades meet. This happens more quickly if the metal at this point is thick and rounded, and this is why a new V tool should have blades which

After some use a tiny hook develops where the two blades meet

meet sharply underneath, and not in a rounded thickness.

Generally speaking, if not too long, this hook is useful because it acts as a snowplough, clearing a path and cutting in advance of the blades. It is also useful when cutting in end grain, as it lifts the chip out more easily.

You only need to remove this hook when it becomes troublesome. To do this, hone it as if it were a tiny gouge in a figure of 8 on the sharpening stone, and then remove the burr so formed with the sharply pointed slipstone. Then re-hone the whole tool as described above.

If you find one of the blades wears faster than the other, this will probably be because the metal of that one has been made thinner than the other, a manufacturing error, or else you are honing with more pressure on that particular blade, for longer, or at a different angle.

In the following article (pages 106-9) I look at how to restore a damaged V tool and how to use it. ■

Zoë Gertner is a qualified teacher and studied anatomy as part of her degree. A professional carver since 1980, she works by commission and teaches woodcarving to people of all ages from eight years upwards, and from all walks of life. Zoë lives and works in Somerset and her work can be found in local churches and in private collections all over the world.

VICTORY OVER THE V – PART 2

IN HER SECOND AND FINAL ARTICLE ON V TOOLS, ZOË GERTNER LOOKS AT RESTORING DAMAGED TOOLS AND HOW TO USE THEM IN CARVING

In this article I shall deal with restoring a V tool, dealing with nicks and damaged or badly angled cutting edges, and how to use a V tool.

Unfortunately, accidents happen, and edges can become nicked or broken. Restoring a damaged V tool is less daunting if you remember it is really just two straight chisels that happen to be angled together, and treat each blade as such.

You may be unfortunate enough to have acquired a V tool which has its cutting edges set angled forward or backwards from where they meet, and not at right-angles to the length of the tool, as they should be when viewed from the side.

Maybe the cutting edges have become badly mis-shapen due to careless sharpening, or pitted with rust. For whatever reason, the cutting edges will need to be squared up by re-grinding them, which usually involves removing quite a lot of metal to get rid of the defect, using an electric grind-stone. Once squared up the two bevels can be re-ground, and the tool honed as already described.

Run the damaged tool edge across the wheel surface, dipping the edge in

....

Damaged or sloping cutting edges will need to be squared up on the grind-stone before new bevels can be ground

cool water between each stroke if your wheel is not water cooled, in case you draw the temper of the tool. Repeat this until the edge becomes straightened and squared off, and no trace of the nick or damage remains.

If you have a V tool with cutting edges leaning backwards or forwards, that is, not at right-angles to the length of the blade when viewed from the side, remove the unwanted metal from each blade by beginning from the tip of the 'nose' (if blades are set backwards), or the upper tip of the blades (if blades are set forwards).

Little by little swing the tool edge round to remove the excess metal until the blade passes across the wheel at right-angles to the wheel edge, and is straightened and squared off.

When viewed from the business end, each blade will appear as a thick straight flat edge. The tool is now ready to have its bevels replaced along each blade. Do not attempt to do this until the cutting edges are truly squared and straight.

RE-GRINDING BEVELS

To re-grind a V tool, treat each blade as if it were a straight chisel, and work forwards from the new heel towards the cutting edge to replace each bevel at the correct angle to make the tool cut.

Generally speaking, the length of the bevel will be approximately half the width of the blade, so begin the re-grinding here, by marking a line at this point with a felt pen for a guide.

Remove a line of metal across just in front of the drawn line, then repeat this, raising your right hand fractionally with each pass across the stone (cooling each time if necessary) and drawing the cutting edge minutely closer to the rest until the very edge of the blade touches the revolving wheel. Repeat this for the other blade.

If the tool has been made from thick metal, you may have to reduce the point where the two bevels meet on the back of the tool by rocking it, as described below.

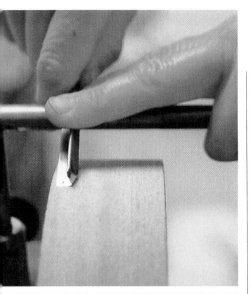

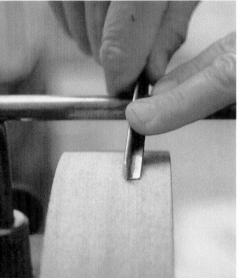

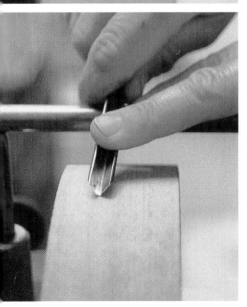

Top left **Rest the V tool so its cutting edge is at right-angles to the grindstone. Draw the heel across to begin reforming a bevel. Advance towards the cutting edge with each stroke**
Centre left **Repeat this operation for the other blade of the V**
Bottom left **If the metal is too thick where the blades join at the V, reduce the thickness on the grindstone. Start at the heel and use a gentle rocking action as you pass the tool across the wheel to produce a thinner, elongated bevel along the exterior angle**

The bevel angle of each blade should be reground back to about 27° then sharpened as already described in my previous article. If need be the two bevels can be extended by carefully repeating the grinding from further back.

Again draw a line as a guide to begin with, and work forwards as before. Both bevels should be identical if possible or your tool will be difficult to control, and one blade may wear faster than the other.

If you should find your tool cuts only when held at a steep and uncomfortable angle, extend the bevel lengths. This will be necessary if the tool has been made with thick walls.

The most comfortable and controlled angle will be when the tool cuts easily when held with your wrist or forearm resting on the work. This is the correct way to use a V tool.

If your V tool still refuses to cut properly, even though you have extended the bevel lengths, it is most likely the metal at the meeting point of the two blades is too thick, which you will see if you look at it from the cutting edges. This is common with thick walled tools.

Carefully reduce this thickness by grinding, again starting at the heel, but this time using a gentle rocking action as you pass the tool across the wheel to produce a rounded, thinner and elongated bevel along the exterior angle.

Be careful not to turn the tool too

Hold the V tool well down the blade for maximum control and rest your wrist on the work

much or you may affect the previously ground surfaces. Then re-sharpen the tool as already described in the previous article.

USING A V TOOL

The V tool has a lot of uses, but because it has two cutting blades it needs to be used with care and thought. Unless the cut is being made in end grain, or directly along the grain, one or other of these blades may tear into the line you are cutting, if this curves across the grain.

The V tool, as its name implies, cuts a V-shaped channel, and is used for initially marking out a relief design before deepening it by removing the background. For this you should use a 60° tool, so you will be given the correctly angled slope to guide your gouge as you deepen the initial outline using gouges.

If you use a 45° V tool for the outlining, the channelling will be too narrow and vertical and you will quickly find yourself undercutting the outline, resulting in messy crumbling edges.

V tools are also useful for marking out details on a figure such as ears, eyes, buttons etc, before refining them. These are really just relief carvings on a rounded surface. It is quite useful for texturing, as well.

USING A V TOOL

The V tool is very useful for marking the outline of a relief. Hold it well down the blade, near the cutting edge, and support it with your thumb

Use a mallet, and cut in a steady unhurried way. You should produce a chip of uniform width. Watch the grain all the time, as you will have to change the cutting direction fairly frequently, depending on your design

Always cut in the grain direction so the outline receives the clean cut side of the V cut. Any splitting then runs into the background, and your design is quite safe

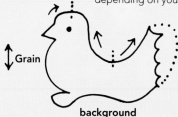

Grain

background

Loop generously round narrow projections. Being cross grained, they will break. They are refined later, using gouges

When starting:

Drop your hand a little, and continue tapping. Don't hurry

Hold the tool fairly steeply, give a tap with the mallet so it penetrates the surface

If you drop too much, the tool scoots off, or the channel is just a scratch

If the chip impedes your view of the line, break it off, but do not lift the tool from its furrow until you have to change cutting direction

Nervous
Too shallow

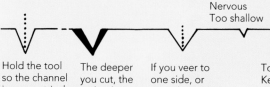

Hold the tool so the channel is symmetrical, and do not waver in its path

The deeper you cut, the wider the channel

If you veer to one side, or twist the tool, the channel will be lop sided

Too deep
Keep the corners above the surface of the wood or it will split

---

To begin with you may find it difficult to use. The secret is to produce a uniformly sized wood chip emerging from the middle of the V, without stopping cutting until necessary. Work without rocking the tool from side to side, while steadily tapping it along with a mallet.

The V tool is better used with a mallet than by hand, as you will have more control. But it is better not to use a mallet with a curved bladed V tool as it is difficult to steer and can break.

You will have most control if you hold the tool close to its cutting edge, so hold it well down the blade, supporting the length of the tool with your thumb along the back, and rest your elbow or forearm on the bench for stability.

Do not cut towards yourself for obvious reasons, but move yourself round so you always cut from left to right, if you are right handed, vice versa if you are left handed, and turn the carving if need be to obtain a more flowing line.

The groove you cut should be of even depth and thickness, the size of the chip being a guide to this. If it varies in thickness you are altering the depth of cut by dipping the tool handle up and down while cutting. If it skids off the surface and will not cut at all, you are likely to be holding it too flat.

If your tool refuses to cut, or does so only when held almost upright, check the state of the blades as described before. You will probably need to extend the bevels, especially along the exterior angle.

When cutting do not remove the tool from its groove until absolutely necessary. But if the emerging chip impedes your progress break it off using your mallet hand and without lifting the V tool from its intended pathway, because it is not easy to continue in exactly the same place as before.

CROSS GRAIN

Unless your tool is razor sharp it will tear when cutting across the grain, which is why a V tool should not be used for lettering. If a channel across the grain is required, or if you are trying to cut a narrow projection such as a stalk, it is better to use the appropriately shaped gouges (nearly always a no 3 or Swiss 2) or bevel chisels when lettering, and cut in from each side, thus safely across the grain, to make the channel.

Although the V tool will cut very well along the grain and in end grain, it is rare that a design is arranged exclusively in this way. Usually the desired line will curve one way or the other and you will have to make two joining V tool cuts, starting from opposite directions to prevent the V tool cutting into the design.

Look at the way the grain runs, mark an arrow on the line showing which way to cut in the direction so any likely tearing will go to the waste side of the line, such as the background of a relief. You should practise making two V grooves meet each other at the same depth and width on some scrapwood so you become familiar with this.

Cutting with a V tool in end grain does not present the same problems as the tool lifts out the fibres, leaving a clean channel. The little hook which develops at the bottom of the V is helpful for this, and I do not remove it for this reason.

As with all mallet and gouge work, begin cutting with a smart tap of the mallet on the handle, then drop your gouge hand while cutting along. Do not cut in much deeper than about a third of the width of the tool, and never so the blades completely sink in beneath the surface. If you do, the wood will split and run ahead of the tool.

Keep the bottom of the V tool at an even depth and do not twist it from side to side or you will produce a wavy-sided channel. Take care when cutting along a curved pathway that you do not lean over to one side like a

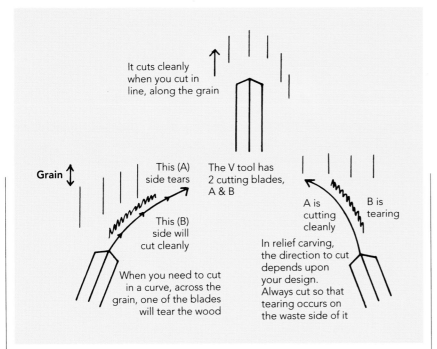

It cuts cleanly when you cut in line, along the grain

Grain ↕

This (A) side tears

The V tool has 2 cutting blades, A & B

This (B) side will cut cleanly

When you need to cut in a curve, across the grain, one of the blades will tear the wood

A is cutting cleanly

B is tearing

In relief carving, the direction to cut depends upon your design. Always cut so that tearing occurs on the waste side of it

motorbike going round a bend or your channel will not be even, and one blade may dig in.

Should your V tool slew from one side to the other and produce an uneven sided groove, check whether the blades have been manufactured symmetrically by looking end on at them.

CARVING RELIEF

Here the V tool is most useful to mark out the outline which is then deepened using the appropriate gouges and chisels.

When marking the outline with the V tool be sure to cut in the correct direction with it so any tearing will run into the waste wood on the outside of the outline, as previously explained.

Make a wide loop around small or narrow projections such as birds' claws or beaks, especially if these lie across the grain. These should be left until later to be refined, otherwise they vanish.

The next step will be to deepen the channel you have made with the V tool around the outline with the appropriate gouges, usually Swiss no 2s or British no 3s of various widths.

Use the slope of the V as a guide. Rest the cutting edge of the gouge against it so you are cutting outwards and away from the design, with the handle of the tool over the design and not held vertically, so the edges are well supported while carving.

Having cut thus all round the design, opposing cuts are made towards the initial ones to create a deeper, wider channel than that of the

V tool. The background can then be safely removed towards this channel without damaging the design. Here we go on to the techniques of relief carving, which have already been covered in a previous article.

CARVING IN THE ROUND

When carving in the round, much use is made of cutting V channels to allow the gouge used for shaping the adjacent surfaces to finish its cut in the gap or space created between the sides of the V. However, the channels are not made by using the V tool, but more safely made with shallow gouges, since most curves will run across the grain at some point, and a V tool would possibly tear.

These V channels are almost always begun by using no 3 gouges (Swiss no 2) of various widths which will correspond with the desired pathway of the channel. This is because in most cases, the channel will be running across the grain and using a V tool can split into the adjacent surfaces. Also, should the cut channel be incorrectly placed, it is possible to adjust and reshape if gouges are used.

Where the curve is tighter use the narrower gouges. Where it is less curved the wider ones will be appropriate. Any gouge with a sweep greater than 3 will cut a fluted edge to its pathway, and you will not obtain a clean meeting cut at the bottom of the V channel, but a ragged mess.

The main use of a V tool when carving in the round is to initially mark out details such as eyes, buttons,

pockets, claws, etc, before refining these with shallow gouges. This is really just relief carving in miniature, on a rounded surface. I also use a small V tool for marking out basket work before establishing the overs and unders of the wickerwork.

In bird carving a V tool is helpful for outlining feathers before detailing them, or depicting animal fur. In this case before attempting to texture the surface of the animal, ensure it is smooth and clean by scraping with either a scraper or the end of a no 3 (Swiss 2) gouge. Then, using a soft pencil, draw on the lie of the hair, not each individual hair, so you have a guide that flows over and around the body of the creature.

Remember the lie of the hair will not be straight but will gently curve around as it covers the creature, and be aware that a deeper V cut will be wider than a shallow V cut so you can give the impression of coarse or fine hair as you wish. Short straight cuts will give a prickled or spiked effect, as used in the hedgehog project in *Woodcarving* issue 13.

Since the V tool will cut cleanly when used directly along the grain, another situation where it can be used effectively is for carving folds in drapery, as in a pleated or gathered skirt or dress on a figure.

To do this, start with a shallow cut and deepen it as you lengthen the fold towards the hem, then refine the edges of the V cut using small shallow gouges to round them over and possibly undercut, and to open up the opposite side of the fold. ●

....

Zoë Gertner is a qualified teacher and studied anatomy as part of her degree. A professional carver since 1980, she works by commission and teaches woodcarving to people of all ages from eight years upwards, and from all walks of life. Zoë lives and works in Somerset and her work can be found in local churches and in private collections all over the world.

It's not surprising that when we think of a walking stick the first thing that comes to mind is the bent handle type handed out by the local hospital; they're made from peeled chestnut. A walk around the local shops or the park will confirm that most people who walk with a stick use the simple bent handle type.

All the sticks I make, I carve rather than bend; I don't much care for the hospital stick, but I suppose it has its uses. So, this is how to carve something a little more elegant, the duck's head handle. This handle also gives the option for different types of finish. If a natural wood finish is preferred use something with interesting grain like yew, walnut, or a burr of some kind. This will make a more interesting subject when finished.

Wood choice

If you want to do a painted finish then a plain grained timber is best. Don't use things like a lime or jelutong, they are too soft and will bruise if the stick is knocked over. I would recommend either sycamore or beech, they are both hard wearing. The more detailed version can be pyrographed and painted, and will make an interesting talking point when out walking.

When you have decided on the bird you want to carve, it is best to spend some time studying your subject in books or, better still, the real thing. It is well worth spending this time, the more you become acquainted with the subject, the more confident you will be when you start to carve.

I have included a drawing for a duck's head handle, you don't have to stick to this but it will help with proportions. Draw the out-

It doesn't have to be a duck, a schnauzer in beech, painted with acrylics

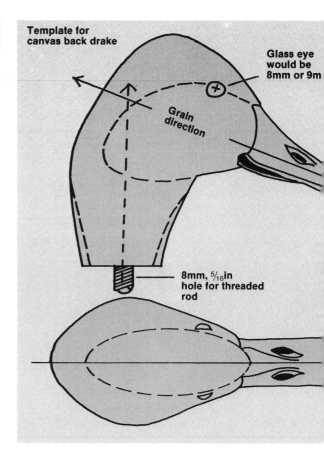

Template for canvas back drake

Glass eye would be 8mm or 9m

Grain direction

8mm, ⁵⁄₁₆in hole for threaded rod

DUCK HEAD WALKING STICK

DARREN ELLERTON

A PRACTICAL AID TO WALKING AND A CONVERSATION PIECE.

Duck head in sycamore with pyrography detail the finish is sprayed cellulose

Rough shaping
started and holes
have been drilled
for eyes and
mounting rod

line on to timber 1½-1¾in, 38-45mm thick and mark on the eye. Cut round the outline with a coping or bandsaw, then turn the handle blank over and mark on the other eye using the drawing. Make sure that the eyes are in line; if they're only a fraction out they will spoil the handle completely.

I use taxidermy quality glass eyes, but you can carve them in if you wish. If you do use glass eyes you have to drill a hole straight through the head, this is best done from both sides so as to get them in line. If the glass eyes are $^5/_{16}$in, 8mm diameter the hole should be slightly larger say $^{11}/_{32}$in 9mm, so the eye lid can be formed.

Mark the exact centre on the bottom of the head, this surface has to be as flat as possible. Then drill a hole $^5/_{16}$in 8mm in diameter as deep as you can without going through the top of the head. Glue a

Mallard in beech, carved, detailed and painted, a matt finish protects the paint

Finished with several coats of danish oil, a canvas back drake in burr elm

The line through the eye forms the top of the cheek, under the cheek has also been relieved

5in, 125mm long piece of all-thread into the neck hole; the rod should be a push fit not a screw fit. Once the glue has set, the pin can be held in a vice, leaving the head free to be worked. Do not glue into the shaft at this stage.

Carving

You should only need basic carving tools, a small gouge about ¼in, 6mm across, a v-tool and a shallow gouge. You can use craft knives, rasps or files, but you will have to spend more time sanding afterwards.

Reduce the bill to the correct width, then start to round off the top and the back of the head. Draw the detail on to the bill and round off the top corners. Draw a line from the top of the bill, through the eye in a smooth curve, to form the cheek. Carve out this line with a gouge and re-round the top and back of the head. Take off the corners from neck and start to round the throat.

Drill a hole down the length of the stick shaft, make this as deep as possible using a $^5/_{16}$in, 8mm

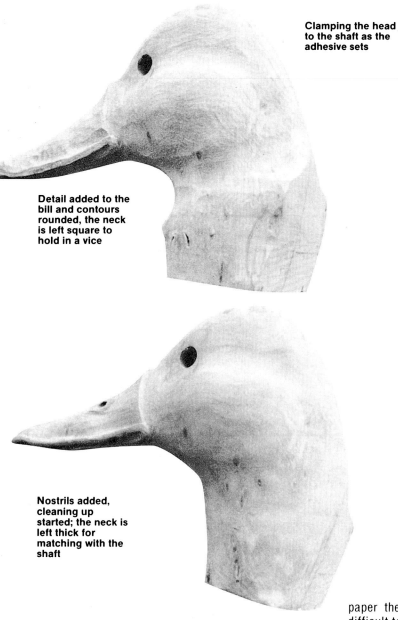

Detail added to the bill and contours rounded, the neck is left square to hold in a vice

Clamping the head to the shaft as the adhesive sets

Nostrils added, cleaning up started; the neck is left thick for matching with the shaft

drill again. You can mount this handle on a 36in, 915mm or 48in, 1220mm shaft. Keep putting the handle to the shaft and carefully match the two together. Check the joint against the light to see if there are any gaps, if so take very fine shavings from the touching parts of the joint.

Keep checking the symmetry of the head by looking down the bill and from above the head. Still do not glue the head and shaft, if you do, later sanding will damage the bark on the shaft.

Carve the fine detail on to the bill, and for the nostrils, drill two small holes backwards into the head; spend a little time lining them up. When you are happy with the overall shape, and the joint is good, start sanding with a medium grade of paper. Remember to go with the grain, if you don't, or if you use coarse grades of

paper the scratches will prove difficult to get out later. Once all the flats and bumps are out, move on to fine grade paper and get as smooth a surface as possible.

Now you are ready to set in the eyes. Use a wood filler to set the eyes in. Fill the hole with filler and push in the glass eyes, the filler will ooze out round the eye and this is carefully smoothed out to form the eye lids. You will have to work quickly as the filler sets in a few minutes.

Finishing

If you have chosen the natural wood finish you can seal the wood with varnish, cellulose, or an oil such as teak or boiled linseed oil. For the textured look use a pyrograph or small v-tool. Try to use small strokes, slightly overlapping each other, to give the effect of the small feathers.

If you wish to paint the hea seal the bare wood with thinne down varnish or sanding sealer use acrylic paints, as they d quickly and you can build the up in thinned coats to give a dee realistic tone. Oil paints will wo just as well, but they do tak much longer to dry. When th paint has dried, it is best to give a couple of thin coats of ma varnish; this will protect the pai and give a realistic sheen to th feathers.

Fit the head to the shaft wit two-part epoxy adhesive, takin care not to get glue on to th finished head. ■

A duck head walking stick ki containing all you need for a 36i 915mm stick, is available fror Darren Ellerton at Church Farn Marton, Nr Macclesfield,Cheshire SK11 9HF (Tel: 01260 224668 price £18.50, inc. P & P.

CIRCUS FOR THE CEILING

E. J. TANGERMAN

. J. Tanger-
man has
probably
e more to help
p woodcarving
e in this century
n any other writer
carver. Certainly
ane has written
e prolifically on
subject nor
velled more widely
esearching it.

wn affectionately
Tange' to his
nerous friends
und the world, he
s been described as
'dean among
odcarving writers'
d 'a dean of
erican
odcarvers'. He is a
t vice-president of
National Wood
rvers Association
d is editorial
nsultant to its
cellent magazine,
ip Chats.

1982 he became
e first American
norary Member of
e Guild of Master
aftsmen – a
stinction conferred
him in recognition
his skill as a
odcarver/whittler
d his long and
stinguished service
the craft.

RELATIVELY SIMPLE TO CARVE BUT TIME CONSUMING TO SET UP, A MOBILE ADDS COLOUR AND MOVEMENT TO A CHILD'S ROOM.

New babies (as well as some adults) spend considerable time staring at the ceiling. This has suggested a suitable mobile to some new mothers, the motif depending upon mother's preference. Through the years, I have carved mobiles of birds, fish, dinosaurs and dancers, to meet this need for entertainment.

My latest is a mobile of 16 wild-animal heads and a dragon wagon — a local circus or wild-animal show. I selected heads rather than complete animals for two reasons: the heads could be to much larger scale, and I avoided the tiresome nuisance of carving the less-interesting and repetitive bodies and legs.

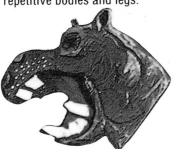

My choice for wood was holly, but any wood can be used, from pine or linden up, depending upon individual preference (babies can be destructive, so I prefer durable wood). Holly, if available, carves well and is quite hard, dense and strong, so the finished mobile is less fragile. For a one-colour mobile, it would be very white, of course, but my figures are all painted with oils to get vivid colour that will attract a baby.

Figures are in ¼" 6mm wood and average about 3" 75mm long or tall. I selected these dimensions to keep the over-all size relatively small, as well as to speed the process of designing from available pictures in books and other sources. Also, I wanted to provide surfaces for vagrant breezes and light over-all weight.

Pieces can readily be carved double-sided, and I added a fillip by drilling through eye pupils in most cases. Modelling is quite low relief and the painting makes elaborate texturing, delineation by carving of such features as a zebra's stripes, unnecessary.

Tools required are relatively few. Blanks are cut with a coping saw. I used an interchangeable-bladed knife with a pointed blade, a ¹⁄₁₆" 1.5mm veiner, a ⅛" 3mm firmer, two small V-tools ¹⁄₁₆" and ⅛" 1.5mm and 3mm wide, and a small flat gouge for roughing out hollows. If you prefer them, engraver's burins could replace the small V-tools. The knife is the most important tool.

I drew in all 18 designs and selected 16 from these for carving.

That number is quite arbitrary — a mobile can consist of only one shape, and I've made some with as many as 21 elements. The number depends on how well you can juggle them in assembling the mobile and your personal preference.

Shapes should have silhouettes that identify the subjects if possible, because a mobile is usually hung against some sort of contrasting background. Also, full profiles of full faces are easier. I only designed two in partial profile — the hippo and the polar bear — in each case because that gave me an open mouth.

The dragon wagon was designed from memory — it is the one circus wagon that has no other use than in parades, according to circus buffs. The only highly fragile elements of these designs are the deer antlers, the hippo's teeth and the walrus' tusks, all of which run with the grain.

Modelling is quite low-relief — ¼" 6mm thickness divided by two is not very great. Texturing is limited to horse, zebra and lion manes, orang-utan hair, elephant trunk, and walrus whiskers, plus a little roughness at the sides of

LION

MOOSE

ELEPHANT

GORILLA

GRIZZLY

GIRAFFE

HIPPOPOTAMUS

WHITE-TAILED DEER

POLAR BEAR

MONGOLIAN

WILD HORSE

Ball-if desired →

ZEBRA

ORANG-UTAN

WALRUS

SEA LION

RHINOCEROS

CAMEL

GIANT PANDA

TIGER

DRAGON WAGON

...he tiger's head and under the camel's chin and whiskers on ...on, sea lion and tiger. Painting ...as in full colour, of course.

The real work in making a ...obile like this is in assembly. ...ly guess was that basic ...ssembly could be in balanced ...airs, two heads being balanced ...n a 2" 50mm whiffletree, and two ...hiffletrees connected to a 4" ...00mm one. This would provide ...ur 4-piece units which could be ...ung from the ends of two 10" ...55mm whiffletrees lashed ...gether to form a cross. However, ...is would be monotonous, so I ...lected to make two of the ...ssemblies of two small heads ...alanced by a large one.

This left the polar bear and the ...ippopotamus to be balanced on ... wider whiffletree — a total of ...ix arms rather than four. All ...hiffletrees were made of piano ...ire, light-gauge for the shorter ...nes, heavy-gauge for the top ...nes. End eyes are formed with ...ooseneck pliers.

Sketches show whiffletree ...hape and design. The curvature ... the natural curve of the piano-...ire coil — elements are so light ...ey cause little deflection. ...emember when cutting the wire ... allow ½" 12mm for each eye.

Begin assembly by taking two ...mall heads (such as the deer and ...e zebra) and suspending them ...om the ends of a short ...hiffletree. I use monofilament ...ylon fishing line for suspension, ...nd tiny jeweller's screw-eyes in ...e pieces, placed so each head

hangs as I want it to. A little practice will allow you to judge screw-eye position, by eye — no pun intended.

Make the nylon about 6" 150mm long initially. Double-knot it through the screw-eye and immediately set it with plastic glue — nylon has a nasty habit of slipping its knots just at the wrong time. The ends going through the whiffletree should have only single knots because they will require adjustment to avoid conflict between the animals.

Make six assemblies like this. Four of them will then be assembled into groups of two by tying nylon filaments at the centre of each 2" 50mm whiffletree, double-knotting, sliding the knot until the whiffletree is horizontal (so the sides balance), then gluing the filament in place. Again, the tops are merely single-knotted to the wider whiffletree.

Now assemble the other two into 3-part harnesses by balancing each against a somewhat larger head and gluing on the filament. The two long whiffletrees (8" 200mm at least) are then crossed at right angles and lashed together with nylon that also provides a loop to hang the entire assembly on. Hang it and shift the large whiffletrees until each balances horizontally, then glue — and glue copiously — because you want the lashings to hold well.

Now begin to adjust heights of the various elements so they do not intertwine or — even better — do not touch. This is a slow, painstaking job, but repays the effort. When the job is completed to your satisfaction, double-knot

For a second great grandchild a different topic for the mobile; this time, leaves, moths and butterflies

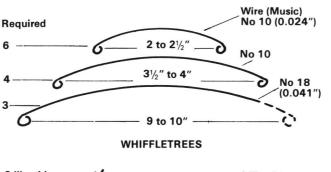

at the whiffletree eyes and glue as before.

Now place the other long whiffletree, with its two heads across the assembly, and lash it in place. You'll find that the final two heads will probably be best on rather short filaments. Tie the dragon wagon in place under the centre, double knot, glue copiously to hold it and the final bar and you're done.

You may want to spray the finished job with a crystal plastic to delay rusting of the wire and ease dusting. Carefully, please!

Other mobile patterns

Any single form, flat silhouette or in-the-round, can form a mobile, and the possible number of elements can be a score or so, although I feel that an odd number and relatively few — say five or seven — pieces are a good choice. I have made at least 20 multi-piece mobiles and described and provided patterns for many in earlier books.

A partial list includes:

Flying Birds (horizontal) from Bali: *The Modern Book (now The Big Book) of Whittling and Woodcarving*, page 42. (I have since made two mobiles using the pattern size in the book.) *Sun-and-planets*, Same book, pages 14 and 15.

Tropical Fish: 1001 Designs for Whittling and Woodcarving, pages 46 and 47.

Dinosaurs: Complete Guide to Woodcarving, pages 106-112. (This has 20 pieces, each of a different wood.)

Ballet Dancers (difficult subject): Tangerman's Basic Whittling and Woodcarving, pages 40 and 41.

Butterflies: Complete Guide to Woodcarving, pages 118 and 119.

A 7-piece mobile of ocean fish, made from carvings collected in the South Pacific, and *a 5-piece mobile of sharks* from the same source: See pages 278-281 of *Woodcarver's Pattern and Design Book*.

Vertical Stylised Balines Birds: Woodcarver's Pattern and Design Book, page 186. ∎

Required

6 —————— 2 to 2½" — **Wire (Music) No 10 (0.024")** · **No 10**

4 —————— 3½" to 4" — **No 18 (0.041")**

3 —————— 9 to 10" —

WHIFFLETREES

2 like this ———   1 like this

├ 2"   2"   9 or 10"

HARNESS DETAIL

WILDLIFE IN ACTION

THERE ARE TIMES WHEN CAPTURING A SENSE OF MOVEMENT MAY BE MORE IMPORTANT THAN ACCURATE REPRESENTATION. JEREMY WILLIAMS EXPLAINS WHY

Despite hours of painstaking effort, at the end of the day, a carving can still retain a 'wooden' look. No amount of surface decoration can change this because the problem lies in the original design concept. In some cases this static treatment may not matter very much. If the subject is recumbent, a dog asleep for example, the feeling of immobility may even be desirable. But where movement, or action, are primary ingredients of a design, a sense of heaviness and lack of animation must be avoided at all costs.

You can achieve the right effect by making the feeling of movement the dominant design factor and suppressing more minor aspects of detail. Think about what you see when you look at a moving object. For a moment, imagine you are standing on a railway platform. An express train rushes through the station. Do you see the minor detail, the spokes of the wheels, the faces of the passengers looking out, or are you just aware of the general outline of the engine and carriages?

What would you draw? All the detail, or a slightly blurred image? My guess is that most people would go for the latter. And that is what should be carved if movement is to be captured.

MAKING A BREAK

In three-dimensional carving it is not quite so simple as just drawing a blurred image on paper. For one thing, the work may have to have some form of base to support it. Then the carving and base need to be divorced visually; whether they are from the same piece of wood, or comprise separate components. It is necessary for eye and brain to travel from one to the other and know that a change of emphasis has taken place.

With carvings that stand on plinths this can be done in a variety of

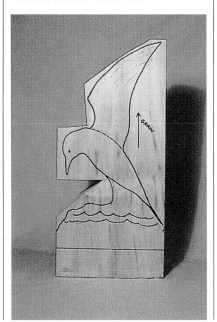
The tern is drawn onto a piece of lime, 4in, 100mm thick, ready for carving

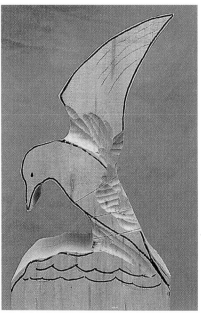
The rough outline of the bird is carved

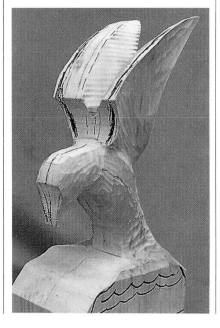
Side view of bird to show wing spacing

ways. For example, a sculpture of an athlete could be modelled to stand on a foot with the heel raised. This would serve as a break line between the plinth and the carving, as well as imparting a sense of movement. For dolphins and birds, stems or wedges made from metal or acrylic are favourite methods employed to 'lift' the work, but sometimes the result can look contrived.

In many ways it is better to just let the carving grow out of the plinth. This invariably means using differing treatments of surface texture to make the visual break between the two, but it does bring a greater sense of flow to the sculptural line. I used this method recently when I had to carve an Arctic tern hovering above, and about to dive into, the seashore waves.

CREATING A BIRD IN FLIGHT

There are three main techniques I used to create the visual impression of an Arctic tern in flight. The first relates to the base. The lower half is quite plain, but the wood above it has been ripple cut. The reason is two-fold; visually to lift the work, and also to give a wave effect. But the 'lift' effect is the more important, since it will help to give more spacial feeling to the carving when it stands on a piece of furniture. In other words for the bird to fly it has to be off the ground!

The shape and the position of the wings also affect the sense of movement. Both leading, and trailing edges rise vertically away from the body, then sweep back to give the impression of being in mid-flight.

Thirdly, I worked on the angle of the beak which is close to the main perpendicular line of the piece. This gives a dramatic effect; perhaps the bird is about to dive. The way the tern is looking down may not be totally realistic, but the primary objective is to emphasise the hovering action.

PRACTICAL TIPS

The practical carving of a bird in this pose is quite straightforward. Personal observation of the subject and a suitable choice of timber were probably the most vital ingredients. The tern illustrated here was carved from lime (*Tilia vulgaris*), 4in, 100mm thick.

During the roughing out process it seemed that the wings would not be sufficiently far apart and that thicker wood, had it been available, might have been a better choice. But once they were reduced to their final thinness,

Carved bird before finishing touches

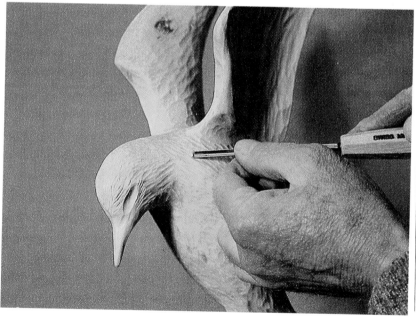

Jeremy in action,
creating a tooled finish

and the aerofoil sectional shape produced, the wing spacing proved sufficient. Importantly the lie of the wings was true to the run of the grain. This gave them plenty of strength without any directional change to the figure-pattern of the wood, which the conventional splicing-in method of construction could have caused.

ARTISTIC LICENCE

When doing this type of carving, it is very easy to be drawn back, even unwittingly, to more realistic interpretation of minor detail. A typical example is in the treatment of the eyes. They might be perceived as round, as you would expect with normal eyes. However, if movement is to be the dominant factor, they would have to become blurred, like the faces looking out of the train's windows. I chose to represent the eyes with two short veiner-cut grooves, which lent strength visually to the head and beak.

Equally important was the way the carving was finished. This required careful thought. For example, individual feathers would not be seen at speed. But whether the carving should be sanded smooth, or given some fine tooling just to relieve the blandness of the lime, was a matter of personal preference. As shown, I opted for the tooled finish. Lime is soft and vulnerable to accidental marks, less noticeable when the surface is textured, and the tern was to go on exhibition before flying to its new home. ●

Finished tern in profile. The angle of the beak is close to the main perpendicular line of the piece

Jeremy Williams started carving at the age of 14 and his family's connection with woodcarving can be traced back to the early part of the 19th century. During the past 15 years he has practised professionally with work sold widely both in England and overseas. Jeremy is a fully qualified instructor and has been running his own courses in woodcarving since 1982.

'FLORAL MOTIF'
by Jeremy Williams
Photographed by Anthony Bailey

EARTHWORKS

THE COMPLEX RELATIONSHIP BETWEEN NATURAL AND MAN-MADE LANDSCAPES PROVIDED TED VINCENT'S INSPIRATION FOR AN EXHIBITION.

These four pieces were done specifically for my exhibition at Chichester District Museum earlier this year. As with previous works, they drew their inspiration from the Rother Valley.

POND LIFE

Within the theme of *Diatoms* I was searching for a form to express the idea of growth. After considering various possibilities, I became interested in using these beautiful, single-celled, microscopic water plants, which are invisible to the naked eye.

Magnified drawings in *The Observer Book of Pond Life* showed them as attractive forms. I thought their decorative shapes and sculpted surfaces with fine lines and textures would present many possibilities for carving.

I selected a number of diatoms of varying shape and complexity, produced a series of drawings on tracing paper, and juggled these around to form a composition.

After exploring various ways of setting the diatoms out in patterns along a 600mm, 2ft stream of water, I decided it would make a stronger image if I made a complex arrangement of shape and form at one end, and led the eye to this along the perspective of the stream.

The stream itself was made by cutting the wood to shape on the bandsaw and by working the surface with a gouge to represent water, making the marks diminish in size as they reached the point.

I made the curved shape as thin as possible to give a very lightweight and visually simple form that provided a background to the more dynamic and complex shape of the diatoms.

Some of the diatoms were carved from the same piece of wood. Others, like the trumpet-shaped, floral motif at the top of the design, were carved separately and glued into place as the composition evolved.

The piece grew as it went along, suggesting to me ways to develop the

Top left **Microscopic water plants are represented as part of a flowing stream.**
Centre left **The sculpture presents many different diatoms as a collage.**
Left **Detail was carved with small gouges and chisels.**

asymmetrical pattern I was looking for. Some shapes were exclusively carved using gouges and small chisels to create various texture and surface details. On some shapes I used a fretsaw to cut lines through the forms, which were then carved in to create a full three dimensional image.

The diagrams I was working from, although fairly detailed, were all 2-D images and gave no account of the depth, so I interpreted thickness in a way that made the composition grow out from the background.

Once I had set out the overall design I completed the carving using small gouges and a variety of burrs and dentist drills in a flexible drive tool to incise and remove deep undercuts in the design.

Because of the level of detail it was important to use good quality lime (*Tilia Vulgaris*) and vital to keep all carving tools sharp and polished throughout the operation.

I have always felt carving was very much part of the decorative tradition, and see this method of working as a way of developing this area in a modern idiom.

FOSSIL FORMS

Buried Fossils was a development in a series of simplified landscape pieces which were distinct from the combined carved and constructed pieces I also produce. As with other pieces of work of this kind, the composition was not specifically pre-planned, just a notion about an undulating surface with fossil forms trapped in the landscape.

I began with a piece of lime 305 x 305 x 50mm, 12 x 12 x 2in. I made no drawing or sketch to begin with but worked initially from the feeling I had developed from a visit to a particular piece of downland.

Using a 25mm, 1in gouge, I established the contour of the hills, which set out the basis of the composition.

When I began to place the fossils in the composition, I used the British

Above **Fossil forms trapped in the landscape.** Right **Hollowing out. A difficult process in this case.**

....

Museum (Natural History) publication *British Mesozoic Fossils* as reference.

Both forms were based on echinoids which conform to a circular pattern, so I drew directly onto the wood with a compass, marking a series of circles radiating out from the centre of each, and used these as guide marks to carve the basic form.

I used a small flat chisel to establish the semi-spherical forms of the echinoid. I finished the surface with scrapers and steel wool to give a well finished form into which I could carve the detail.

I marked out the divisions that made the surface pattern and the holes in the centre in pencil, and this cut into the surface, following the pencil line with a very sharp, thin scalpel blade so as to not break out.

Then, using a small, flat chisel, I removed sections of the wood to give a very low relief. I wanted to keep the detail as subtle as possible and removed only about 1.5mm, ¹⁄₁₆in. Any blemishes were removed by scraping.

The decorative holes in the centre of each fossil were achieved by first drilling a pilot hole of 13mm, ½in, then carving away the insides of the fossils from behind with a gouge.

I had to be careful at this point, as the wood where I had carved from the inside of the form was very thin, to give the feeling of the delicacy of the fossil against the robust nature of the surrounding landscape.

This was an important part of the composition as I intended to exhibit the finished work on a hollow plinth, so spectators would look into deep blackness through the holes. The void formed a strong part of the design.

I paid attention to making the shape of the holes exact, achieving a crisp edge with knife and needle files. The surrounding landscape was carved with various sized gouges, finishing to a smooth, continuous surface with scrapers.

I find a cabinet scraper is a versatile tool which, unlike sandpaper, does not clog the grain so you can achieve a very clean surface. I finished the surface with two coats of sanding sealer rubbed down between each application with 0000 wire wool.

As well as looking at my work, people like to touch it, and the tactile quality of this piece was just as important as its visual appeal.

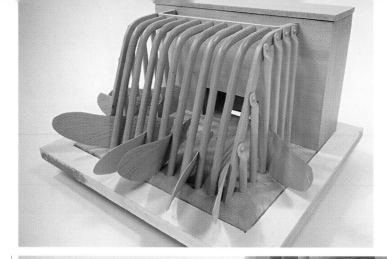

DRAGONFLY WINGS

This piece combined a variety of techniques of carving, shaping and fabricating, and was made from lime taken from the same plank of timber to ensure evenness of colour and surface. I developed the idea from observing a sluice gate where various fragments floating on the water had become caught in the bars.

As this was a fairly complex structure, I first made a maquette in cardboard. Although this gave only an overall idea, it saved a lot of time and costly material. I can develop an idea so far using drawing, but I find the hands-on experience of the model gives a full and informed picture of the idea.

Once I had decided on a set of dimensions, I began the job by making the bars of the cage. Using the bandsaw I cut a set of blanks, which I sanded to a round cross-section, keeping a close eye on the shape, particularly at the bend.

I took them to their final dimension with a curved scraper. It was important they were accurate and of the same diameter, as they all had to fit into the same size holes in the base.

The next stage was to make the water base. This first had to be cut to shape to fit with the wall to which the cage was connected. Once the holes had been drilled to accept the bars, I carved the pattern of the water, giving the impression of it rushing towards the sluice and tumbling down through it. The box representing the wall was a simple structure with holes cut to receive the cage.

Having made most of the components I came to the more delicate and detailed work of the dragonfly wings. I made some card templates, traced from drawings I had done of the wings of a dead dragonfly, and used these to mark out the eight separate wings.

I cut them from a fairly thick, 25mm, 1in piece of lime, which allowed me to sculpt each one with a

Top **Dragonfly wings, inspired by detritus stuck in a drainage grille.**
Centre **The wings give the impression of being held against the grille by water pressure.**
Above left **Carving the wings.**
Above right **Building the grille.**

twist in it, giving a greater feeling of three dimensions than if they were flat. I shaped them on a drum sander attached to a De Walt radial arm saw, finishing them as thin as possible with a curved cabinet scraper.

Once I had arrived at the right curvature and thickness, I marked out the pattern of the ribs on both sides of each wing using tracing paper. I first

followed the pencil line with a scalpel, being careful not to cut too deeply as the wings were very thin and I was cutting on both sides.

Then, using a 1mm, $\frac{1}{32}$in gouge and the scalpel line as a guide, I cut lines to represent the pattern of the wings. I did all eight wings in succession, keeping the gouge very sharp throughout, to ensure a crisp cut and flowing line. This gave a complex organic rhythm that played an important part in the composition, providing contrast to the regular, severe pattern of the bars of the cage.

Having assembled all the components, I gave everything two coats of sanding sealer, rubbed down with wire wool, and assembled and glued together all the parts.

I placed the wings trapped between the bars to give the feeling they were being forced by the pressure of the water towards the weir.

MOVEMENT

As with the *Dragonfly Wings*, I had a specific idea of the image I was after for *Waterfall*: water falling from a hole in a wall. The focus was very much on the water and the form it made as it gushed out. I took lots of photographs of my subject at various shutter speeds, capturing the movement and frozen effect of the water.

To create the water, I began with a large piece of lime 760 x 150 x 150mm, 30 x 6 x 6in. This was a clean and well seasoned piece purchased

Below left **Water pouring through a hole in a wall.**
Above left **The wood was cut right through at the bottom of the fall.**
Above right **Fitting the waterfall.**

from W. L. West's of Petworth, who provide very good quality English lime.

I first removed the concave shape that would form the back of the waterfall, initially using a large gouge and mallet.

Having created what I regarded as a satisfactory shape, I turned my attention to the front, following the curvature set by what I had removed from the back to a basic shape. Again using a large gouge, I carved the front of the waterfall, then working from the top downwards, using first a 13mm, ½in gouge, I created an overall pattern.

Next, using two small gouges I cut marks to represent the flow of the falling water, piercing through the thin wood as it got nearer to the ground to represent the water breaking up. I then worked the back in the same manner.

I wanted to present the water in a particular way, isolated, not quite touching the ground at the bottom, and flowing from nowhere at the top. To achieve this effect, I built a neutral box which was painted white and, in effect, formed the plinth out of which the water flowed.

The front and a small part of the back were made from lime with a brick pattern incised into it. Not only did it represent a material but it also gave a clear idea of scale.

The square hole the water flowed from became a focus in the design, and I carved a stream to run through the plinth, giving the feeling to the spectator of an underground spring that fed the waterfall. ●

De Walt (Elu Power Tools)
210 Bath Road, Slough,
Berkshire SL1 3YD
Tel: 01753 576717

W.L. West & Son Ltd (timber merchants), Selham, Petworth, West Sussex GU28 0PJ
Tel: 01798 861611

Second hand tools from Leeside Tool Shop, Burntell Road, Yapton, West Sussex BN18 0HP
Tel: 01243 554056

Ted Vincent is a senior lecturer in the School of Three-dimensional Design at Kingston University, Surrey. He is happy to advise anyone entering an education in 3-D design. His exhibitions, sponsored by the Environment Agency, John Blake Hydraulic Engineers and Canon UK, are held at Chichester District Museum. Tel: 01243 784683.

BODY BUILDING

IN THE FIRST OF TWO ARTICLES ON SCULPTING THE HUMAN TORSO, DICK ONIANS BEGINS WITH A STUDY OF ANATOMY

The idea of sculpting the human torso without head and limbs would probably not have occurred to man if he had not been attracted by the wreckage of ancient civilisations such as Greece and Rome.

The torso is the most solid and compact part of the body and therefore most likely to endure intact.

Seventh Century BC Greek figures look like modern wood sculptures where front and side profiles are cut out with a bandsaw and the corners rounded.

But in 300 years the Greeks shook off the rigidity of their first attempts and produced lifelike figures.

Their aim was a god-like perfection, and mathematical proportions were seen as divine. The result was, as each carver tried to make his sculptures more alive than his master's

he also made the forms as close to the ideal as possible.

It is also easier to plan a sculpture if there are set proportions for the parts of the body.

With the Greek example in mind, carvers wishing to represent the human form should try to improve upon, rather than copy poor sculptures.

The best way to start is to make a thorough study of the figure by life drawing or modelling. An excellent aid to this is anatomical study.

This helps to show how the various lumps and hollows are formed, which parts can change shape and which are hard and soft.

Though fat, fascia tissue and skin soften the details of bones and muscles, they cannot hide them altogether, nor can clothes.

SKELETON

Carvers of the human figure should know the basic skeleton and the main muscles visible at the surface. They should then be able to avoid making square, disjointed and impossibly contorted figures.

A good way to start is with modelling the torso, since the armature is uncomplicated and there are no arms to get in the way of the ribcage and its muscles.

True modelling involves building up from the inside, not carving excess clay from a block.

When modelling a torso you do not usually work from so far in as I do here, but it is worth doing once to learn why the surface is as it is.

The spinal column or spine keeps the shoulders apart from the pelvis so we start with that. It is made up of 33 or 34 *vertebrae*, with *inter-vertebral discs* between those above the pelvis.

The bumps which you can feel down the middle of your back are long *processes* which grow backwards from

The armature of the spine made from square aluminium wire. Note the curvature of the side view with the pelvis sketched in clay, showing the iliac crest sloping down to the anterior superior spine at the front.

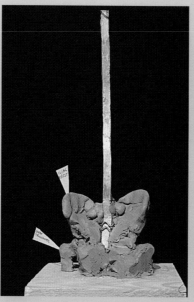

The spine and pelvis, front view. the iliac crest is held on a wire armature. Note the relationship between the iliac crest and the great trochanter and the position of the anterior superior spine.

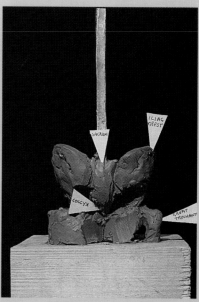

Back view of the pelvis showing the sacrum between the halves of the pelvis.

every *vertebra*. They are known as spines, which can be confusing.

The spinal column seen from front or back is a straight line, but seen sideways is gently S shaped. At its base in the small of the back or lumbar region it curves backwards.

Five *vertebrae* are here fused together to form the *sacrum* which continues the same curve tapering into the *coccyx*, which curves forwards again.

Above the lumbar region the spine curves backwards as it ascends and then forwards from near the top of the ribcage or thorax.

It returns more or less to the vertical at the top of the neck where it fits under the middle of the skull. Seen from behind, the *sacrum* is roughly triangular and links the two halves of the pelvis.

PELVIS

The pelvis forms half a cup to hold the intestines and other organs. But the parts that interest the sculptor most are the outer rim or *iliac crest* that runs from the *sacrum* up, around and down at the front to the *anterior superior spine* at each side, the bony lump just in from the side of the body below the waist, the *symphysis pubis*, the lump which we do not see because it is behind the genitals but to which are fastened some of the *adductor* muscles that we use to pull the legs together, and the hip socket (*acetabulum*) in which the top of the thigh bone, the *femur*, sits.

The *acetabulum* is also invisible because the ball on the head of the femur is on the end of a short stalk almost at right angles to the main shaft of the bone.

On the outer side of the bone at the top is a big lump called the *great trochanter*. Lumps (or *processes*), ridges, spines and plates of bone are where strong muscles are attached.

The pelvis is composed of large plates with thick rims and, being in the middle of the body, has numerous powerful muscles attached.

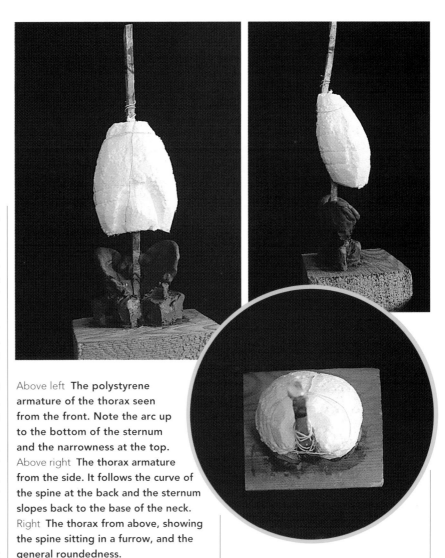

Above left **The polystyrene armature of the thorax seen from the front. Note the arc up to the bottom of the sternum and the narrowness at the top.**
Above right **The thorax armature from the side. It follows the curve of the spine at the back and the sternum slopes back to the base of the neck.**
Right **The thorax from above, showing the spine sitting in a furrow, and the general roundedness.**

....

The gap between the highest part of the *iliac crest* and the lowest rib is about a finger's thickness. It is possible to build the thorax rib by rib, but it is safe to regard it as basically egg-shaped, with the little end at the top, and the bottom end cut off.

The ribs curve in towards the spine and appear to form a valley down the back with the row of *vertebral spines* standing out in the middle.

If the back is well muscled these spines barely project unless the back is bent forwards. The two bottom ribs at each side float in front.

Above them the ribs are linked at the front by cartilage which arches up to the *solar plexus* which is at the bottom end of the *sternum*.

The *sternum* is a jointed bone that runs from this point to the top of the thorax. From the front it appears dagger-shaped, but viewed sideways it curves and slopes backwards to the neck.

The top five ribs are joined to it by more or less horizontal strips of cartilage, which flattens out the middle area.

THORAX

On my model I made the thorax out of expanded polystyrene as it is light, easily shaped and, when anchored with wire to the spinal column, stops the clay from sliding down. I was also able to push some wire through it to support the tops of the arms.

The arms are easily moved in many directions because they are joined to the thorax only by muscles and where the collarbones (*clavicles*) rest at each side of the top of the *sternum*.

The shoulder blades (*scapulae*) are attached to the back by muscles. They are roughly triangular plates, curved to fit the thorax.

Near the top, which is the short side of the *scapula*, there is a ridge (spine) that slopes across to the outside corner and projects beyond, forming the *acromion process* which the *clavicle* rests on.

At the front there is a similar projection, the *coracoid process*. The head of the upper arm bone, the *humerus*, sits in a socket on the corner of the *scapula* below and between these two.

Top far left The thorax with clavicles, showing how their angles change as the arms change position.
Left The side view of the thorax with clavicle, scapula and top of humerus.
Below far left Back view of thorax with scapulae. Note the left scapula's position. Its spine is at a steep angle and the bottom corner swings around to the side. The clay above the pelvis is simply a core.
Left Top view of the shoulder girdle showing the way the clavicles are S shaped, following the curve of the thorax and swinging forward to the shoulder joints. The spines of the scapulae also slope forward to the shoulders.

You should be able to feel the *clavicle* and the *processes* when the arm hangs naturally. You can also feel the *great tuberosity* which sticks out on the side of the *humerus* opposite the joint and lower than the *acromion process*.

TOP VIEW

The most important view of a sculpture is from above. If you look at the skeleton from above you can see how the curvature of the thorax makes the edge of the *scapula* nearest the spinal column project.

The result is there is a slope forwards from there to the arm when the shoulders are relaxed. The *clavicles* seen from above curve around the top of the thorax, then swing forward to the front of the *acromion processes*.

From the front the *clavicles* present a virtually straight line unless the arms are raised.

On my model I have raised the left arm to show how the *clavicle* and the *scapula* move and the muscles change when the arm stretches upwards.

There are interior muscles and organs that affect the surface form, but I assume you know the general shape of the body well enough for me to miss them and concentrate on the superficial muscles.

They contract, harden and change shape when they are used. By adopting various postures and pushing and pulling you can feel what most of them do.

I start at the bottom with the *gluteus maximus*, the big muscle that we sit upon. It is the body's strongest muscle, used in making the body erect and in bending the thighs.

It attaches to the back of the *iliac crest* and emphasises the triangular area at the top of the cleft of the buttocks caused by the *sacrum*.

It slopes diagonally forwards and outwards from the back of the *iliac crest*, joining the rear part of the *ilio-tibial* band behind the *great trochanter*.

Seen from the side this band of fascia tissue is Y-shaped. It runs tapering down the outside of the thigh and is attached to the top of the shin bone at the knee.

The *great trochanter* sits in the angle of the Y. The front arm of the Y is joined to the *tensor fasciae latae* which continues up to the *anterior superior spine* of the pelvis.

MUSCLES

The *gluteus medius* is a fan-shaped muscle which springs from the *iliac crest* between the other two muscles with its point on the *great trochanter*.

Because there is usually some fat on the hips and buttocks, the grooves between these three muscles are softened, but the *great trochanter* either stands out or sits in a hollow, depending on fat and posture.

Also attached to the *anterior superior spine* is a long thin muscle, the *sartorius*, which seen from the front runs diagonally across the thigh to the inside of the knee.

Between the *sartorius* and the *tensor fasciae latae* is the *rectus femoris*. The *sartorius* creates a groove between this and the group of *adductor* muscles, which form the inside of the thigh.

The main muscles of the back are the *latissimus dorsi* and the *trapezius*.

The *latissimus dorsi*, literally 'the widest of the back', is attached to the lower half of the spine, including the *sacrum*, and the back of the *iliac crest*.

It swings upwards and outwards, crossing the bottom corner of the *scapula* and twisting up into the armpit to attach to the front of the top of the *humerus*.

You can feel and see it when you raise your arm. From behind it makes the back seem to taper from the armpits to the waist.

The *trapezius* is a huge kite-shaped muscle with its bottom point in the middle of the back overlapping the two *lattissimus dorsi* muscles.

It forms a V shape up to the inner ends of the spines of the *scapulae*, runs along the tops of these spines to the meeting with the *clavicles*, then up to the base of the skull and down to the clavicles at the front.

It is the muscle that makes the shoulders slope up to the neck and makes the base of the neck wider at the back.

Attached to the underside of the outer third of the *clavicle*, to the *acromion* and to the underside of the spine of the *scapula* is the *deltoid*.

This attachment is like the base line of the triangle, the apex of which is almost halfway down the *humerus*.

Slotting up under the *deltoid* at the back is the *triceps* muscle which runs down the back of the upper arm.

The muscles of the side and front consist mainly of the breast (*pectoral*) muscles, the *external oblique* muscles and the *rectus abdominis*.

RIBCAGE

The *pectoral* muscle is a large plate-like muscle which is attached to the inner part of the *clavicle*, the *sternum* and the cartilage below. Its head twists to a point which is inserted under the *deltoid* onto the *humerus*.

If you push your fingers up between it and the *latissimus dorsi* you can feel the ribcage sloping up to the base of the neck. The nipple sits on this muscle near its lower outer edge.

Emerging from under the front edge of the *latissimus dorsi* and sloping

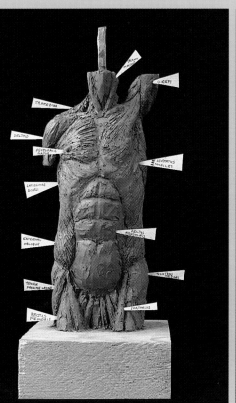
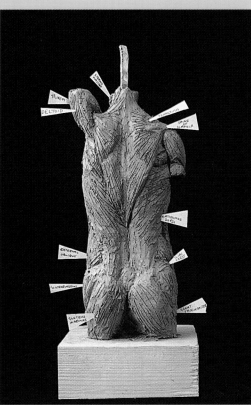

Far left **Front view of the torso without skin, fascias and fat.** Left **Back view in the same state. Note how the left scapula shows through the muscles and pushes out the latissimus dorsi at the side.**

127

Right **Three quarters view of left front showing the armpit and the adductor muscles on the inside of the thigh. Note the deep hollow between the pectoral and latissimus dorsi muscles that forms the armpit.**

Far right **View of the right side. Note the small bump formed by the great trochanter in the hollow below the gluteus medius with the gluteus maximus behind and the tensor fasciae latae at the front. The Y formed by the ilio-tibial band and the last two muscles contributes to the hollow.**

Below **The genitals in place in front of the symphysis pubis and the adductor muscles.**

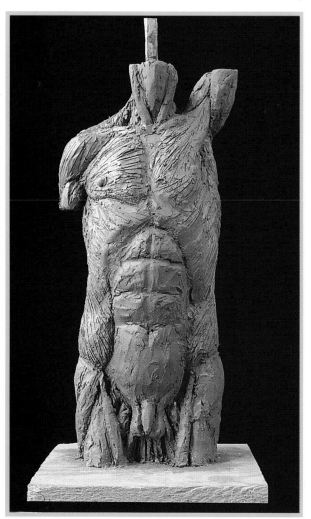

downwards to the front of the thorax is a row of fingerlike heads to a muscle called the *serratus magnus*.

They form a zigzag groove where they slot into the *external oblique*, a tall muscle that is attached at the bottom to the *iliac crest* and at the top to the lower eight ribs.

It particularly swells out above the *iliac crest*. It is joined to its pair by a large flattened tendon or *aponeurosis* which completely covers the *rectus abdominis* from top to bottom.

At its bottom edge it joins the *Poupart's ligament* which runs from the *anterior superior iliac spine* to the *symphysis pubis*, immediately behind the genitals.

This ligament forms the curved furrow between the abdomen and the thigh. The *rectus abdominis* is an oblong muscle running from the arch at the bottom of the thorax down to *Poupart's ligament*.

When well developed it presents a great column with a groove down the middle to the waist with three horizontal grooves, the lowest of which crosses just above the navel.

At the top of the *sternum* the windpipe runs up in front of the spine surrounded by the *thyroid* and the *thyroid cartilage*. From the side this makes the front of the neck slope up and forwards repro-

ducing the slope at the back.

However, at the front the two *sterno-cleido-mastoid* muscles come down from the *mastoid processes* on the skull just behind the ears to the top of the *sternum*.

From each one another head swings out near the bottom to join the *clavicle*. This means where the *trapezius* is tapering out to the shoulders the front of the neck tapers in the opposite way.

The female torso differs from the male mainly in having breasts, a wider pelvis and different fat distribution. ●
In my next article, on page 14, I describe how I carve a torso in wood, bearing in mind the bones and muscles.

Dick Onians is senior carving tutor at the City and Guilds of London Art School. Since 1968, as well as teaching, he has been working as a professional sculptor in wood and stone. He inaugurated the City and Guilds Institute Creative Studies course in woodcarving. He also teaches a part-time woodcarving course at Missenden Abbey Adult Residential College in Buckinghamshire. His book, *Essential Woodcarving Techniques*, is published by GMC Publications.

VASED IMPROVEMENT

RATHER THAN LET A BAD BACK PUT AN END TO HIS INTRICATE CARVED VASES, MICHAEL KORHUN DESIGNED AND BUILT AN ADJUSTABLE WORK TABLE

Above **A selection of carved vases.**
Below **Already turned to shape, the vase is scribed with a compass prior to carving.**

When carving I rarely use a knife. I do all my carvings with chisels and gouges which I have designed for each specific job. They are made of tool steel, either old knives and saw blades filed down, or something as simple as the grooved spokes of an old umbrella.

My chisels are short, with the handles not more than 200mm, 8in. long. The blades range from 25 to 70mm, 1 to 2¾ inches in length. The width of the chisels can be anywhere from 5 to 13mm, ³/₁₆ to ½in. The skew angles of these chisels can range from 45° and 60° to 90°, and from 1.5 to 20mm, ¹/₁₆ to ¾in in size.

This wide variety of chisels enables me to create designs of various degrees of complexity, each one unique. In all I own approximately 200 tools, including 15 knives.

CONTROL

In carving I prefer to work with shorter chisels because they allow me greater control and stability. I not only push the tools with my hands but also my shoulders which gives me greater control of the chisel.

After completely covering a turned vase with a coat of polyurethane and wax, I place it back on the lathe to carve circumferential lines. Steadily, I place a 5mm, ³/₁₆in chisel on a rest leaning toward the vase.

I carefully turn the vase with one hand using the other hand to guide the chisel applied against the vase to draw the preliminary lines.

On completion of the horizontal lines on the vase I remove it from the lathe and place it vertically in a workholder. This allows me to turn the vase, so I can divide its area with a compass, vertically, depending on its size, into four, six, or eight evenly spaced sections, and from there I begin to create a design.

PATTERNS

I never plan any preliminary designs, and a lot of the time I have no idea how the final pattern will look, though certain elements will be fixed when I'm doing the initial turning.

It is important to divide the vase into equal and precise sections because problems may otherwise occur as you proceed with the work.

Above **Symmetry is all important at this stage.**

When I have sectioned off the vase I begin to chip carve out the design. As I carve notches, edges, angles, curves, squares, lines and so forth, I make sure all the angles and ends meet correctly and accurately.

With an angular chisel, I begin the notched, jagged, or tooth-like design of

The finished object, in mahogany
(*Swietenia macrophylla*), padauk
(*Pterocarpus spp*), poplar (*Liriodendron
tulipifera*) and ebony (*Diospyrus spp*)
430 x 305mm, 17 x 12in.

Cutting and parts

Table	Qty	
top (26 x 18in)	1	25¼ x 17¼ x ¾in
top frame	2	26 x 3 ½ x ¾in
	2	18 x 3½ x ¾in
base (20 x 13¼in)	1	19¼ x 12½ x ¾in
base frame	2	18 x 3½ x ¾in
	2	13¼ x 2½ x ¾in
lifters	8	2¼ x ¾ x 24in
side bars	2	2 x 2 x 13in
inside slide		
aluminium angle	1	6 x 2 x 2 x ¼in
slider	1	17 x 8 x ¾in
slider rails	2	13 x 1 x ¹³⁄₁₆in
back plate	1	13 x 10 x ¾in
front plate	1	10 x 7 x ¾in
feet	2	6 x 4 x ¾in
winder	1	¾ x 12in diameter
	1	¾ x 4in diameter
worktop	1	28 x 26 x ½in
sides	2	26 x 3in
sill	1	28 x 3in
ratchet	1	20 x 2 x 2in cut at 1in intervals.
stand	2	18 x 2 x 2in
Parts		
table	4	⅜in bolts, 2½in long
	6	⅜in bolts, 1½in long
	4	⅜in machine bolts 2½in long
slider	12	no.10, 1½in wood screws
	3	no.10, 1¼in wood screws
winder screw	1	30 x ¾in

a repeat pattern and proceed to the
end. I have to keep in mind how much
space I have remaining.

I slightly increase or decrease the
size of the teeth in the design to create
the appearance of uniformity. I have to
avoid having space for only half a tooth
at the end of the pattern.

Working on a piece covered with a
finish can be extremely difficult as it
does not allow for mistakes. If a mistake
is made it is obvious and is quite difficult
to correct as the finish is broken. I experimented with many variations before I
settled upon this system.

The outside coat on the vase,
finished in a dark-coloured stain,
creates a contrast to the carvings on the
wood. The carvings give the impression
of inlaid work rather than carving.

I buff the carved area with a stiff
brush to eliminate all unwanted
fragments, wood, dust, and small particles
that might be caught in the corners.

POSTURE

With my injured back I find it difficult
to work in a stooped position. I do
most of the work sitting down, but
carving in the sitting position also poses
a problem for me because each piece I

work on is a different size and height.

It is feasible to carve plates of
varied diameters on a table top in the
sitting position. However, carving a tall
vase poses problems.

I looked at commercially available
stands but none were exactly what I
was looking for, so I built a table to my
own specifications.

I can lower it to a height of

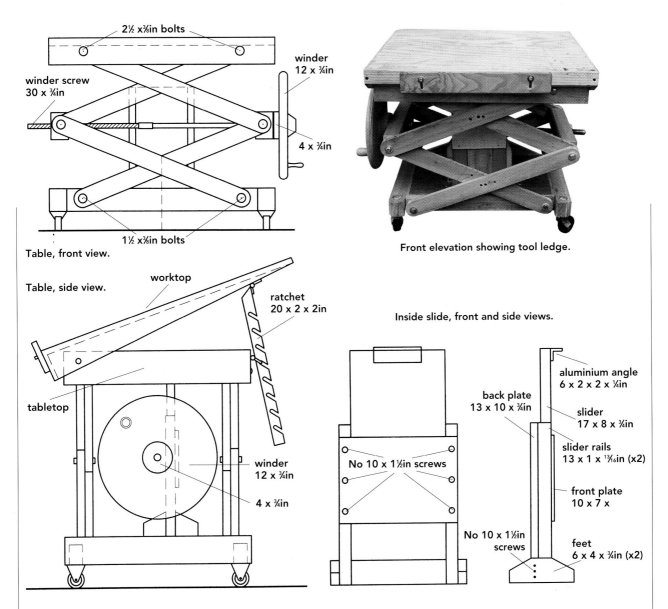

2½ x ⅜in bolts

winder screw
30 x ¾in

winder
12 x ¾in

4 x ¾in

1½ x ⅜in bolts

Table, front view.

Front elevation showing tool ledge.

Table, side view.

worktop

ratchet
20 x 2 x 2in

tabletop

winder
12 x ¾in

4 x ¾in

Inside slide, front and side views.

aluminium angle
6 x 2 x 2 x ¼in

back plate
13 x 10 x ¾in

slider
17 x 8 x ¾in

No 10 x 1½in screws

slider rails
13 x 1 x ¹³⁄₁₆in (x2)

front plate
10 x 7 x

No 10 x 1½in
screws

feet
6 x 4 x ¾in (x2)

Side elevation showing winder.

Rear elevation showing angle and height adjusters.

432mm, 17in or raise it to a height of 815mm, 32in depending on the subject to be carved.

This table, incorporating criss-crossed legs fastened together with a centre screw, allows me to set the table top at any desired height, and to carve in comfort.

It also makes the whole process easier, especially on cross-wise designs.

The chair I sit in also adjusts to various heights. A pair of locking castors allows for full mobility or firm immobility as required. ●

Michael Korhun was born in Jazyny in the central Poltava region of the Ukraine in 1924. His family were farmers, but his father was a craftsman who made violins. After the war, when he was a prisoner in a work camp, he studied sculptural carving with Russian carver Arkadi Lapsenkov. In 1952 he moved to Troy, New York, USA, where he still lives, and worked as a toolmaker.

BODYWORK

IN HIS FINAL ARTICLE ON SCULPTING A HUMAN TORSO, DICK ONIANS COMPLETES THE CARVING IN WOOD

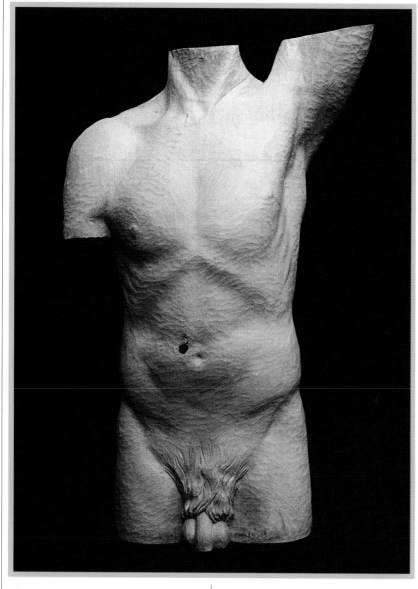

One of the most pathetic objects I have seen, yet one of the most instructive, was a plaster cast of the torso of a girl who had drowned in the Seine during the 1890s. There must have been a time when all art schools had a copy.

What struck me most was the flatness of the forms. From a distance

Finished carving from the front. Note sterno-cleido-mastoid muscles forming a V around the windpipe, not quite symmetrical because of the raised arm. The right clavicle is visible with hollows above and below. The left clavicle is mostly lost behind the pectoral. Note the rhythms formed by shadows.

they could not be read, but all merged together without defining shadows.

When Rodin submitted his *Age Of Bronze* sculpture of a male nude to the Paris Salon it looked so lifelike he was accused of taking a mould from a real person.

Eventually the jurors were convinced he was right as, like all good sculptors, he had omitted some details and exaggerated essential forms to create the shadows needed to make it readable.

In modern art schools this skill is seldom taught, and because the emphasis is now on ideas and not on execution, it is fashionable to take casts from live models.

I find this sad, as the rigorous demands of looking, understanding and interpreting are avoided and the figure produced is more bland and eerie than impressive.

Because it is normally clothed, the torso needs special study if we are to carve it.

There is a good chance, too, that if we look and discover things about its structure for ourselves, some of the excitement of discovery will transmit itself to the finished carving.

Life drawing is a quick way of looking and seeing. Modelling in clay is slower, and carving is the slowest way of learning how natural forms behave.

One short cut is to learn anatomy, as I demonstrated in my previous article (see page 6). This is no substitute for drawing and modelling, but makes it easier to see what is going on.

My account of carving the torso will be more intelligible if the anatomy article is read first.

CYLINDRICAL

At first glance the body appears cylindrical with cylindrical arms, legs and neck, but if you make a body like this, even if you notice grooves and bumps and put them on, it will look wrong.

The first will be a symbolic body,

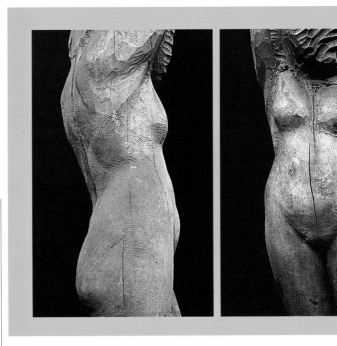

the second a symbolic body with surface decoration.

If after roughing out your carving you realise the underneath of the buttocks is lower than the crutch, or the armpit is well below the top of the shoulder, it may be too late.

If, however, you know the shapes of the pelvis, the spine and the hip joint, you will get the right relationship between the crutch and the buttocks.

If you remember the thorax is like a slightly flattened egg with the little end at the top, and how the clavicles (collar bones) and scapulae (shoulder blades) fit on it, the waist and shoulders will be recognisable.

If you know the scapula has a spine that runs across the back to the outside of the shoulder you will not, as some carvers do, make a groove that follows the inside of the arm right up to the top of the shoulder, effectively separating the arm from the body as on a doll.

Anatomy makes sense of the lumps, ridges, hollows and grooves of the body, but sometimes the combinations of muscles produce unexpected results.

Besides, variations in the positions of bones and muscles used differently cause changes in shape.

For this reason I have raised one arm. By cutting off the hanging arm at the armpit the shape of the relaxed ribcage is revealed.

FEMALE

The photographs of the carved female body show how putting the weight onto one leg makes the pelvis tilt and the buttocks change shape.

They also show how the different distribution of fat on the female body, the wider pelvis and less pronounced musculature, make the shape differ from a man's.

My purpose in carving this torso is to show how to carve down to the essential bones and muscles, and how to develop the forms to give the sculp-

Side view of a female figure left unfinished when I was a student. It has been out of doors for 29 years. The muscles of the hips are usually softened by fat on a woman. You can see the latissimus dorsi swinging up into the armpit and how the breast is flattened by the raising of the arm.

tural depth which an exact copy from life would lack.

One aspect that cannot be reproduced is life: the breath and the heartbeat. Nor can even the most cunning replica maker reproduce every pore, hair and variation of the surface.

You have to compensate for their absence by simplification and exaggeration, even when making a representational carving.

Having accepted you are using a different material from the original, and acknowledged you are incapable of copying it absolutely, you should resign yourself to being an artist and give the world something of your own unique understanding and vision.

Having said that you should also treat this as an exercise in getting to know the structures, so later you can take informed liberties with them.

It takes so long to carve a torso you cannot expect a model to pose for you while you do it. It is essential to attend a life class to learn the shapes of the body. Then quick reference to anatomy books while you work should fill any gaps.

If your own physique does not appeal to you, you could imitate the ancient Greeks and idealise the human

Front view of the female torso showing how the left side of the pelvis drops and the great trochanter on the right pushes out as the weight is taken on the right leg.

form, as I have done with this carving which is based on my own torso.

SYCAMORE

I used green sycamore (*Acer pseudoplatanus*). There was a slight spread at one end of the log which seemed suitable for the raised arm, so I could get a torso almost two thirds life size.

To make it as big as possible I left some bark on the outside of the hanging shoulder and lost a little width on the hips, particularly as some men are narrow there.

I used a simple way of scaling down to any proportion. For this method you need a pair of callipers that can measure the largest dimension on your body. They are fairly easy to make from plywood or sheet metal, or you can buy them from Alec Tiranti's.

You also need a board and large sheet of paper or a stretch of wall, and a long straight edge.

Draw a base line at least as long as the maximum dimension on your body and with one point of the callipers resting on one end describe an arc from the base line upwards.

From its intersection with the base line and with the callipers set at the maximum length obtainable from the wood (compatible with the other two dimensions), draw another arc to cross the first.

The method for scaling down showing the extended callipers resting against the base line. The base and long diagonal lines record the actual measurements. The short parallel diagonal lines give the scaled-down sizes.

....

With the straight edge you now join these intersections and the end of the line to create a triangle. It is easy thereafter to mark off on the base line and the diagonal the distances on your body.

MEASUREMENTS

If you then connect these points you will find you get a series of parallel lines. By noting what measurements they record you can quickly check your carving as you work in towards the finished form.

It is incredibly boring and will make for a lifeless carving if you take every measurement. Helpful distances to record are those between the anterior superior iliac spines, between them and the crutch, between crutch and navel, navel and bottom of sternum, and length of sternum.

Useful, too, are the width and depth of the thorax at particular points, the width outside the heads of the great trochanters, the interval between the dents where the posterior iliac spines meet the sacrum, and the width between the backbone and the outer ends of the scapulae.

All these points should be marked on the wood and redrawn as they are cut away.

You may not realise until you measure it how much the shape of the neck varies from the top of the sternum to underneath the chin.

You will probably have other surprises. In my case I was surprised to find the dimensions of the raised shoulder somewhat larger than my neck below the chin.

The positions of the nipples are also useful as are the lower edges of the pectoral muscles at the front, the latissimus dorsi and trapezius muscles on the back and the gluteus maximus and medius and the tensor fasciae latae on the buttocks and hips.

ROUGHING OUT

When roughing out the sculpture leave about 12mm, ½in, waste all around. In some places it will be more. If one arm is raised it is best at first to keep the interval between the neck and the body as small as possible to allow for changes of plan and accidents.

I used a chainsaw to quickly create profiles with the neck, the raised arm, the cut off hanging arm and the slopes of the spine forward to the neck and in to the small of the back. It also marked the hollow formed by muscles on each side of the spine.

I used an Arbortech Industrial to further shape the waist, hips and shoulders, but because the wood was green it was easy to carve by hand. Further roughing out was done with an 18mm, ¾in gouge.

Once the positions of major forms had been established I used a hand auger to drill holes as far up inside as I dared to allow the wood to dry from the inside and to reduce weight.

I bought a second-hand Hydraclamp universal vice, and although the carving was really too heavy for it, it did enable me to move the piece around more freely.

Without it I should have had to screw a block onto the base so I could hold it in a vice or with clamps.

I did most of the detailed carving with a 12mm, ½in No 11 gouge. This

● Front of the sycamore block after chainsawing. The neck and raised arm a not yet separated. A block has been lef for the genitals.
● Front view after further roughing out with the Arbortech and some carving wit a large deep gouge. The auger used to drill up inside it is shown. Lines show the outline of the thorax, the right clavicle, the position of Poupart's ligament runnir down from the anterior superior iliac spines (heavily marked), the navel and a vertical line running down the sternum towards the crutch.
● The wood has changed colour after being left for several days. Detail is now carved in with a 12mm, ½in No 11 goug

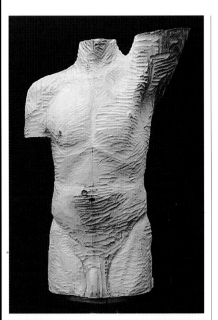

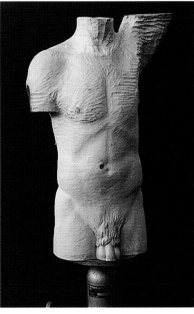

ainsawn block from behind showing
e for the spine, the hollow in the
e back and the scapulae sloping
b the shoulders.
iew at the same stage showing
the posterior iliac spines and the
by them and the sacrum. Spine
ht scapula is marked running onto
der.
ck at the same stage showing the
d diamond formed by the
alis muscles from the cleft of the
to halfway up the back.

● **Right side of the chainsawn block
showing bark on the upper arm, the
pelvis marked, and the clay model
showing the muscles.**
● **Right side at the same stage showing
positions of iliac crest, great trochanter
and gluteus medius.**
● **Right side at the same stage. The
grooves around the gluteus medius are
visible on the hip and the bottom front
edge of the thorax is defined.**

Top **Front showing further development of the external oblique and
pectoral muscles. Positions of the
nipples are marked and the left armpit
begins to appear. Only now is the neck
separated from the raised arm.**
Above **Lower parts finished with a bull-
nosed No 3 gouge, showing the dent of
the navel and the pubic region. Raised
arm is still waiting to be developed.**

was used principally to carve across the grain working around the forms, but some forms were outlined with grooves first to fix where the lowest parts were.

Deep hollows demanded a No 8 or 9 spoon bit gouge of about the same width.

SURFACE

I refined the surface with a bull-nosed No 7 gouge and finally with a bull-nosed 12mm, ½in No 3. The rounded ends made it easier to use the gouges in hollows as the corners were less likely to catch in the wood.

Occasionally it was necessary to use a flatter spoonbit in deep hollows, and in one or two places I used a 30mm, 1¼in Swiss No 2 gouge flute-down to create a smoother effect.

On a piece of this size a very smooth finish is not needed. Indeed I found the worked surface more exciting.

Not only does it have a softer look, like skin, it also holds the light and shade and emphasises the modelling of the form rather than bouncing light off and drawing attention only to the surface.

....

Bull-nosed No 3 gouge being used to finish the front edge of the latissimus dorsi as it swings up from the lower back over the bottom of the scapula into the armpit.

Above **Look for lines that echo or reflect others. The trapezius muscle is just discernible.**

Above right **The all important top view. It shows the curvature of the thorax, the angles between it and the shoulders. The left clavicle is in the front hollow on the shoulder. The hollow behind it is where the spine of the left scapula runs into the deltoid muscle. The slope of the spine of the right scapula to the shoulder is clear. Note cross section of the neck.**

....

Linseed oil would have made it too yellow, and wax would have been caught in any roughnesses, so I sealed this piece, inside and out, with one coat of Danish oil.

You will find consciously or, more likely, unconsciously, you are developing patterns out of the anatomy.

For instance, if you look at the photographs of the back of the finished torso you will see the diamond formed by the sacrospinalis muscles, that run under the aponeurosis of the latissimus dorsi muscle beside the backbone, from the sacrum to between the scapulae, and the way the inward slope of the buttocks is in line with the top sides of this diamond.

At the front there is a correspondence between the bottom of the relaxed pectoral muscle and the external oblique, and between the bottom edge of the thorax and the hollows of the groin. In later sculptures these patterns could be developed further.

If you do as I have done you should complete an attractive object and will certainly have great excitement making it and acquiring skill and knowledge which will prove useful even beyond carving clothed figures. ●

Alec Tiranti Ltd, 70 High Street, Theale, Reading RG7 5AR. Tel: 01189 302775.

Arbortech Industrial available in the UK from **BriMarc Associates, 8 Ladbroke Park, Millers Road, Warwick, Warwickshire CV34 5AE. Tel: 01926 493389.**

Hydraclamp available in two sizes from Tilgear, 69 Station Road, Cuffley, Hertfordshire EN6 4TG. Tel: 01707 873434 Or contact the manufacturers Spencer Franklin, part of Smiths Industries Hydraulics Co. Ltd., Windrush Industrial Park, Witney, Oxfordshire OX8 5EZ. Tel: 01993 776401.

Dick Onians is senior carving tutor at the City and Guilds of London Art School. Since 1968, as well as teaching, he has been working as a professional sculptor in wood and stone. He inaugurated the City and Guilds Institute Creative Studies course in woodcarving. He also teaches a part-time woodcarving course at Missenden Abbey Adult Residential College in Buckinghamshire. His book, *Essential Woodcarving Techniques*, is published by GMC Publications.

WORKING THE BLOCK

IN THE FIRST OF TWO ARTICLES, ROGER SCHROEDER FINDS OUT HOW FIGURE SCULPTOR ARMAND LaMONTAGNE ACHIEVES HIS STARTLING RESULTS

In May and June 1995, issues 16 and 17, I profiled Armand LaMontagne and featured his highly detailed and realistic portraits of famous American sportsmen including Babe Ruth, Ted Williams, Larry Bird and Bobby Orr.

He revealed some of his philosophy, how he goes about planning and preparing his figures, and spoke about some of his tools and techniques.

For these two articles I questioned LaMontagne about the details of wood preparation, making patterns, cutting techniques and tool selection.

I noted that LaMontagne, like many great wood sculptors before, preferred basswood (*Tilia americana*) for carving and wondered whether he had ever tried another wood.

He said he had used freshly cut white pine (*Pinus strobus*) which he dried himself. When it came to painting he stained the flesh areas to let the grain show through, but he had a problem with that.

"The grain took away from what I was trying to say. Basswood is the only wood I use now, and I don't stain it."

He obviously worked with some massive blocks of glued-up basswood for his life-size sculptures of athletes, and I asked where he obtained his blocks.

He does a major sculpture once or twice a year, so he does not need his own huge glue press. Instead he uses people who do it for a living.

"If I did this myself I would end up not having the right clamps and not enough hands. Until I find a tree that grows its own laminated, kiln-dried wood, I go to East Coast Lamination in

....

A glue press like this laminates the basswood blocks that LaMontagne turns into life-size sculptures. Photo by Ken Franckling.

Rhode Island where they have hydraulic presses. The cost is negligible when I know that I get the job done right."

The block has to be square. The company laminates a block with boards of the same thickness, usually 75mm, 3in basswood, so it comes out square.

SQUARED BLOCK

LaMontagne squares off one end with a chainsaw and hand plane so it rests evenly on the floor. It is nearly impossible for a shop to put a 2,000lb block on a table, saw and square the ends. There is no blade that big, and it is not easy to pick up a block that large.

The massive glued-up blocks are moved into his studio horizontally on rollers and then have to be set upright. This is done with a two-ton block and tackle that he attaches to a large iron hook sunk into a heavy oak beam that runs across the studio ceiling.

Even the largest glued-up block cranks up with a little effort. But he puts a steel noose on the top half of the block with a choke chain. The overhead beam does not budge.

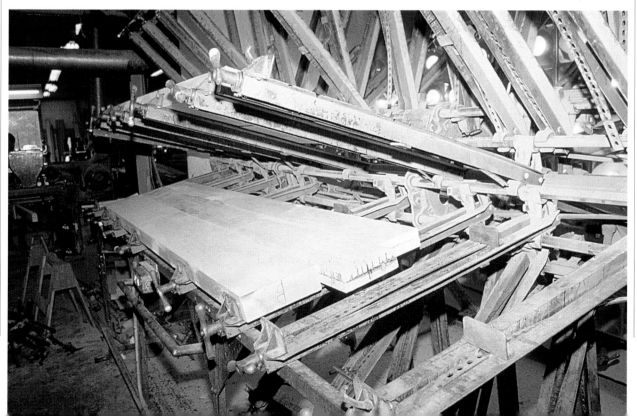

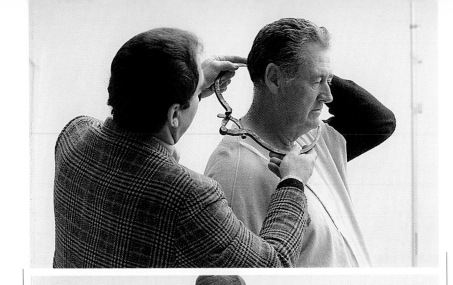

Top right **Many measurements are required before a pattern can be created. Here LaMontagne uses callipers to take a dimension off the head of baseball star Ted Williams.**
Right **LaMontagne takes a dimension from hockey great Bobby Orr.**

"I am only picking up part of the weight since the lower half is resting on the floor. The mechanics involved are not unlike what the Egyptians used. But I do move one of my work benches under the rising block so that even if it slips, the bench will stop it and it won't come through my floor."

PATTERN

I next asked about getting the pattern on the block. He usually works with a life-size portrait of his subject as a reference, and I asked if the pattern came from that.

He said, "When I can, I rely on photographs taken of my subject, usually from every angle. Getting a pattern from photographs is very tricky because photos lie.

"You cannot take a slide and blow it up to get your pattern. There is foreshortening. And therein is the lie. What helps eliminate that is to have the photo taken at belt level with a telephoto lens. This creates the fewest distortions.

"Even then the projected photo will be inaccurate. The camera does not compensate for depth of field, though the human eye does.

"Here's an example of the problems I have encountered. I take the measurement of a person's head, using callipers to get the outside distance between the ears. I then project the image of the body until the head fits within the measurement I have marked off on my pattern paper.

"The head is right, but the body comes out over 2m, 6ft 8in. The athlete is really 1.8m, 6ft 1in tall. If I projected the image so the body projected within the 6ft 1in limit, the head would measure an inch too narrow.

"I have learned to compensate for these inaccuracies. This means I need dimensions of other aspects of the image.

"For example, I will have taken and recorded the size of the numbers on an athlete's jersey. I will use the size of the basketball or football my subject is holding.

"This is why it is so important to have as many references and measurements as I can when I create a pattern.

"So my pattern is really a rough sketch based on these various focal points. And when in doubt I go bigger. And I always go bigger. That is my insurance policy.

"To rely too much on a projector is a mistake. The projector is only a tool. So sometimes it helps, sometimes it does not help at all. There is no one perfect tool. It is a combination of tools."

The pattern is therefore not the most important factor in creating life-size sculpture, yet LaMontagne still uses one. So I asked how he transferred the pattern to the block.

This is elementary for him. He perforates the outline with a pounce wheel, which is a perforating tool. He then takes the pattern to the block and uses chalk line powder which he pats onto the pattern.

The laminated basswood block for basketball star Larry Bird. A front and side profile have been established on the block that weighs nearly a ton. The cross-hatched lines in the upper part of the side profile indicate where the first chainsaw cuts will be made.

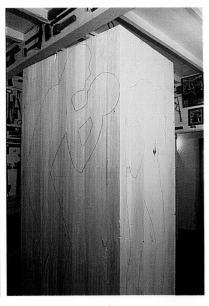

This makes its way through the paper and leaves an outline on the wood. Carbon paper is too cumbersome and too messy. This is a method artists have used for centuries.

FIRST CUTS

Next comes the question of where to start cutting away the wood.

Says LaMontagne, "Some carvers think that as long as you are cutting wood, wherever that is, you are doing okay.

"I think about cutting wood a long time before I actually cut it. I have to carve with my brain.

"Where to start has to do with how much wood I can remove in the shortest amount of time. It's being able to take a 200lb piece of the block off in five minutes with the chainsaw.

"It's not chipping wood away with the chainsaw. It's getting as much wood off as quickly and as accurately as possible. 100 years ago the poor sculptor had to take wood off with a hatchet and a roughing chisel and spend three days doing what I do in five minutes."

I took this to mean that if LaMontagne were slow he could be sloppy with his sculpting, and he agreed.

"Usually the slowest typist makes the most mistakes, and the fastest makes the least mistakes. The latter has an aptitude for typing.

"Perhaps this is why only a few people shine at what they do. It's having the aptitude.

"I often make these pronounce-

LaMontagne removes as much wood as possible in large blocks. Here he tackles the block for his Bobby Orr sculpture. (Protective gear should be worn when chainsawing). Photo by Ken Franckling.

....

ments about speed, but 100 years from now, the average person looking at my work is not going to ask how long it took to complete.

"The only important thing is whether the work is good or bad. Speed, then, only matters to me."

I asked LaMontagne to explain what he meant by the term panning to describe one way he uses the chainsaw.

He said panning was a method of roughing, of taking wood off a surface.

....

Below **The results from rough carving with the chainsaw. This is the sculpture of football player Harry Agannis in progress.**

Below right **Even after chainsawing and roughing with a large gouge, LaMontagne keeps the sculpture noticeably overweight. This allows him to make corrections in the position of the anatomy as he continues sculpting.**

He could do it with a roughing chisel, but preferred to use a chainsaw held perpendicular to the wood.

"There you have a thousand chisels at work. I slide a blade back and forth. When I get nervous that I might be taking too much wood off the block, I stop."

CHAINSAW

So when does the chainsawing end and the chisel work begin?

"It is when I go from rough-rough to finished-rough. Rough-rough describes the basic rounding and shaping. Finished-rough describes the wood after is has been carved to its final shape and sanded, though it still lacks the fine details.

"When the chainsaw is starting to bring me too close to the finished shape, meaning I won't be able to

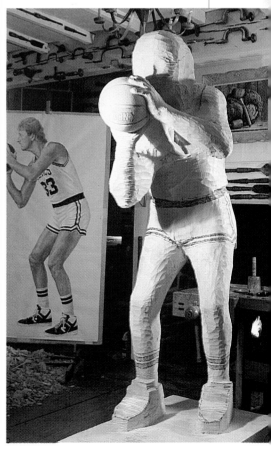

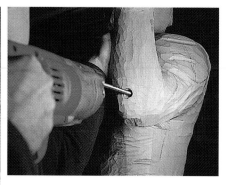

adjust the anatomy later on, that's when I quit with the saw.

"Remember, this is subtractive sculpture. If I were working with clay, I could make things bigger. With wood I have no options if I take off too much wood."

LaMontagne uses air-powered chisels only when it suits his purpose, when it helps him achieve a faster result. But this does not necessarily replace hand tools. It is just another available tool.

Asked if he had a favourite hand sculpting tool he said, "That's an easy question. The answer is a sharp tool. One of my favourite quotes is: 'A dull tool is the wrong tool'."

When it comes to keeping his tools sharp he does not go with the book-taught sharpening methods. No stone can maintain a flat surface, and oil makes a mess, he says.

He uses an aluminium oxide wheel and rocks his gouge back and forth on it to get a small burr on the concave side.

He then goes to 220 grit sandpaper, laid over a milled steel surface, and strokes the gouge across the paper until it is smooth.

The next step is the buffing wheel. He holds the tool vertically with the steel down and removes the burr on the concave side.

REINFORCING

I noticed with many of LaMontagne's sculptures that some of the anatomy looked fragile, especially extended arms. I asked if these areas were reinforced.

He said, "If my sculptures were like the real tree, there would be no problems. All extensions of the tree are reinforced with the grain and how it changes direction. The body does the same thing, with bones.

"But in a wood sculpture, the opposite is true. The grain does not change for an extended arm and there are no bones in the wood, until I put them there.

"I use threaded rods. A bonus with them is they compensate for the wood's expansion and contractions. The threaded rods actually stop that movement. So when the wood shrinks and swells, the rods make the anatomy even stiffer, much as reinforced rods in concrete do."

LaMontagne found he could not insert the rods with a traditional lubricant. Oil would come out through the grain and affect the paint applied later.

The solution was Teflon which creates very little friction. Teflon does not come in liquid form so he had to think of how to get it on the rod.

"I called engineers who recommended using solid bar Teflon. I could then run a heated rod through the Teflon.

"But I came across another problem. Even using a high-speed, powerful drill, I could only get the Teflon-coated rod in so far before the drill slowed to a halt.

"I realised that even with the Teflon, there was enough resistance to create a lot of heat. I was compressing air inside the wood and there was no way for the air to get out immediately.

"But after a while the heated air got out through the pores of the wood. Then I could advance the rod some more."

LaMontagne drove the rounded, threaded rod into wood against the resistance by putting two nuts on the end of the rod and locking them.

He then tightened the drill chuck on the nuts. The only other way would have been to grind the rod square, but that would weaken the rod and probably round it over.

He also makes a larger hole where he inserts the rod so he can get the chuck below the surface of the wood and countersink the rod.

Once the rod is in he takes the nuts off and bungs the hole with a basswood plug.

SCRAPS

LaMontagne's sculptures produce quite a bit of scrap wood. He burns the small pieces and turns the larger pieces into mementoes with his lathe: basketballs, footballs, hockey pucks, baseball bats.

Scraps from the sculpture of hockey player Bobby Orr made 2,800 hockey pucks which he was able to sell.

"This is one of the reasons I take such sizeable chunks off the block. They maximise my spin-offs." ●

In the following article LaMontagne describes the tools and techniques he uses to get an accurate likeness of a face.

PORTRAITS IN WOOD

IN THE SECOND
OF TWO
ARTICLES, ROGER
SCHROEDER
DISCOVERS HOW
ARMAND
LaMONTAGNE
GETS SUCH
ACCURATE
FACIAL
LIKENESSES

For my second article on American wood sculptor Armand LaMontagne I questioned him to discover how he achieved such realism in his portraits of famous sportsmen.

LaMontagne had often said in previous interviews that the faces of his sculptures were the most challenging aspects of his work, and I asked him why that was.

The real challenge of LaMontagne's sculpting is capturing the essence of a person in wood. This is Harry Agannis, an acclaimed US athlete of the 1950s.

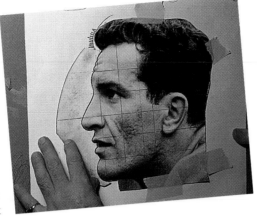

He said the most difficult thing for an artist to do was an individual human face. Not just any face, but a face that could be recognised at a particular age, in a particular frame of mind.

"Sometimes I see myself as a palaeontologist who has nothing but bones to work with, yet has to reconstruct the animal, including the surface details", he said.

For his latest sculpture of American athlete Harry Agannis he had to recreate his face with nothing more than black and white photographs that left much to be desired. From that he had to recreate the man, give him texture, colour, and put emotion into the face.

"The dinosaurs died 65 million years ago. Agannis died 40 years ago, but it may as well have been as long. It was not the ideal situation."

LaMontagne said the ideal situation was to have the real person sitting in front of you at the age you want to sculpt him. "That's the ideal, and for me the ideal is usually the exception."

He admired the work of Antoine Houdon, an 18th century French marble sculptor whose portraits were extremely accurate.

"But he worked from life masks. He did not have fuzzy photos to work from, nor did he have to put someone's face into a time machine and remove the years as I sometimes have to do.

"But despite the limitations placed on me as the sculptor, the head always remains the critical thing."

PHOTOGRAPHS

I asked LaMontagne how important photographs were in his work.

He said every sculpture was different and there were no set rules for what he did with the face.

With the Agannis face he had the black and white photos blown up life-size. There was one acceptable front view and one from the side, but he had

LaMontagne never met Agannis, who died in the 1950s at the age of 26. Though he was commissioned to do a sculpture of Agannis, LaMontagne had only a handful of photos to work from. But from them, as with this life-size side profile of the face, he was able to generate patterns and templates.

to alter the side view because it was not a perfect profile. It was turned 10–15° toward the camera.

From the altered photograph he made a template using an exterior outline of the profile.

"When I do a portrait in wood, I aim for a particular age, a particular attitude, a particular feeling that I want to capture in the face.

"There may be no photograph available that has all that. That is where the art comes in, but in the meantime there are an awful lot of engineering techniques involved."

I asked LaMontagne about those techniques. I had noted, for example, he left a block on top of the sculpture where the head would be, even when he shaped and detailed the rest of the body. Why not carve it to shape early on?

He said a block that had been squared off and given a smooth surface provided a canvas in wood.

The head was left until last, leaving atop the shoulders a squared-off block on which he drew accurate front and side profiles.

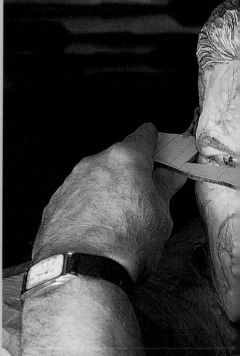

Top **This template, generated from the photograph, was used to check on the accuracy of the sculpted face.**
Above **LaMontagne devised this visor, held in place with a rubber band around the back of the head, to locate accurately the exact position of the eyes. LaMontagne's work calls for extreme accuracy.**

"This block is a precise thing on which I can draw my profiles later on. This allows me to separate the rest of the body, the easy part, from the difficult part of the anatomy.

"I cannot over-emphasise the degree of difficulty doing a portrait in subtractive sculpture. I have no room for error because I am locked in to

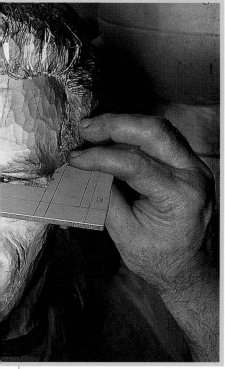

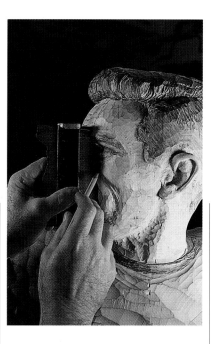

particular does what nature does, it divides the face from side to side.

"Nature separates the face into two slightly different halves. I do the same, and it is fundamental to my sculptures. Maintaining that centreline, not only vertically but also horizontally, is as critical as anything I do.

"In fact they are so important I refer to them as my genetic codes, my strands of DNA."

I asked what the horizontal centreline accomplished, and LaMontagne said the line went through the centre of both eyes. "The eyes are the centre of attention on any human face. They help provide that look that makes you different from Agannis or anyone else.

"I maintain the horizontal centreline as perfectly as I can. That is a very difficult thing to do since I am dealing with a rounded object."

As centrelines, horizontal or vertical, got carved away quickly, I asked how he replaced them on the wood, especially as the block lost its flatness.

He said there were two important tools for working on the face, a profile gauge and a visor.

The profile gauge had steel pins which, when pushed against a surface, conformed to the shape of that surface. When he pushed the gauge against the roughed-out face it provided an edge against which he could move his pencil and re-draw the centrelines.

The visor was a template which could be pushed up close and perpendicular to the face.

"I do it on something rigid like masonite (hardboard). The key lines I draw on that visor, which is really my gun sight, are those that locate the centres of the eyes.

"As I remove wood, leaving the nose out in front and setting the eyes back in the head, I want to know those eyes are going to retain the measured distance between them.

"Without a guide, if I am off ¹⁄₁₆in on the surface, I can be ¼in off as I set the eyes back into the head. If I am that far off, I have carved the wrong person.

"With the visor I can maintain that critical distance because I know I am going in dead centre.

"Before working on the Agannis sculpture, I took the eye measurements from the few photos I had available."

CALLIPERS

I asked LaMontagne why he did not use callipers to mark off the eye locations from the vertical centreline.

He said you could use callipers on a flat surface. That was how he got his distances from a photograph. But you could not use them on a contoured surface which was changing shape, as the distances would never be the same.

I commented that even in the rough stage of the face there was an identifiable person starting to emerge.

LaMontagne said he asked himself what characteristics made a person who they were. There were specifics you look for such as the shape of the nose, mouth and hairline.

"When I am roughing out, I try to emphasise some things in particular. The nose that helps make Agannis' face unique takes on some shape early on. Even if it is exaggerated or over-sized, the basic form is there.

where the ears are going to be, where the nose, the eyes, the mouth will be located, where the back of the head will be situated. I am committed on all sides of the head.

"So to begin this task that requires such extreme accuracy, I need to start with a block that has 90° corners. If I know the corners are precisely square I will know where I am going as I remove wood because I know where I am coming from."

CENTRELINES

When I asked what were the key tools or techniques in doing a portrait in wood, LaMontagne said centrelines were the critical tools in doing the face.

"The vertical centreline in

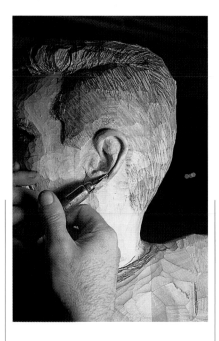

Ears are as unique as fingerprints. Here LaMontagne works on one of Agannis' ears using a custom-made V-tool.

"Ears are as unique and individual as fingerprints. And they are as different from one side to the other as they are from one individual to another, though at a quick glance they appear to be the same.

"I have yet to find two ears identical on the same person. Ears have a lot of character, so they are something I zero in on when sculpting the head. I even make templates of the side and front profiles of the ears."

TEMPLATE

I asked how he transferred the template profiles to the wood. He said he used a technique called chalking and rubbing.

"It's an old method, a meticulous and time consuming operation, but very important when you get close to where you are trying to finish up.

"I put pencil lead on the face of my rigid template which I then push against the wood.

"Here is another place where centrelines are so important because they give me the locations for my templates.

"I move the template ever so slightly to leave a black mark. I then proceed to trim the dark spots away. I will do this many times before I arrive at the right place.

"I do this only when I am close to the finished size. This keeps the measurements accurate in a mechanical way."

I asked why LaMontagne often

sanded the face smooth, even before it had reached its correct size and shape. I thought sanding would leave grit which would dull his tools.

"Rough chisel marks bother me. They are distracting and do not give me a feeling for how the face is emerging. They give a false look to the face.

"I break all the rules. I did not get into this business to save chisels. I sculpt wood to use my chisels and wear them out.

"Most amateurs are fascinated by having a large tool collection, but they do not know how to use them or they have to spare them.

"I am not fascinated by the tool. I am fascinated by what I can do with the tool. I realise I am going to have to re-sharpen my tools more often when re-carving sanded surfaces."

LaMontagne said when he was working on a face much of what he did was skimming the wood. A mallet was okay for the early roughing, but he had more control with his hands.

"I use a wide but shallow gouge for this and pare the wood down. Sand and pare, sand and pare, until I get to the finished surface.

"I am dealing with fractions of an inch. I have to remove the wood slowly and methodically while at the same time emphasising what makes that person's face I'm sculpting unique.

"Don't think I discount the body, because the body has to reinforce the face. There has to be an overall integrity, but the face is still the most difficult."

WRINKLES

I asked LaMontagne what tools he used to make pores and wrinkles. He said wrinkles were pressed in with a rounded tool such as an awl or even a nail, but it had to be very smooth to press into the wood.

"End grain takes details better than side grain. I try to make my creases with one stroke, but sometimes I have to re-do them, though I try to avoid

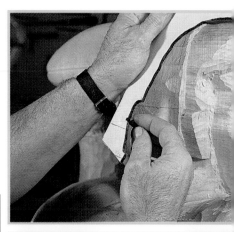

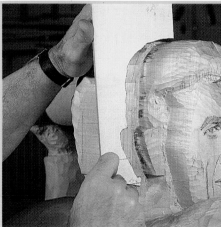

Top **LaMontagne applies pencil lead to the edge of this rigid template.**
Above **By pressing the template against the surface of the wood, he learns how much wood to take off and where to take it off because of the marks left.**

that. The variety gets lost and the creases look stale.

"The pores on a face are pushed in with a sharp object like an awl or a nail. This is tedious work, but it all contributes to the realism I have locked myself into.

"When it comes to tools for the head I use whatever works best. I found a piece of emery board cut to a point is the best sanding tool for the corners of the eyes.

"A long, narrow gouge does a good job removing wood from inside a nose. Or a thin file can work the areas between the teeth.

"It is not the tools but the sculptor using them and adapting them that makes for great art or mediocrity."

LaMontagne had a ping-pong ball on his workbench with an eye pencilled on it's surface. He used it when carving an eye as a reference as it was very close in size to the real human eyeball. It gave him a guide for the circumference.

Noting the sculpted look of the

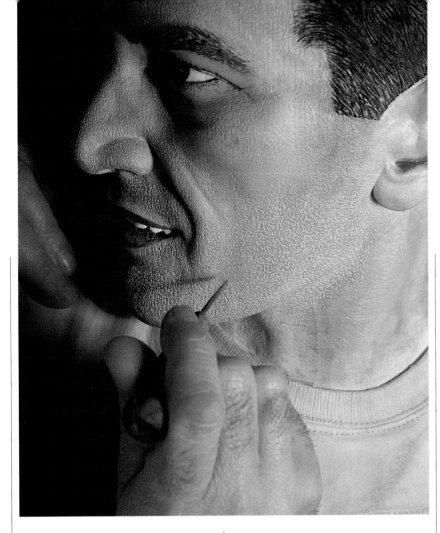

LaMontagne uses a variety of tools to create textures, including an awl to press in pores on the face.

hair on his figures I asked him if he had ever tried burning in the strands of hair as bird carvers burn in feathers.

HAIR

He said hair was important to a person's look, as Hollywood and politicians knew. More time was spent on hair styles than on anything else.

"It's one of those things that can change your appearance overnight.

"Hair is soft, variable, not an easy thing to duplicate in wood. But I still try to achieve a natural flow and you cannot really get that with burning.

"With certain feathers there is a stiffness that comes with lines that have to be parallel. But with hair there is an in and out flow. The only way you can get that is by carving it.

"That carved flow is more important than individual strands. It lends itself to a more vibrant look.

"Even though I do not like burning, I will do it for certain areas, say at the back of the head where the hair feathers into the neck. There you want some real fine lines.

Sculpting hair is done with the aid of a custom-made V-tool, which can literally split hairs. LaMontagne darkened the hair and eyebrows with pencil dust to highlight them, a visual aid which gave him a preview of how the finished head would look.

"Also for the eyebrows. When you try carving these fine hairs you are carving across the grain, and there is a tendency to rip or tear out the grain.

"A real problem with burning is that it produces dark lines. That does not help when you are doing a person with blonde hair. You end up using a lot of paint to cover the burns and you lose the fineness you were trying to achieve.

"Also, burning tends to make things look flat and shiny and too smooth, which hair is not."

To achieve the strands on his sculptures LaMontagne used a V-parting tool specially made for him by a machinist. It was shaped from high-speed steel on a diamond wheel.

This was one of his smallest tools and he pushed it by hand. It could literally split hairs.

"Making realistic wood sculptures is a process that requires a million adjustments to make a unique individual at a particular age.

"It is one adjustment at a time, and each chip I remove is an adjustment. Yet each is a final adjustment, because there is no bringing the wood back.

"You could say a wrong adjustment leads to disaster, but that never happens with me." ●

Roger Schroeder is a prolific writer and lecturer on woodworking, construction, sculpture and carving, as well as a cabinet-maker and amateur carver. He combines these activities with a full-time job as a high school English teacher, specialising in teaching creative writing and research.

FANCY FOOTWORK

TED OXLEY SHOWS HOW TO MAKE BIRDS' FEET WITHOUT USING SOLDER

Carved song birds need good strong feet if they are to stand or perch properly and give a realistic pose. Here is my method of making feet from brass rod without having to use solder.

You will need some 5 x 2mm brass rod section. This can be bought from good model shops in metre lengths. You will also need some cutting off discs to cut the brass rod, a mandrel to mount the discs on in a power tool, plus some Milliput putty.

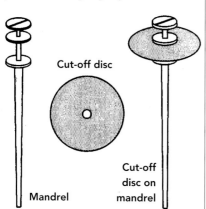

Cut-off disc

Mandrel

Cut-off disc on mandrel

Above left and above **Finished feet fitted to a robin**

The cut-off discs cost about £7 for 100 thin 22mm diameter discs, and a steel mandrel is about £1.80. Meisinger is a good make. Do not use a brass mandrel as these can bend. Milliput putty costs around £2.60 for a 4oz pack.

The marked up brass rod. Cut through the brass along the dotted lines, taking care not to cut into the area marked A

Mark out the brass rod as shown in the diagrams and cut through the rod along the dotted lines with a cut-off disc, taking care not to cut into the area marked A.

Cut-off discs are very thin and require careful use, but because they are so thin they make only a minimal cut between the toes.

A jeweller's piercing saw is the equivalent hand tool. Piercing saw blades can be used in some fretsaw frames with blade holding clamps.

Cut away the shaded areas as shown on the diagrams, leaving the toes the correct length. At this stage the patterns for both legs are identical and you need only turn one pattern over to make the opposite leg.

Cut away the shaded areas leaving the toes the appropriate length

Tarsus

The toes cut to length. Leave the tarsus extra long to enable fixing into the bird

HEATING

Soften the brass by annealing, or heating, until it is cherry red and leave it to cool slowly. This lessens the risk of the brass breaking. Then separate the toes by inserting a small screwdriver between them and prising them apart.

After heating and cooling, the toes can be prised apart. This shows the right leg

Carve the claws to shape with a small barrel-shaped steel or tungsten cutter with a cross-cut or hatched, diamond pattern. It is important to use a cross-cut pattern as a straight cut pattern can throw out sharp slivers of brass into your eyes or clothing.

Always wear a full face shield or protective goggles for all grinding stages as the discs are brittle and break easily.

Use pliers to continue the bending and shaping of the toes and tarsus, or ankle and heel bone.

Cover the leg and toes with a thin layer of Milliput putty. When this has set hard, carve it to shape.

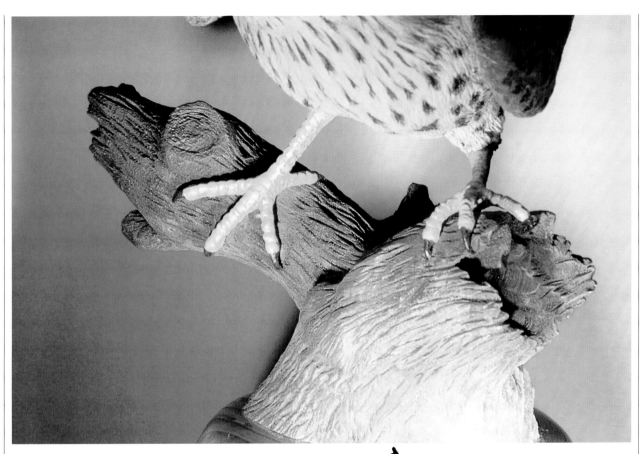

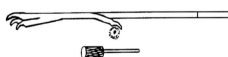

Carve and shape the claws with a cross-cut pattern cutter. The tarsus is long to allow for fixing into the bird

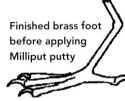

Finished brass foot before applying Milliput putty

Above **Larger feet fitted to a kestrel**
Below **Extra material can be added and textured for webbed feet**

If the feet are to be attached to a branch or other object you may need to put a small pin through the foot. If this is to be soldered on, this should be done before applying the Milliput.

Obviously, for larger birds you can use a larger brass rod section and cut it with a bandsaw or fretsaw rather than a cut-off disc.●

Cut-off discs and mandrels available from Bill Bragg, 9 Plowmans, Hambro Hill, Rayleigh, Essex SS6 8BT Tel: 01268 776409
Milliput putty available from Pintail Carving, 20 Sheppenhall Grove, Aston, Nantwich, Cheshire CW5 8DF Tel: 01270 780056

BEGINNING WOODCARVING **147**

OWLING SUCCESS

TERRY MOSS TELLS HOW HE CARVED THE FIRST IN A SERIES OF BRITISH OWLS

When I was a child I lived with my family in a pub which overlooked the river at Ross-on-Wye, and I spent many happy hours doing what children do along river banks. One day I noticed some birds flying into little holes in the river bank opposite and I wondered what they were.

I went to ask my mother, but she was busy with a customer and somehow the question remained unanswered. A couple of days later when I returned from school I found a small book, the *Observer Book of Birds*, on the kitchen table. The customer who heard my question had bought the book for me. It cost 2s 6d, a fortune to me.

I owe a lot to that lady, whose name I do not know, and often wish I could thank her, for it was a parting gift and I never saw her again. It has resulted in a life-long interest in birds, a great love of wildlife and of books.

I have carved several birds at different times and am still fascinated with the range of shapes and forms that birds come in. I only wonder why God gave them such spindly legs, a real problem for woodcarvers.

Another problem when starting a new carving is reference. Relying on observation is fine if you are blessed with a photographic memory and good eyesight, but neither of these were given to me.

It is inevitable that observation has to be backed up with good photographs of the subject, so the collection of books containing photographs of birds and wildlife are among my many treasures on the bookshelf.

Some time ago I decided to do a series of carvings on a given subject, and I came up with the idea of carving the indigenous owls of Great Britain. The poor old owl has long been a favourite subject for the carver and has

Little owl with a squat shape and large head (Athene noctua)

The Little Owl in walnut with a yew
base (560 x 190mm, 22 x 7½in)

suffered many interpretations through
the years, so now it was my turn to pay
my respects to these effective hunters.

The first problem was ascertaining
the exact number of indigenous
species, for the little owl was introduced in the 19th century and the
snowy owl only occasionally nests in
Shetland. So I decided the snowy was
out, little owl in, with the tawny, long-
eared, short-eared and barn.

LIVELY CUTS

My current thinking about finishing
carvings is to keep the tool cuts. The
idea behind this is generated from the
energy that seems to emanate from the
cutting tool. This seems to impart life
into the subject and is the way I intend
to produce all the carvings in the series.

There also seems to be a special
quality in very old carvings where all
the tool marks are showing. You feel
the carvers have left something of
themselves in the marks on the wood.

Much modern work is finished
with careful sanding, wiping away all
trace of the woodcarver's dexterity and
personality, for we all cut differently
with favoured tools.

I am not advocating that sanding

should not be used, I've done enough
of it in my time, but after many years
behind the gouge I love that certain
quality of finishing with tool cuts.
Many old church carvings have a sense
of life and movement, and I wanted to
impart some of these feelings to all the
carvings. The word used by bird
watchers is the 'jizz' of the bird.

I decided to apply the cuts in a
sort of sketchy way, much like
drawing. Not carving every detail, but
leaving areas unadorned to counter-
play with places where detail was used.
If the quality of the cuts was vigorous
and it was not finished with great
delicacy everywhere, I felt it would add
to the sense of life.

PICTURE POWER

Normally I produce a working
maquette, modelled in Plasticine, and
because many of the subjects are
difficult to see in real life, I rely on
photographs, taken either by myself or
other people.

I use them, as I suspect many
carvers do, to provide me with access
to subjects I probably would have little
chance of seeing in their natural
environment. Of course one photo is
never enough, there is always the bit I
can't find, and have to call upon my
memory and imagination.

As well as making a maquette, I
usually draw the subjects, either from
life or using photos as a source to
create the particular image I am trying
to achieve.

This has two advantages. It helps
to clarify the image I am after, but
probably just as important, it makes
me look at the subject. I find there is
nothing quite like drawing to make the
powers of observation work properly
and get all the information possible.

It also helps to clarify the design
and solve problems in the difficult
areas of the piece. When the final
carving is under way, it is reassuring if
you feel those 'problem' areas have
been thought through and worked out.

CARVING PROCESS

The first carving in the set was the little
owl. It was carved in walnut (*Juglans
regia*) with a beautiful colour and,
being made from the intersection of a
branch, had varying figure.

The fork caused a small problem
towards the end with splitting, but not
enough to detract from the carving. In
fact the splits have become a feature of
all the carvings, another natural event
to add to the effect.

The base was in yew (*Taxus
baccata*) with the ivy leaves carried
down into the base to unify the design.
I have employed this idea in the other
two carvings. The surface was left with
tool cuts, as I intended, and I applied
several coats of an oil mixture which
gave a dull gloss to the walnut and
brought out the figure.

The second carving was the barn
owl which was based on a photograph
I particularly liked and developed in
the maquette. This was then enlarged
to give a side view of the bird and a
front view, rather like an engineering
drawing. This gave the essential areas
of material, making sure it was in the
right place to produce the carving.

It was carved in English oak
(*Quercus robur*), a 300-year-old tree
damaged in a storm and built up from

three pieces glued together. The wood was still so wet I was unsure if the bond would hold.

To overcome this I glued it temporarily to enable me to carve it. When it had dried out I took it apart and glued it more permanently, and so far this has worked successfully.

The colour range of the wood was very good, from deep chocolate brown through to a golden straw colour. This colouring was the result of a fungus which produces the much coveted

Long eared owl (*Asio otus*)

brown oak. The drawback is the fungus can eventually rot the wood, and cause it to hold water. In fact it was so wet I found it impossible to stop cracks appearing when carving so I decided to use them as part of the design.

....

Sleeping Long-eared Owl **in brown oak (560 x 190mm, 22 x 7½in)**

I managed to get two pieces of brown oak from the tree. One was very good and I used part of it to carve the long-eared owl. The other piece was a little wetter, but had fine graduation from brown to straw. I decided to use it as the base.

The third owl completed in the series of five is the long-eared, inspired by yet another photograph of one

sleeping in a tree. Of all the owls I have completed so far, I had the greatest trouble in finding good reference material for this one.

It took me some time to finish the first three, but now I'm over half way I hope they will soon be completed. So now it's out with the owl books and back to safaris in the deep dark places with sketchbook, drawing hand a-quiver, and the short-eared and tawny owls waiting. ●

After many years as a freelance illustrator Terry Moss now works as a lecturer in illustration, computer graphics and woodcarving at Brunel College of Arts and Technology in Bristol. He started carving in 1962 as a continuation of model making, drawing and painting. He also takes part in the annual Sculptree event, carving large trees which are auctioned for TreeAid. He is available for commissions at 10 Old Manor Close, Charfield, Wotton-Under-Edge, Glos GL12 8TS. Tel: 01454 260656

STONEWORK

DICK ONIANS COMPARES THE TOOLS AND TECHNIQUES FOR CARVING STONE AND WOOD

If you have carved only wood you will find carving stone changes your understanding of wood and your way of working, opening your eyes to new opportunities. It is also immensely rewarding in itself.

For the carver the main difference between wood and most carvable stones is stone has no noticeable grain. When you begin carving wood, grain is all important. You naturally carve along the grain, frequently changing direction.

But after only a few days of stone carving I found when I returned to wood I carved it as freely across as with the grain. I was working around forms and in better control of their shapes and was also getting faster results.

Many carvers in the past, including Veit Stoss and Tilman Riemenschneider, worked in both wood and stone. Grinling Gibbons, Henry Moore and Barbara Hepworth carved in both materials. It is a good tradition.

If you are trained as a stone carver it is frustrating to begin woodcarving because the grain slows you down, the chisels are more numerous and sophis-

Beakheads copied or derived from 12th century originals in various limestones by first year and part-time stone carving students at the City and Guilds Art School. The shape of each stone was carefully masoned to fit in the arch.

ticated and their sharpening so much more time-consuming and skilful.

Traditionally, people wishing to learn both skills have started with woodcarving.

Obviously carving stones vary in hardness but the commonest used in Britain are carved faster than wood.

Stone is removed in larger pieces, and because of the absence of grain and fewer tools, is shaped faster.

Nor do you need to be a giant. While it is traditional to use a heavier hammer or mallet, it is possible to produce results, albeit more slowly, using lighter ones.

Nowadays much professional stone carving is roughed out with an angle grinder and cut with a reciprocating cutter on a flexible driveshaft or air line.

The pitcher is a thick chisel which has a flat end about 6mm, ¼in thick, slightly bevelled to present an angle of 75° at its tip. This is used for removing large lumps of stone.

The roughing out is done with a punch, although on soft stones this is not always needed.

The punch has a narrow chisel edge which has been rounded into a bull nose. Mine are mostly 230mm, 9in long but many are shorter.

The rough furrows left by the punch are ironed out with a claw, which may be a chisel which has had its end cut into teeth or it may consist of a replaceable bit held in a slot cut in the tapered end of a bar of steel, a claw holder.

Carvers usually at least have ones of 25mm, 1in and 12mm, ½in.

Finishing is done with a chisel. For general purposes 25mm, 20mm, 12mm, 6mm and 3mm, 1in, ¾in, ½in, ¼in and ⅛in chisels are used.

Carving into hollows is done with bullnosed chisels or with gouges, probably of similar widths.

The thickness and length of tool varies according to the hardness of the stone and the fineness of the detail required. Granite demands very stout tools but letter cutting and fine detail are carved with slender ones.

The tools are cheaper than woodcarving chisels although large tungsten-tipped ones are expensive. Tungsten tips keep their edges far longer than 'fire sharp' tools and will hold up well on granite, sandstone and marble.

Some tools have rounded, mushroom heads. These are for use with a mallet, nowadays often of nylon but also still of beech.

These mallets are used mostly for soft stones as they give a gentler shock. The mallets are round like woodcarvers' mallets only much wider.

Other cutting tools have heads which taper when new but are quickly bushed by the use of a steel lump hammer, usually weighing about 2lb.

Above **Marcia Bennett chasing lettering with a fine tungsten-tipped chisel on a column which she has masoned.**
Far left **A good range of stone carving tools. Back row, left to right: pitcher for use with hammer, followed by mallet-headed tools, 2 chisels, 2 claw holders with bits and a bolster or broad chisel. Front row, left to right: 2 gouges, 2 fishtail claws, 2 bullnosed chisels, 2 straight chisels and 2 tungsten-tipped chisels. Note the tapered heads of the hammer-headed tools.**
Above left **Dummy mallet, small lump hammer and beech and nylon mallets.**
Left **The stoneyard at the City and Guilds Art School. Carvers work under cover with good light and air circulation. They sometimes use large blocks of stone as bankers (benches).**

However, it must be said levelling the surface of a piece of stone by hand takes longer than on wood as only very soft stones may be hand sawn.

TOOLS

Another major difference between wood and stone carving is the shape and size of the tool are not so crucial to the shapes of finished details.

The stone carver can manage with few tools. The basic tools are pitcher, punch, claw and chisel.

Right **A block having one surface levelled by ledges drafted from corner to corner. Two boning blocks are visible on the banker. They were used in carving the corners into the same plane. The carpet under the blocks protects finished surfaces.**

Below **This piece of York stone was sold as Portland. It was a cruel trick to play on Gill Green, who has almost finished it. The iron stains show the bed of the stone. By making slots across the bed with a stone cutting disc large lumps could be split off along the bed but it blunted the tools very quickly.**

Light work is often executed with a dummy, rather like a small woodcarver's mallet made of soft steel.

Fire sharp tools are usually sharpened on a piece of sandstone (mostly York stone) with water. Oil could mark the carving badly.

The only way of sharpening tungsten is with a green grit stone or a diamond so these are increasingly used, particularly the diamond.

STONES

There are many stones suitable for carving. In England **limestone** is the

Above **This dragon, designed by Alan Llewellin, is having its side profile accurately masoned. He has plenty of experience so will avoid a square dragon. The stone is Maltese limestone which is soft and finely textured.**

....

commonest and most used.

Sandstone and **limestone** are sedimentary rocks, that is they were built up over the ages by particles settling in layers on prehistoric seabeds.

Some have marked layers which means they de-laminate easily and

Above **A life-sized head in alabaster, carved by Sylvia Worthington in a week. The red is shale and the white is bruised stone.**

....

therefore are not suited to carving, but others are virtually the same strength in all directions.

It is only when stone is used structurally or outdoors that the natural bed direction is important.

Some of these rocks enclose fossils such as hard pieces of shell and often have intrusive deposits of other hard materials such as calcite.

Above **A point being used on the marble carving of a shell by Lesley Powell. Note how it cuts vertically to the surface and bursts the stone off.**

These are stone's equivalent to knots and can be very annoying when carving detail. Sometimes there are voids or soft crumbly pockets in the stone.

Like wood, stone can have shakes, often caused during quarrying.

Marble is limestone that has metamorphosed under pressure and heat. It becomes crystalline often with coloured streaks. It is harder to cut and is usually carved with a different technique.

Slate is metamorphosed shale, some varieties being hard, some soft, but all easily break away in layers. It lends itself to lettering and shallow relief.

Granite, an igneous rock, is far harder but resists the weather longer than other stones.

Soapstone and **alabaster** are other stones used extensively. These are comparatively soft but present their own problems.

HOLDING

As with woodcarving it is essential to be able to hold the work firmly. A small irregular piece of stone will need to be cradled in a box of sand.

If one surface is flat it may be stuck to a larger block with plaster of Paris.

A wooden frame fixed to the work surface will steady larger pieces before final details are carved, but unless the finished sculpture is intended to have no flat surfaces it is best to start by masoning a flat surface for it to stand on.

For masonry all surfaces are usually cut flat at the correct angles and even rounded mouldings and columns are shaped by first squaring and then regularly facetting blocks.

If the stone is heavy enough it will stay steady while the first surface is cut. On softer stones a saw may be used. There are special ones, some with tungsten teeth. I use old cast off wood

saws, which can be bought cheaply in junk shops.

Other ways of taking off large lumps are to knock them off piecemeal with a pitcher or, more economically, to split the stone by drilling a series of holes and then driving in special wedges.

Another slow way is simply to draw a line around the stone and tap a chisel along it aiming it always towards the line on the opposite side of the block. Eventually the shock causes a fracture and a surprisingly clean break can result.

From this it is worth noting that frequent cuts directed into the stone in the same way can set up a line of weakness which may cause an important part of the carving to fall off.

To make a flat surface a line is drawn around the stone and little flat areas are made at four approximate corners.

Cubes of wood, boning blocks, are placed on each flattened area and with the guidance of straight-edged bars or rulers the platforms are cut into the same plane.

Lines are then scored between them and chisel cuts are made along the lines to create ledges linking the little platforms.

The rough area in the middle may then be reduced with a punch, making furrows at about 25mm, 1in intervals followed by a claw and then a broad chisel until the surface is even.

With practice the cuts become regular so the surface is gently textured. If it is necessary to make the surface absolutely smooth it may be scraped with a drag, a piece of metal like a large cabinet scraper, or rasped, then abraded with wet and dry paper of various grit sizes.

The carving then follows the same processes as in woodcarving.

RELIEF

In carving a relief the ground level is established. For work in the round

Above centre **Roughing out a piece of Portland stone with a punch.**
Above **Main forms being shaped with a claw.**

large pieces of waste stone are cut off using a pitcher or a punch.

Smaller pieces, depending on the hardness of the stone, are carved away with the claw or the chisel.

As with wood there is a danger, if profiles are cut at right angles to one another, that the sculpture ends up looking square.

Also as with woodcarving it is not sensible to carve the inside forms until the outside ones are made except in the case of a carefully planned relief when, as with wood, a drill may be used to set the depth of a ground and give a space for waste stone to move into.

Stone is a brittle material and has its limitations. Although large lumps may be carved off it in any direction, more may come away than you expect.

As with wood, if you carve up to an edge more stone may break out than you wish, so it is always sensible to work from an outside edge inwards.

A difficulty with stone, rather like that encountered around wood knots, is a tendency for some stones to pluck. As the chisel passes across it may drag up some of the stone below the cut.

This can happen if the chisel is blunt or if you attempt to cut off too large a lump.

Limestone and sandstone may be carved to a finish with the chisel and gouge or bullnose. As most stone carving is displayed out of doors and is probably seen at a distance it does not usually need a smoother surface.

Rasps, rifflers and abrasive papers are far more likely to be needed on stones that crumble or bruise too easily or where beautiful figure in the stone is revealed only by refining the surface.

Some people like to start with alabaster or soapstone because they are soft. Pure alabaster is hard to obtain in lumps in Britain as most is crushed and heated to turn it into plaster of Paris.

Some deposits have inclusions of shale which is very brittle and dark, quite out of keeping with the luminous almost waxy appearance of the polished stone.

The natural stone contains some chemically bound water which makes it feel resilient when carved with hammer and chisel.

It is less likely to be bruised if you remove large lumps with a saw and carve it with rasps, putting in details with cheap woodworking chisels. Alabaster also dissolves in water.

Soapstone can be worked in the same way but is crumbly.

Marble also bruises, particularly as one of the conventional ways of cutting it is to use a pointed punch which you hit vertically to the final surface.

This means a skin has to be left which is carved away with a sharply pointed claw followed by chisels and abrasives.

DUST

However it is worked, stone is dusty and it is easy to get particles in the eyes and lungs. Stones with silica or mica in them are particularly dangerous.

It is best always to work where a draught can carry the dust away and to wear eye protection, especially when striking the tools hard.

Always wear a mask to protect nose and mouth when creating much dust or using a poisonous stone.

For the beginner I recommend starting with a piece of limestone. Portland or Bath are readily available.

Portland is hard and may contain large shells but will take fairly fine detail, whereas Bath stone is softer, consists of large grains and crumbles on sharp edges.

If you can get one of the French limestones such as Caen you will find it a soft, finely-textured cream-coloured stone almost too good to be true. ●

Kara Belmont using a chisel to chase the surface of a copy of a piece of 18th century French acanthus leaf.

Stone carving tools available from:

Avery Knight & Bowlers Engineering Ltd, James Street West, Bath, Avon BA1 2BT
Tel: 01225 425894

Alec Tiranti, 70 High Street, Theale, Reading, Berkshire RG7 5AR.
Tel: 0118 930 2775
and 27 Warren Street, London W1P 5DG

B.I. Crawshaw, 3 Silverwing Industrial Park, Horatius Way, Croydon, Surrey CR0 4RU
Tel: 0181 686 7997

Dick Onians is senior carving tutor at the City and Guilds of London Art School. Since 1968, as well as teaching, he has been working as a professional sculptor in wood and stone. He inaugurated the City and Guilds Institute Creative Studies course in woodcarving. He also teaches a part-time woodcarving course at Missenden Abbey Adult Residential College in Buckinghamshire. His book, _Essential Woodcarving Techniques_, is published by GMC Publications.

PASSION FOR PANELS

IN THE FIRST OF TWO ARTICLES, SPECIALIST ROSS FULLER DESCRIBES THE DELICATE RESTORATION OF CARVED OAK PANELS AT ST MARY ABCHURCH IN THE CITY OF LONDON

I began restoring the pierced pew panels of St Mary Abchurch in 1992 and have been doing so on and off ever since.

First I photographed and catalogued all 98 of them, sketched freely to familiarise myself with their characteristic forms, and produced working drawings to scale from squared photocopies of my prints.

I had to confer with the architect, reassure the clergy, liaise with the police about parking, and move my workshop into the church at intervals to install the restored panels.

The process has been a protracted dance, waltz, jig, hip-hop and sometimes a limp.

Craft work at the bench is necessarily isolating, and contact with the world outside always vivid. Bringing the two worlds together is the greatest craft.

Mary Abchurch is a Wren church on a medieval site near the Bank of England. A dome on a cube with a spire, it is set in something like a Venetian piazza with an inlaid pavement.

The wooden-clad interior is extensively carved, and the reredos by Grinling Gibbons shows the pelican in her piety, piercing her breast to feed her young, a symbol of divine love and sacrifice.

Beneath the box pews the gentry kennelled their dogs while they said their prayers. The panels date from the 1680s and are by several distinct hands.

Authentic traces of the influences on native art, from Celtic interlace to Renaissance acanthus were carried in the subconsciousness of the English craftsman to be reproduced here. The church is indeed a treasury of 17th Century art.

OAK PANELS

The panels are let into the pews at the chest height of a man kneeling at prayer. They are formal symmetrical compositions of abstract foliage, stems, leaves and flowers, carved on both sides in 19mm, ¾in oak (*Quercus robur*) boards with the grain running horizontally.

The vertical uprising direction of the design is active and crisp, the lateral is passive.

Each side is achieved out of an effective depth of 8mm, ⁵⁄₁₆in, but through skilful foreshortening appears more fully three-dimensional. The average size is 510–535mm, 20–21in long by 180–200mm, 7–8in high.

After my euphoria at getting the commission faded, I had to look at each panel in detail, appraise the damage and face the particular difficulty. No two difficulties were the same.

Many of the panels were warped and twisted. In some the design was asymmetrical. I noted the tension of line and surface, moving everywhere in one of the six directions.

Copying from the masters was a traditional way to learn, but there is a great difference between dead copying, or reproduction, and emulation. You need to study as if you are immortal and work as if it is your last day on earth.

I laid each panel in a cradle cramped flat on the bench. This was a board with battens glued and screwed to frame a space slightly larger than the work so it could be held firmly with pairs of folding wedges. If the panel was warped I supported it underneath.

If work is not properly held you cannot apply the correct force to the tool.

For the repairs I used 18th–19th Century oak from pews which were being discarded from St Sepulchre-without-Newgate.

In the following account I will take a panel at a time, as I did at the bench, and give my notes on each, which should be read with the photographs in view.

PANEL 48

With panel 48 there were two missing stems. The replacements had to be finally attached to the original with slender glued surfaces, but carving them would involve some force, so the mother block had to be held strongly in

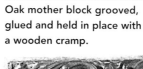
Oak mother block grooved, glued and held in place with a wooden cramp.

Panel 48 with the two missing stems.

place by increasing the gluing surface.

I reduced the irregular broken-edged gap to one with straight edges by paring them square with a No 1 chisel. I also grooved them.

Access to the inside edge for grooving while holding the fragile, slightly warped panel was awkward. I wrapped the panel in a cloth, put it in a wooden-jawed vice, and used a fine-toothed Japanese dovetail saw and

straight chisel to mark the sides, lifting out the waste with a small front-bent grounding tool.

I visualised the final result and squared and shaped the oak mother block, leaving enough spare wood, and grooved the edges.

I cut and inserted a false oak tenon and glued and cramped it using the gentle pressure of a Klemsia wooden cramp.

For this job I used white PVA glue because the surfaces mated well and it does not damage chisel blades. Cascamite resin type glues are gap filling but will damage a sharp tool.

After about four hours I began carving the stems, referring to the undamaged other side.

Whether simple or complex, good carving always depends on the clarity of visualisation in three dimensions, or four if you can manage it. Then, just when you are being carried away, there is the other side to carve.

··

Above left **The mother block fixed and ready for carving.**
Left **Carving progresses to match the original.**

PANEL 51

There was so much damage to panel 51 it was best to cut the panel in two and completely re-carve one half. As there was such a large gluing surface I did not need to groove the block edges.

My working drawing reproduced here shows the details of the design

Top **Panel 51 was so badly damaged it had to be cut in half.**
Above **A new block of oak glued into position on the remaining half of the original.**

7

6

5

4

3

2

0   11   12   13   14   15   16   17   18½

Above **The working drawing for panel 51. The left half shows the profile to be carved.**

and the work involved. The drawing was done from a squared photocopy of my photograph of the original.

The photocopy and the paper were divided into a grid of the same number

Below **The finished panel.**

of squares, with those on the paper having longer sides. This enabled an accurate working drawing to be made from a small photograph.

PANEL 56

On panel 56 I made as small a window as possible to include the missing detail while maximising the gluing surfaces. I laid on straight edges and masked the window with tape.

I drew the design on paper with intersecting compass sweeps and transferred the cut-out, slightly oversize, to the new wood block.

Next I cut a window in the carved panel along the taped lines with a fine-toothed dovetail or Japanese saw and trimmed the edges square with a flat chisel.

I grooved the edges of the window, prepared and grooved the mother block and fitted a tenon as with block 48.

PANELS 91 AND 94

With panels 91 and 94 I began as before by reducing the gap of the missing parts to a regular shape. I measured the length of the edges, took diagonal measurements with dividers and transferred these to the new wood and cut a mother block.

On these panels there was enough gluing surface without the need for grooving the edges or inserting false tenons.

With the mother block glued and cramped up I painted it with white emulsion and drew on the design profile in pencil.

The central missing parts of these panels were reconstituted by studying the characteristic patterns of the surrounding panels. The drawn profile was lost as the third dimension was entered.

Carving is essentially vision, passion and force with tools. It is a process always teetering on the brink of implosion and dissipation.

It is vital to see the invisible, intermediate forms and to risk using the largest possible tools, which saves energy. A depth gauge can be used, but the understanding eye is more sensitive.

Chisels must be sharp as only

Below **Panel 91 with a mother block glued in place, painted white and with the design drawn on.**
Bottom **The finished restoration.**

The mother block was then inserted in the panel and the whole put in the cradle with wedges for gluing up. It had to be weighed down because of a warp in the panel. Then the carving could begin.

It would have been possible to carve the replacement part first, before fitting it to the panel, but I preferred my method of working in situ as I could refer to the adjacent profiles and forms.

From top to bottom
Panel 56 with the taped-off window round the damaged part.
The replacement block is in place, marked out and wedged in the cradle for gluing up.
The replacement block has been carved to match the original.
The finished panel.

sharp tools obey and free the force of hand and mind.

Your own discoveries are irreplaceable. The old carvers interpreted forms with freedom and panache. We see only outlines and shrink from spoiling them.

Outlines are important because they contain the movement between the planes which cannot ordinarily be seen, but can be felt and sensed.

There were traditional craft exercises for vision, such as closing the eyes and 'seeing' what the finger tips touched. Also for rhythm, by reducing a block in even-sized chips.

CARVING STAGES

There are established, common-sense stages to a carving. These are not my ideas, so they can be trusted.

Having transferred a design profile onto the wood you must begin either by stabbing down onto, or chasing around, a two-dimensional line. I prefer the dagger to the spoon.

Then follows grounding, setting-in, bosting or roughing-in, modelling and finally undercutting, refining vision and re-drawing the profile as you proceed.

I tend to see what is wrong with what I am doing continually and am driven by personal discomfort until the last stage when there is no more wood to remove and it is too late.

By that time the work has either become a whole, invisible to the restless eye, or not. At the end something is revealed, the inevitable result of thousands of small decisions.

Having been revealed it must be disguised. The restorer tries to discern the original forms and merge his work totally in them, but when this takes place he feels bereft if he has become fascinated by his own creation along the way.

His lot is to lose sight of his horse at the last fence. In finishing the wood to conform with the whole effect his effort is consigned to oblivion. Restoration work is successful if it is invisible.

The Mary Abchurch panels had been coated in Victorian toffee varnish. I made experiments with stains, aniline dyes and spirit varnishes but the colour did not prove light-fast.

Eventually I settled on a mix of black and red French polish over a dark oak stain, rubbed through and dressed with deep brown antique wax. It was acceptable.

INSTALLATION

The process was completed by installing the panels. With one I broke the pews open from the top, lifted out the top rail and dropped the panel in from above.

With another I knifed out the mouldings, which are integral with the rail, inserted the panel from the front and pinned the mouldings back in place around it.

Joinery in the 17th Century was by rule-of-thumb, not micrometer. The dimensions of either side of the pew frame window into which the carvings were fitted were never quite the same, so the panels had either to be trimmed on site, or the mouldings scribed to fit the carvings.

Each panel was a different problem to fit, as it was to restore. On site everything had to be done immediately,

whether I felt like it or not, with whatever tools I could lay my hands on.

Standing back and looking anxiously at the fitted panels the tension dissolved if the work blended into the venerable ensemble of the church. It did, finally.

Installation is not really the end of the process, nor even is the arrival of the cheque. The experience of one job may enter the next. Everything is in movement.

The Mary Abchurch carvings still dance. ●

In the following article I describe the carving of a complete replacement panel.

Ross Fuller was born in Farnham Royal, Buckinghamshire, in 1946, from a line of joiners and cabinetmakers. He attended Cardiff and London Universities and the Institute of Historical Research and gained a first class honours degree in History. In 1985 he gained his doctorate in medieval spirituality and religious thought.

He studied woodwork, antique restoration and gilding in private workshops before setting up as an artist-craftsman in 1975. He subsequently studied woodcarving and sculpture at the City and Guilds of London Art School at Kennington.

He has travelled extensively in Europe and the Middle East studying ancient sacred sites and the works of art associated with them.

He is registered with the Conservation Unit, The Council for the Care of Churches, and architects and diocesan advisory committees throughout the country. He specialises in restoration carving, design, sculpture and letter cutting.

Studio: 23 Rosecroft Avenue, Hampstead, London NW3 7QA. Tel: 0171 435 4562.

Klemsia cramps and Japanese saws available from John Boddy's Fine Wood and Tool Store, Riverside Sawmills, Boroughbridge, North Yorkshire YO5 9LJ. Tel: 01423 322370.

Helpful book: *Practical Woodcarving and Gilding* by W. Wheeler and C. Hayward, published 1973 by Evans, London. ISBN 0 237 44516 6.

PANEL PIECE

IN THE SECOND OF TWO ARTICLES ON RESTORATION CARVING AT ST MARY ABCHURCH IN THE CITY OF LONDON, ROSS FULLER DESCRIBES THE MAKING OF A COMPLETE NEW OAK PANEL

This article is a commentary on a complex series of actions and decisions which became, through experience, properly unconscious.

Carving, like driving a car, cannot safely be entrusted to the mind. Thought initiates the movement, which then passes into the body. If it does not pass, the mind will interfere and bring the action to nought, because thought is too slow.

This is difficult to describe, but every craftsman knows of its existence and explores it in their own way.

Panel 43 at Mary Abchurch was missing, so I had carte blanche. From the beginning my eye had been drawn by the panache of two panels on the north side, sinuous rolling acanthus forms in perpetual motion like waves breaking.

I chose the lesser of these two designs for the first complete replacement carving, which I installed in 1992.

I saved the greater for panel 43 which I intended to carve at the end of the job. But I made an almost finished

Below **The working drawing for panel 43 based on the design of an existing, original panel.**

drawing of it before attempting any of the restorations to familiarise myself thoroughly with their style.

I produced a full size working drawing from a squared photocopy of my photograph, changing the dimensions to fit those of panel 43.

The way you draw is a personal matter, but it is the conception of what follows. It is an investigation of what you see, not a description.

A pretty picture is beside the point. If you will not draw, you cannot see, and if you cannot see, what are you doing?

I am sure there are many ways to work, but this has been my experience.

At best, drawing is the contemplation of three-dimensional forms, four even. By representing them in two dimensions, we square the circle, which will be useful later.

Drawing is about bodily posture, relaxation and tension, a preparation for wielding the chisel. The cut edge must be as alive as the drawn line.

You must struggle with the drawing to taste the refusal of this live movement in your body. A great sensitivity can appear in this struggle. Something is distilled.

OUTLINE

Four years later I began to carve the panel. I transferred the outline of the drawing onto lay-out paper and then traced it over carbon paper onto an oak (*Quercus spp.*) board of the right thickness, which I had previously painted white.

After all that time I was impatient to start, but forced myself to stop. Before plunging in there was a chance to reappraise the design, to look at the heights, depths and intermediate forms, not just the two-dimensional profiles of the outline.

As soon as you set a chisel into the surface the outline disappears, so it is crucial to keep a vision of the whole for as long as possible so you can return to it.

With a clear head I tried to foresee what could only be done at that stage. I marked the centre line and final thickness of the edge of the tongue with a marking gauge while the surface of the board was still intact, thus establishing the vertical limits of the material within which the design would be accomplished.

The lateral limits were established by the tracing. The carving could then start in earnest.

Using mallet and chisels of a curvature appropriate to the profiles, I stabbed down close to the final depths, and in the case of the frets stabbed right through. I left 1.5mm, ¹⁄₁₆in or so around the profiles at this stage.

I used the mallet as long as possible, to forestall the descent into mindless dentistry.

SCALE

I moved over all the panel reducing the wood equally, doing the work of one scale before passing to another, not losing a sense of the whole.

The appearance of dentistry at this stage would show this sense was weak. I always used the largest tools possible, those which embraced the limits of the intended cut.

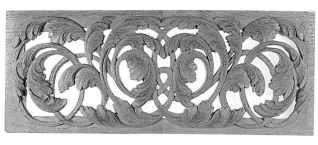

I cleared the margins (the tongue) by chasing along the edge, and by stabbing down around the forms and lifting out the waste with a front bent grounding tool.

It was important to keep seeing depths, not profiles. At a definite moment, I risked moving into the third dimension, losing the surface drawing and abandoning the safety to which the small mind clings.

I looked from an angle across the forms of the panel, not just straight down upon them as if they were two-dimensional.

I was emulating something beyond me. Appreciation of that fact came and went. When it was there I was learning.

A process of intuition began regarding the methods and approach of the old craftsmen which is difficult to put into words. With what flair and economy of effort they translated a linear design into three dimensions.

At first I approached Mary Abchurch carvings as art, which they of course were. I luxuriated in their subtleties, but as I proceeded my work became simpler, less emotional, more direct. I understood better how they were originally done.

I began to take down the stems, bearing in mind their overall linear movement, the unders and overs, the interweaving, whether it was rising or falling at any point.

Nothing is static in this kind of design, which is based on the observation of nature by generations of people who lived far closer to it than we do.

WHOLE

It was important not to forget the whole. I had to look at the whole sea and not just the froth on the waves. I looked, could not see, changed something and became able to see something else.

Thus I moved step by step,

inevitably towards a completion in which all the details blended in a unity.

Nothing was flat except the margins and they were tilted. There the carving ceased, or rather blended into cabinet-making.

The margins became tongues which fitted into the groove between the two sides of the moulding worked on the edges of the rails and stiles of the pew frame.

As the carving proceeded, I realised anew everything had to take place between the high and low points, that was within just 8mm, ⁵⁄₁₆in.

I took down the tips of leaves which were obviously lower, measuring everything against the datum of the margin's ground scribed on the edge before carving began.

I noticed the angle of the leaves downwards tilt, breaking the forms down mentally and visualising the concave and convex.

I chose the largest gouges appropriate for the 'invisible' intermediate forms, Nos 3, 5 or 7, and worked overall, redrawing profiles where they were lost, and stabbed down.

These forms were invisible because they had recognisable profiles only in their unseen cross-section.

I had to avoid being drawn into premature detail. I referred to the working drawing for exterior dimensions, then separated the leaves from one another and pushed down the tips

and edges further towards zero.

I had to simplify and be free. I measured depths from the centre of the thickness, remembering what had to be done on the other side of the panel.

Observing, remembering and note-taking for this article altered the way I worked. Such sensitivity was bound up in the physical process of carving and everything tried to interfere with it.

INVISIBLE

Restoration must be invisible. It is said anonymous blending and intentional conformity is good for the soul, but if it were automatically so restorers would be the best of men.

I began to work more finely, restoring outlines of leaves that had been pushed down to their proper level, but had become distorted (fatter) in the process.

I measured from the working drawing to rectify profiles, and turned the chisel and freed my mind to find the flick and tension of growing leaves.

I had to visualise the relationship of profiles as they changed and avoid picking. The body repeats what it knows automatically as the mind goes to sleep. Then the body tires and the mind interferes, trying to do what does not belong to it.

'Carving is labour-intensive, and as your energy runs out the work slows. When you lose what you are doing you must stop, rest and start again.

I worked systematically over the surface from left to right as a discipline when my mind flagged. I had to keep looking and see that everything was relationship.

The course of a carving is a sequence of seeing what is not there, and revealing it. The finished carving is actualised in the tension between the high points and the ground.

In the intervals of forgetting why

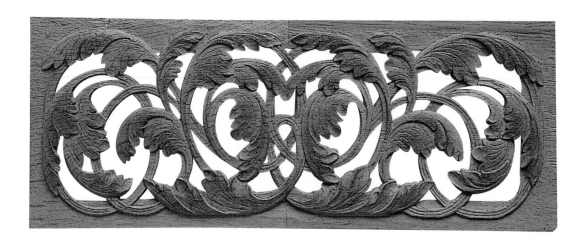

you are making the effort, rest on the fundamental techniques of stabbing down and lifting out the waste and of chasing the surface in broad sweeps to establish the intermediate forms. The meaning will reappear.

I used a few tools repeatedly, 2s, 3s, 4s, 5s 7s, 8s, fish-tails, veiners and back-bent gouges, to establish clarity and unity of form.

The confidence with which these were employed distinguished .the old work from the contemporary. I could see the wonderful way convex forms passed into concave, which so puzzled me when I was trying to think it, before I found out how it was done.

HARMONY

I could see where the slow movement of the coiled stem sprang from and followed it round to the high point. Again and again I realised everything in these traditional designs was a matter of relationship and harmony.

In the wood it took place within 8mm, ⁵⁄₁₆in. Inwardly there was another scale. If the rest of me could not obey these quick perceptions, my work would be dead on its feet.

I began to work ever more finely, closer and closer to zero. Measuring from the centre-line of the edge, I feathered the panel's outer margin which had to slot into a narrow, sometimes collapsed, 17th century groove.

If one thing changed, everything changed. I had to adjust the heights of outer leaves to correspond to the new margins, and re-check the two-dimensional height and width of the carving from the drawing.

Carving on site was a problem, but I had to remember that either side of the window was not necessarily the

The other side, not a mirror image but a reversal of the design.

....

same dimension. I had to be prepared to scribe mouldings to fit the panel rather than the other way round.

I noted the way the outside ground dipped down around the tips and edges of the leaves and stems to give them extra height.

Redrawing as I went, I refined profiles and the rise and fall of the intermediate forms. I noticed the high point of the outer leaves was slightly lower than those adjoining so the design built to the centre.

This was subtle but made a big difference. I tested heights by placing a straight-edge across.

This lowering made carving the reverse side difficult as the panel tipped when downward `pressure was applied, so I used wedges to support.

LAST STAGES

The last stages required an observation both intensely specific and global. I had to keep noting the sweep of the foliage and the force of its movement, deriving from the original carver's arm, mind and tool.

Bringing anything to a real conclusion is difficult. Usually you just flake out, but staying with it to the end, suddenly a unity looks back at you and you wonder how it came about.

Whether the result is good or bad, if the effort has been genuine you have participated in a mystery. Something is there which wasn't before.

But this was not the time for self-congratulation. I was only half-way through.

Next I had to turn the panel over and begin again on the other side. I traced the profile on the back of the

layout over carbon paper.

Of course it was not a mirror image because the design was reversed on the other side. Leaves that went under went over and so on, but it was a guide which I interpreted as I went.

In the case of this panel either side of the aperture was not the same, so I had to take exact measurements and trim edges, taking up any slack on site by trimming mouldings.

I could not do final modelling on the first side until the other side had been brought to the same stage, as depths could alter as I got closer to the final thicknesses.

Then I completed modelling the leaves on both sides (concavities and parallel channelling) and veined them and the stems.

Note the order of veining. On the fast side of a curve it was convex, using front-bent chisels. On the slow side it was concave, using small 3s.

The oak was brittle, but the effort was worthwhile. It imparted further life to the surfaces, unifying them, enabling them to be seen altogether.

If the edges broke I lubricated them with white spirit. I had the habit of doing this throughout the carving as it helped me to see the surfaces.

Lastly I undercut on both sides, throwing the forms forwards into visibility.

I am grateful to the architect Anthony New, the churchwardens Messrs Lowman and Henman, and the Rev Oswald Clarke for their support throughout this restoration. ●

WHICH WOOD?

GRAHAM BULL DISCUSSES THE MERITS OF VARIOUS TIMBERS FROM AUSTRALIA AND SOUTH EAST ASIA FOR CARVING

I am asked more questions about wood than anything else, what kind to use or how to get it to behave itself once the carving is started.

It is one of the most perplexing subjects but, like most things, it can be reduced to a set of basic guidelines which, once understood, can take care of most of the problems.

After all, any wood can be carved, but some are more difficult than others, and some are more appropriate than others for a given application. Knowing how to choose which wood for a project is the key to the problem.

The first thing to accept is there are no rules. It's a bit like the weather, every time the wind blows it's a bit different from last time. There are patterns and generalisations, but nothing hard and fast.

The same tree will yield wood with different behaviour patterns depending on where in the tree it came from. The shape of the bevel on your chisel will dictate the behaviour of the wood, as will the ambient humidity level. The variables are extensive, and so are the outcomes.

So, in an attempt to put it all into some kind of perspective, I will go through the most common wood characteristics you will need to take into consideration, and then carve a few samples from different countries.

APPLICATION

We first need to ask what the carving is for, as the end application will often be the deciding factor for choice of wood.

If it is for a decorative wall plaque you will not want a wood so heavy it will fall off the wall, whereas if it is for furniture it will need to be strong and durable and denser than the wall plaque. If it is for the exterior of a boat it will need to be weather resistant, and if it is to be highly polished it may need to be finer grained than otherwise.

Colour may be an important consideration, not only from the point of view of the surrounding decor, but also if the carving is a design with a lot of shadows, then a light coloured wood will show them off better than a dark colour.

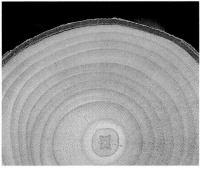

From top to bottom
Jacaranda (*Bignoniaceae*).
Boree or true myall (*Acacia pendula*).
Malaleuca (*Myrtaceae*).

Make a list of the prerequisites for the finished piece, and this will go a long way towards the determination of the right wood to choose.

The next question is what kind of design is to be carved? If it is deep you should choose something not too brittle and prone to breaking off.

Does the pattern change direction a lot indicating you would best use a fine straight-grained wood that does not chip easily?

Does it have large areas without detailed patterns that need to be completely unblemished for best results, indicating a wood that scrapes or sands cleanly without any tear out?

DESIGN

Would the design be improved if the wood was wavy grained or striped in colour, or knotty or figured in some other way? If this is so, be careful the figure in the wood doesn't adversely affect the way it behaves.

Knots can be difficult to handle and may chip your chisels. Wavy grain can tend to make the wood brittle or prone to tearing, and heavily striped woods can have different density, hardness and grain strength in the different colours, making life difficult.

Is the colour of the wood important? Quite often it is, and unfortunately quite often the best carving woods for the design and the application are the wrong colour.

The best, usually meaning the easiest, woods for carving in Australia tend to be pretty boring as far as wood goes. They are figureless, straight grained and generally grey such as beech (Australian and Pacific Island varieties, *Gmelina* family), kauvula (*Endospermum medullosum*) from Fiji, or yellow such as cheesewood (*Alstonia scholaris*) and jelutong (*Dyera costulata*) from Papua New Guinea and Indonesia respectively, or light brown like bollywood (*Litsea reticulata*) from northern Australia.

In this region, woods with colour and figure that polish well and look great tend to be denser than is ideal for carving. Often the figure patterns we all like make the wood want to tear and break if we try to work them by hand to fine detail.

In some cases these challenges can be overcome by altering the design, or if we definitely want to use a difficult wood we may need to alter the way we shape the bevel on our chisel. This can have a major impact on the ease of working the wood.

It may also be necessary to carve the wood wet, before it is seasoned, as unseasoned wood is generally softer and more pliable than dry wood.

DENSE

This is particularly the case with very dense fine-grained woods like Gidgee (*Acacia cambagei*), an Australian inland desert wattle that weighs about 1330 kilos a cubic metre. It is basically impossible to do much with it when seasoned, but generally workable when wet and carved with a correctly bevelled chisel.

In the following examples I look at some of the species which can be carved from countries around South East Asia. They are not all ideal carving timbers, but they cover a range of associated challenges and each one has different characteristics.

For each timber I carved a simple eucalyptus leaf pattern, of the kind that sometimes decorates furniture in Australia. It is not of any actual species, but a generic gumleaf.

Each example has the same finish, two coats of clear artist's shellac, scraped with a knife, and one coat of unrefined beeswax dissolved in gum turpentine with resin.

AUSTRALIAN WOODS

I will start with woods from Australia. **Rose mahogany** (*Dysoxylum fraseranum*), is commonly known as **rosewood**, and the average dry density is about 720 kg/cm.

This is used for furniture and panelling and tends to be flaky and brittle where sharp rises occur, so the design needs to take this into consideration.

The grain is wavy, so to help stop it breaking you need to chisel it diagonally across the grain or along the waves, within reason, changing direction frequently.

A very sharp slim chisel such as a fishtail with a long bevel, giving a low approach to the wood, is best. Take fine shavings for best results.

When the wood has this wavy characteristic, the coarser the fibres the greater the likelihood of breakage. Rosewood tends to be comparatively finely grained, and this

reduces that problem.

It is a fairly gummy timber, and while this can make it even more brittle when it is dry, the natural resins enhance its ability to develop a beautiful polish.

Rose mahogany or rosewood grain, working and finish.

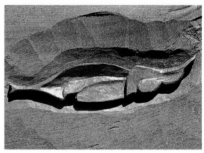

Silver Ash (*Flindersia bourjotiana*) has an average dry density of about 670 kg/cm and is commonly used for furniture and boat building.

It is not often carved, but it has characteristics that cover a large number of timbers, so it is worth including in this study.

Any timbers that are good for steam bending, like silver ash, generally have a long fibre which is conducive to bending. Short fibre timbers tend to fracture more easily. This characteristic can also make the carving process harder.

In the case of silver ash, it is a hard wood with long, wavy, sometimes interlocked fibres that tend to want to grab the chisel. There can be a lot of tear and it is easily splintered.

When carving, do not try to take out too much at once, either in width or depth. Try using smaller chisels than you would normally, and cut diagonally across the grain in the direction of the grain for best results.

Ensure the chisel is very sharp, and try a slightly more convex bevel than normal if tearing and breaking occurs.

Silver ash grain, working and finish.

Jarrah grain, working and finish.

Jarrah (*Eucalyptus marginata*) has an average dry density of about 820 kg/cm and is a relatively coarsely-grained timber with slightly interlocked grain.

It is a general construction timber, and was commonly used for railway sleepers and fence posts and was exported to the UK for use as road pavers. It is now commonly used for furniture in Australia.

It is reasonably hard, splinters easily, but cuts cleanly with a sharp, well controlled chisel, cutting along the grain. It will tear out cutting across the grain, as will most Australian eucalypts.

If you are carving a large piece in most hard woods like jarrah, it will be necessary to alter the angle of the bevel on your chisel to reduce the likelihood of serrating or chipping its cutting edge.

Try increasing the angle anything up to 10° if chipping occurs. Re-grind progressively until you find the best angle that interferes the least with the cutting action of the tool.

An alternative is to put a secondary bevel on the inside of the tool, thereby increasing the strength of the cutting edge without altering the behaviour of the chisel.

PAPUA NEW GUINEA WOODS

Kwila (*Intsia bijuga*) is also known as **merbau** and has an average dry density of 850 kg/cm. This is a slightly interlocked grainy and greasy wood with a highly irritant sanding dust, and is used for furniture, panelling, boat building and carving.

The yellow substance visible in the photograph is capable of staining fabrics and concrete.

The grainy nature of the wood makes it unsuitable for detailed carvings, and as with most grainy woods it is best to test the design in the wood first before committing yourself to carving it.

One benefit of grainy woods is they often glue well, so if you do break part of the carving off it can generally be repaired easily.

Always ensure with grainy timbers like this that your design is not presenting a weakness along the grain, such as an animal's leg that might break off if any stress were placed across it.

Kwila is grainy enough to sometimes crumble to a coarse powder.

Kwila or merbau grain, working and finish.

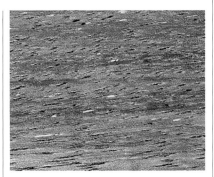

NEW ZEALAND WOODS

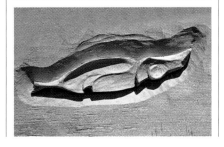

Rimu (*Dacrydium cupressinum*) has an average dry density of about 600 kg/cm and is a fine, even, straight-grained textured timber used for flooring, furniture, panelling and plywood, and is good for steam bending.

It has long, stringy fibres that tend to grab the chisel, like silver ash, and this can make it difficult to exit the wood easily.

It cuts fairly cleanly along the grain, but if you are not careful the long stringy fibres may splinter. Like many long fibred woods, Rimu is also prone to tearing across the grain, so avoid a design that requires a lot of cross grain cutting.

If this is not possible, once again try re-grinding the bevel on your chisel making it rounder or more convex than you would normally have it. This will help the chisel to move upwards out of the wood rather than digging into it.

Rimu grain, working and finish.

PHILIPPINE WOODS

Light Red Meranti (*Shorea spp*) is categorised as light by its density and is known in Australia generically as **Pacific maple**. The average dry density is between 400 and about 640 kg/cm.

Meranti machines well and is generally used for light construction purposes such as doors, windows, architraves and skirting boards. It has a coarse interlocked grain that tends to be stringy and spongy, and demands a sharp chisel to avoid its characteristic woolly tearing.

Because it is soft and coarse it has little substance and does not easily give a crisp finish. The ends of the fibres are easily raised when applying water or spirit-based finishes, and therefore need scraping or papering to clean them up.

Poplar (*Populus eramericana*) is a commonly carved timber which behaves in much the same way as meranti.

Light red meranti, or Pacific maple grain, working and finish.

MALAYSIAN AND INDONESIAN WOODS

Jelutong has an average dry density of about 400 kg/cm and was used commonly in the past for engineering pattern making. It is now also used for

Jelutong gum pocket in grain, working and finish.

rocking horses, door cores, and drawing boards. The latex is used for chewing gum.

Jelutong is brittle if carved against the grain, and certainly is subject to significant breakage if used for finely detailed carvings, particularly with

sharp or steep rises.

It has characteristic gum pockets that can be several inches deep and not always apparent on the surface.

With care, crisp and finely-edged carving can be achieved with Jelutong. While it's lack of strength makes it generally unsuitable for such carvings, its crispness and low density make it ideal for gesso or gilded finishes such as large picture frames. ●

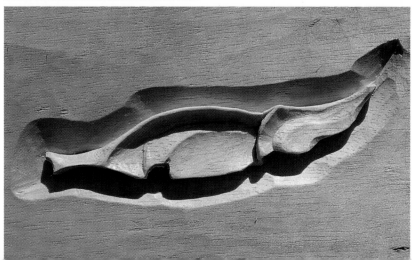

Graham Bull is proprietor of the Whistlewood Studio and Craft Barn in Sydney, Australia. Self-taught, he has been a woodcarver for some 34 years and teaches carving in all its forms to about 100 people each year, from schoolchildren and hobbyists to professional woodworkers.

GET A GRIP

DICK ONIANS' GUIDE TO THE BASICS OF WORKHOLDERS, CUTTING TOOLS AND SHARPENING STONES

In some cultures it is common to hold carving in the lap, with the feet or one hand. However, in the western tradition (when using chisels) the work is held on a work surface of some kind by a special device, leaving both hands free to control the tools.

Unless you are forced by some powerful circumstance to sit down to carve, you should always stand. This means you have mobility and can put your weight more fully behind the chisel. It follows that the bench should be of a height that allows you to stand without bending your back.

For relief carving a good rule is to have the top of the bench just below elbow level. For work in the round it is wise to choose a height appropriate for the majority of your work. The bench should be sturdy and not dance around the floor.

It is tempting to rush straight into carving without planning how the work is to be held. I have known students who have neglected this advice, and as the work has progressed the class has been disrupted by the sounds of carvings hitting the floor and cries of dismay, if not of pain. It is worth mentioning here that you should always wear stout shoes when carving. Sandals and thin shoes give no protection against falling objects, which may include chisels.

CLAMPS AND CHOPS

Countless means of securing work to the bench are now available. To allow for the use of a cramp (or clamp) there must be an overhang of at least 35mm, 1½ins, to allow a grip to be obtained. Room must also be left below for the tightening mechanism to be turned. At least one corner of the bench should be accessible so work can be clamped more firmly at opposite sides. Work may swing if anchored by only one clamp.

A clamp should be strong and have its heads in line. It should have adequate reach and ideally should be easily adjustable. If it has a fine thread it will take longer to adjust and is more suitable for metalwork. When buying second-hand clamps, make sure the buttons are not going to fall off.

The traditional woodcarver's vice or 'chops' is expensive unless you make it yourself, and kits are available for that purpose. The chops can be held with a

Student standing at a carving bench with the elbow level and body leaning to exert weight on the chisel. The carving is held on scrapwood by a paper join and the block is clamped to the bench.

bench screw which allows it to be swivelled. Naturally, this means you need a hole in the bench top. The jaws are lined with cork and felt to ensure a good grip.

A conventional bench vice can also be used, but this limits the angles at which the work can be held. It is always useful to have one if only for preparing wood. Vices with a quick release are more expensive but pay for themselves in convenience.

If there is provision for a dog to be fitted to the moving head, and if dogs can be fitted on the bench, then panels can be held without the need for clamps. This makes planing the carving easier as there are no obstructions above the work.

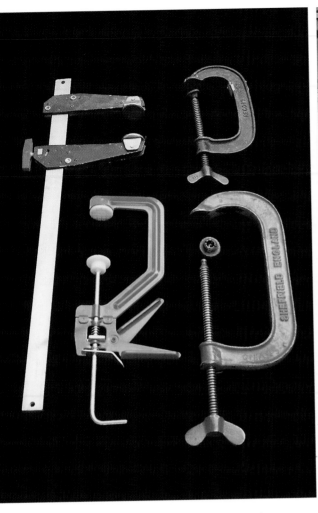

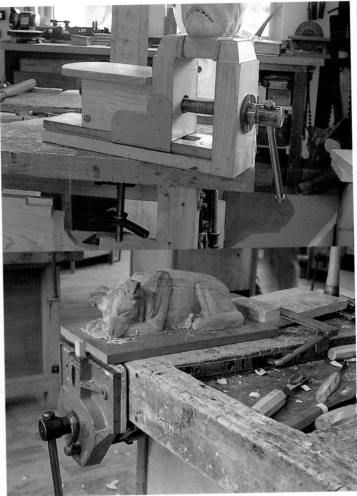

Above **Clamps (reading clockwise from left): Long reach Jet clamp heads on a 670mm, 26in bar, G Clamp with loose button, single-handed clamp**

Top **Carver's chops with square block left under the carving to make it secure**
Above **Bench dog comprised of a thin metal bar holding a bench hook**

Clamps and vices demand that the workpiece has at least two parallel sides. If the piece is irregular in shape at the bottom and can bear it, a rectangular or preferably square, block can be screwed onto the base, but the block and the workpiece must both be flat where they meet.

At least two thick screws are needed if the workpiece is to be carved with force. The lengths of the screws and their positions must be noted so they do not get in the way of the chisel or leave ugly holes on the finished article.

USEFUL DEVICES

Another traditional way of holding wood, which allows it to be easily worked from every angle, is the bench screw. The pointed tip is screwed into the underside of the piece, then the body of the screw is pushed through a hole in the bench and fastened by a wing nut underneath. The work may be raised by adding a block between it and the bench.

Large pieces of wood may be so heavy they need no restraint. They may be workable when lying on the bench or on the ground. A saw horse may form a solid cradle which allows the work to be seen all round and rotated easily. Webbing clamps are excellent for gripping awkwardly shaped pieces.

Increasingly popular today is the ball and socket type of clamp with the work screwed down to a faceplate which can be rotated through 360° horizontally and 180° in the vertical plane. The ball and socket joint is locked by mechanical or hydraulic pressure. A good one is expensive but very effective. It is possible to screw wooden bars onto the plate with sash cramp heads to hold panels or even to screw a carver's chops on.

An old device which is still available is the bench holdfast. This enables work to be clamped from the middle of the bench. It usually comes with two collars which are let into the bench in different positions. The largest readily available holdfast in Britain will clamp wood up to 250mm, 10in thick and has a reach of about 185mm, 7¼in.

RELIEF WORK

You can prevent a relief carving from sliding by using a frame which can be nailed or clamped to the bench. The panel can be wedged while carved, but moved around quickly. Alternatively a frame can be made on a board which is then clamped to the bench. In commercial workshops thin strips of mouldings are usually. nailed to the bench. Another method is to glue a sheet of newspaper to a flat piece of scrap and then glue the work-piece to the paper. This is particularly good with delicate pieces of relief. When

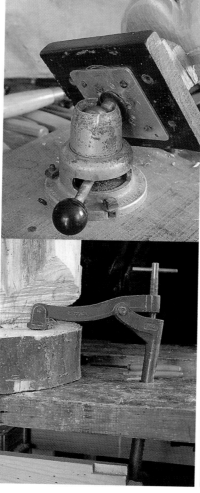

Top **A bench screw**
Above **Webbing clamp holding an awkward piece on a saw horse**

Top **Ball and socket clamp with home-made faceplate. Work is screwed on from underneath**
Above **Holdfast in use**

Above **Tirolean carving horse from the carving school at St Jakob**

finished, the carving is gently prised off with a broad straight-edged chisel. You can also use double-sided tape.

Many carvers have their own solutions to the problem of holding. I once saw a good example at a carving school in the South Tirol. It was a simple horse with a carving table held against a post by a threaded bar with a handle. This passed through a slot in the post and allowed the table to be raised or lowered and tilted. The work was fastened to the table by a bench screw so it could be rotated.

ANCHORING FOR ADHESION
Holding is important whenever you need to glue wood, whether building up a block before carving or repairing a break. In the latter case, the surface is often irregular or in danger of being bruised by the head of a clamp.

An old furniture restorer's trick is to cut sections out of an old bed spring and straighten them out to form rings. The cutting usually leaves the end of the metal sharp and when the ring is opened out it will grip on an uneven surface. But beware, this will leave a mark unless the wood is protected.

The Jet Clamp is another useful device which will grip on an uneven surface, and because the heads can be loosened, the surfaces do not need to be parallel. In addition, the heads have rubber pads which reduce the risk of bruising and slipping.

The cam clamp has wooden jaws with cork padding. This is quickly adjusted and has a soft grip, useful on delicate objects. The single-handed clamp derived from the mastic gun is cheap and effective too. It does not exert as much pressure as a G clamp

but is it good for light work or in conjunction with another clamp.

TOOLS AND ACCESSORIES
Once the work-piece is firmly anchored, you need chisels and a mallet. Carvers' mallets are round. The best are made of *lignum vitae* as even a 50mm, 2in diameter model will be quite weighty and last well. They are also made of beech (*Fagus spp*), apple (*Malus sylvestris*) or other tough woods. A soft steel dummy used for delicate stone carving may also be used.

Rasps and rifflers are useful accessories. Handcut ones last longer and cut well. Surforms and dreadnoughts also help in shaping regular curves especially on end grain. But they are all best followed with a chisel finish as they can scratch the work deeply. The alternative is the lengthy, boring and

detail-blurring process of sandpapering down through several grades of paper.

There are now many machines available to speed up the work: chainsaws, bandsaws and rotary discs, burrs and sanders attached directly to drills or on flexible drive shafts which can rough out and finish carvings particularly in difficult corners. The effects they produce are different from those left by chisels, often less attractive. They are also expensive, noisy, dusty and less safe.

SHARPENING STONES

It is impossible to carve well without sharp tools. Equipment for sharpening should be bought with the first chisel. When starting out, unless you have access to a grinder and a buffing machine, sharpening has to be done the hard way by hand. You will need a coarse stone, a medium stone and a finishing stone to hand.

Oil stones are most commonly used. The usual size of a bench stone is 8in, 200mm long by 2in, 50mm

Above **Bed spring clamp holding part of a badly damaged outdoor sculpture**

wide. The synthetic and slate stones are 1in, 25mm thick but hard Arkansas, which is the best finishing stone, is very expensive and is now usually ½in, 13mm thick. The coarse and medium stones may be bought as a combination stone, coarse on one side and medium on the other. The orange, India stone is an excellent medium stone. The cheaper oil stones are too soft to last.

Twenty years ago there were clearly differentiated Washita and Arkansas stones. Although of the same mineral from the same source in the Washita mountains in Arkansas, the Washita stone looks porous and is much softer.

Now, perhaps because Arkansas is a well known name, the cheaper stone is also labelled Arkansas and the unwary purchaser may buy the poorer kind by mistake. Genuine hard

Top right **Jet clamp showing the head fitting well on an angled surface**
Above right **JA cam clamp**

Arkansas is difficult to find. It is translucent, particularly when wetted. Washita stone is not. The black stone seems slightly faster cutting, producing a better edge, than the hard white Arkansas. It is not translucent. Hard Arkansas stones last more than a lifetime unless dropped.

In addition to the bench stones, you need at least one fine (preferably Arkansas) slip stone. Slips come in various shapes and sizes. The rule is to make sure you have one which will fit inside your smallest gouge. It will do for your big ones too, although you may prefer to have different thicknesses for wider tools.

I like to grind an inside bevel on most of my straight gouges, but even if you do not want this bevel you may at some time be forced to grind inside. Therefore, keeping a carborundum or India slip as well will save time.

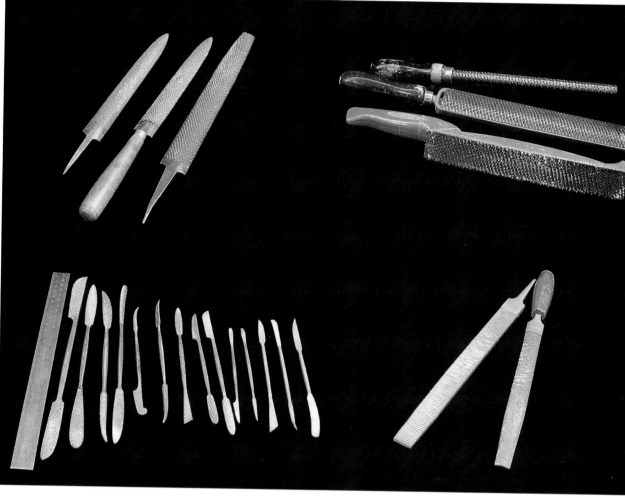

Top right **Rasps: the two on the left are hand cut and typically pointed. The other is a standard half round bastard rasp**

Above **Assorted handmade rifflers shown against a 305mm, 12in ruler**

Top **Three surform rasps: standard flat, half round and the very useful Roundfile**
Above **A dreadnought and a half round Aven Trimmerfile**

SAVING ON STONES

There are various ways of saving money. A biggish Arkansas slip stone can be made to double as a bench stone if it is set into a block of wood. Slate bench and slip stones are adequate for finishing. They are cheap but cut the metal very slowly. Also particles of grit or bits of discarded burr can get caught in the surface and scratch the chisel's edge.

Japanese water stones are excellent at removing the metal, indeed the finishing stones quickly produce as good an edge as an Arkansas. They are comparatively cheap. They work on the principle that the surface is constantly worn away to expose fresh sharp grit.

Another disadvantage is that you need to dry the tools thoroughly, and any oil that finds its way onto the stone spoils it. For finishing carving chisels a 6, 000 grit stone is quite sufficient and

is far cheaper than the 8, 000 grit stone. The slip stones tend to wear into bumps and constantly need reshaping.

Removing the burr after sharpening and keeping the edge keen are best done on a leather strop. A piece of hide will burnish the metal eventually but a dressing of chrome polish such as Solvol Autosol or Autoglym which can be bought from car or motorcycle accessory shops quickly removes the burr and polishes the metal to a mirror finish and the keenest edge.

When the paste dries out it falls off the leather so it is best to rub some tallow or vaseline into the flesh side of the leather and then smear the abrasive paste in afterwards. A little will then last a long time.

In acquiring equipment it is a false economy and can be very frustrating to buy second rate stuff. It is better to start with a small selection of good tools. ●

Dick Onians is head of the carving department of the City and Guilds of London Art School. Since 1968, as well as teaching, he has been working as a professional sculptor in wood and stone. He inaugurated the City and Guilds Institute Creative Studies course in Woodcarving.

THE GREAT AUSTRALIAN BIGHT

PETER FLETCHER SHOWS HOW TO GET YOUR TEETH INTO CARVING TAGUA NUTS

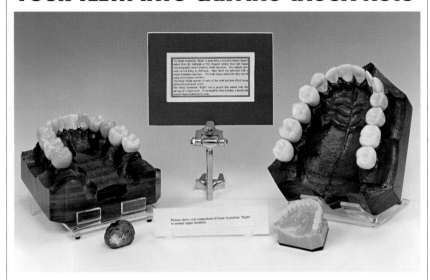

The completed Great Australian Bight, tagua nut and normal false teeth for size comparison.

The idea for this project, *The Great Australian Bight*, came to me after I had carved a single tooth in olivewood (*Notelaea lingustrian*). To make a complete set of teeth I set about trying to find the whitest wood available locally.

From previous woodturning projects I knew red river gum (*Eucalyptus camaldulensis*) would be suitable for the jaws, and this had a variety of colour variations.

I experimented with many light-coloured woods, including olivewood, Huon pine (*Dacrydium franklinii*), acacia (*Acacia cambagei*) and bottle brush, or tea tree (*Melaleuca leucadendron*).

I eventually came across some tagua nuts (*Phytelephas macrocarpa*) which had a design carved on them. This carving revealed what I was looking for.

Tagua nuts are native to Columbia, Ecuador and Peru in South America.

The size of these teeth is approximately seven times normal dentition. Therefore, allowance had to be made for selection of the tagua nuts suitable for the teeth to be carved.

A single upper central is about the same size as your thumb to the first joint.

When selecting the nuts I had to first grind part of the protective shell away to reveal the colour underneath. I bought twice as many nuts as I needed so I could find the whitest, creamiest to closely

Great Australian Bight, articulated.

resemble a normal tooth.

I bought the tagua nuts by mail order from Supreme Wood at St Albans in Victoria, Australia.

GRINDING

Once I decided which tooth was to be carved and the nut which would suit, I began to reduce the size by grinding a rough shape using a belt sander. I find this is the fastest method and gives me more control as I visualise the tooth taking shape.

One problem I encountered while grinding tagua nuts was the very fine dust created. It is essential to wear a mask and visor if an extraction system is not installed.

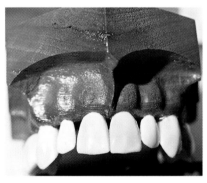

Close up of upper teeth and gums.

Once the roughing was completed I began shaping in more detail, using a suspension motor, handpiece and tungsten carbide dental burrs.

A lot of the anatomy of the tooth was from memory but I occasionally referred to a dental workshop manual for particular landmarks.

The tagua nut is ideal for carving using burrs because it is very hard and dense with no grain as such to worry about. On close examination there are growth rings but these are close together so it makes carving easy.

I now appreciate why the native South Americans used tagua nuts in the past for carving buttons, chessmen and dice as a substitute for ivory.

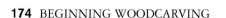

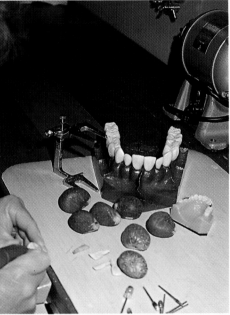

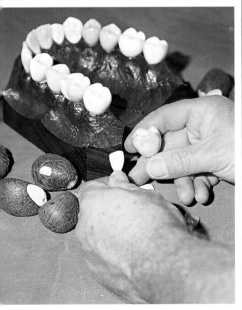

CAVITY

The nut itself is not completely solid but has a cavity in the centre which can pose a problem. Depending on which tooth is to be carved, I overcame this by making a feature of the cavity and filling it with tooth coloured dental acrylic which was cured in a dental hydroflask (small pressure cooker).

Once the acrylic had cured I was able to continue carving the detail, and when complete the tooth appeared to have had a filling.

At this stage I prepared the upper and lower jaws. These were made from an old redgum railway sleeper salvaged from the Adelaide to Port Augusta railway line in South Australia.

I was able to purchase this sleeper from the Railway Sleeper Company at Reynella in Adelaide, South Australia.

To construct the jaws I first used an Arbortech rotary cutter fitted to my angle grinder. This was ideal for removing the initial waste and shaping some of the detail.

The more intricate carving was achieved using the handpiece and burrs once again. Extra care was needed when setting the teeth in the arches so the mesial (middle) and distal (outer) surfaces would contact each other.

On this project I completed all the upper teeth and jaws before attempting the lower. When I was satisfied with each tooth's detail I polished the nut with dental pumice and tripoli.

Because of the hardness of the nut, the burr marks were removed by the pumice and the surface remained smooth.

ARTICULATED

I then began the lower arch and tagua teeth and completed them to suit the opposing upper dentition. Some allowances had to made when articulating the jaws together by grinding the occlusal surfaces, that is the surfaces of the teeth when closed together.

The plain line articulator was modified to suit the oversize jaws, then

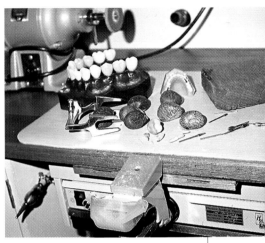

The tools and materials used for the project. There is a dust extraction vacuum unit below the bench.

sandblasted and polished. I also sandblasted the tissue areas of the redgum jaws to achieve a dull and more natural looking effect. The top, bottom and sides were fine sanded and finished smooth.

I then gave the tagua teeth a coat of clear gloss enamel to protect them from discolouring. I gave the jaws coats of satin for the tissue areas and full gloss for the top, bottom and sides.

The final stage was drilling, positioning and cementing the teeth in situ.

I added a plaque and furniture tacks to protect the base and top, and The Great Australian Bight was complete. ●

Peter Fletcher is a dental and maxillo-facial technician by trade. He enjoys woodturning and woodcarving and makes a feature of his work with the addition of coloured acrylic which adds character to projects.

Arbortech supplied in the UK by BriMarc Associates,
8 Ladbroke Park, Millers Road, Warwick CV34 5AE.
Tel: 01926 493389.

CHAIN REACTIONS

JOHN BEASLEY SAYS A CHAINSAW CAN BE USED SAFELY AND EFFECTIVELY FOR WOODCARVING, BUT HE STRESSES THAT VIGILANCE IS ALWAYS ESSENTIAL

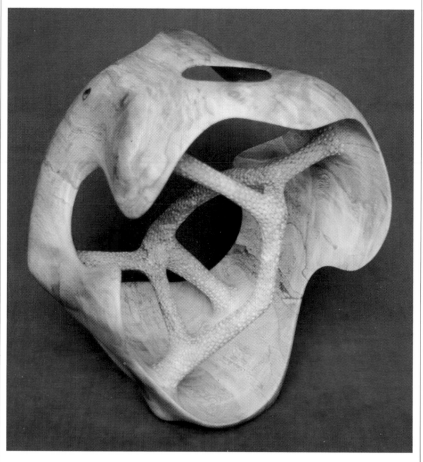

Before I start, I must emphasise that the benefits of using the chainsaw come at a cost – constant vigilance. Although it is a wonderful tool, it can also inflict severe injuries. Most chainsaws on sale today come with detailed instruction manuals, and these should be read and understood if you are new to the tool. Take time to develop confidence and a feel for your saw before attempting more difficult techniques.

The techniques I describe here have been developed over time, and with experience I have become confident in using them. However, someone new to the chainsaw may encounter difficulties I do not mention. So although I have tried to describe as clearly as I can what I do and the likely safety implications, it remains your responsibility to use the chainsaw with caution at all times. In particular, remember that if the upper part of the nose comes in contact with an object, it will cause kickback.

STRAIGHT CUTS

Chainsaws are designed to make straight cuts through timber; the flat bar more or less dictates this. (Sometimes a badly sharpened saw, or one with damage to one side of the teeth, will cut in a curve, often jamming in the cut as the curve tightens.) Straight line cutting is useful for removing large blocks, squaring the base of the sculpture, and so on, but it takes one only so far.

As a sculptor, I remove the bumper spike from my chainsaw, partly because of the damage it can do to an almost completed piece, but also because I can produce a more accurate straight cut without it. This is because

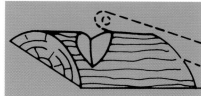

Two straight cuts can meet to remove a wedge of timber

levering the saw through the wood using the spike also causes some sideways twisting movement which is inclined to skew the cut.

Two intersecting straight cuts can be used to remove a wedge of timber, though it takes practice to get the cuts to meet accurately. This is a good time to develop the skill of watching both ends of the bar as the cut proceeds. If you focus on one end only, the other end is likely to cut too deep, perhaps ruining the whole project.

Keep a mental 'no go' zone around the part of the sculpture you are shaping. I tend to leave 10-20mm, about ½in, depending on the situation. Then if you do lose control of the saw the resulting damage is likely to be to this safety buffer, preserving the desired form.

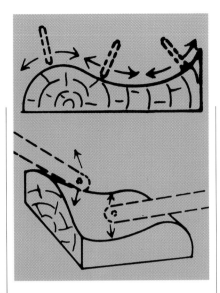

PARALLEL CUTS

It is possible to produce quite complex curves using only straight cuts with the chainsaw. Make parallel cuts about 20mm, ¾in apart, if possible across the grain. Then knock out the intervening pieces with a hammer or the back of an axe in free-splitting timbers, or use a mallet and gouge.

This is quite a safe technique, and can be combined with the floating technique described next to tidy up the admittedly rough surface produced. Again it is wise to leave a buffer zone to accommodate any errors you may make at this stage.

In very soft timbers I find I remove wood as shavings and sawdust rather than in pieces. I often cut slice after slice with the saw as described above, but leaving no intervening pieces to be knocked out later. Having the correct chain fitted makes this much easier: some chains are difficult to hold in position and tend to jump off the cut into the previous slot.

FLOATING

The technique I call floating consists of moving the bar from side to side across the surface, lightly enough to remove a thin layer of wood but not allowing the

Floating across a surface, the bar moving from side to side while the angle of the saw is adjusted to keep the bar perpendicular to the surface

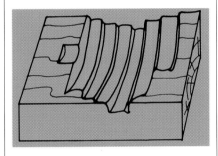

A series of parallel cuts with the intervening pieces knocked out

saw to pause and cut in at any point. This is a useful technique for removing bark or sapwood, and for refining any surface that has already been roughly shaped.

Initially you will find it difficult to prevent the bar digging in and cutting, and perhaps ruining the surface. With practice, a light touch and fluid rocking of the bar from side to side will give good control. By varying the direction of attack you can make the surface true if required. Also, if you have cut an unintended slot, varying the direction of the cut will allow the chain to float over it and not drop in and deepen it.

With a sharp chain and a light touch, a lot of timber can be shaped with this technique, especially on the outside of a piece. Complex curves can be accommodated, using the nose of the bar if necessary to enter hollows (see below). The finished surface can be true enough to move directly to sanding.

There is one important rule when floating: keep the bar at right angles to the surface being cut. This means the machine will need to be rotated with your wrists to follow the curves. Allowing the bar to lean over on the wood may result in it biting or bouncing, with resulting damage to the surface. Some chains are more forgiving than others in this regard.

Floating demands total concentration, and as it puts a lot of strain on your wrists it is best done in short bursts. It is not particularly dangerous, though if you are using the nose of the bar in a deep hollow do not allow the top quadrant of the nose to touch any overhang as this could cause kickback.

CUTTING CURVES

To cut curves the trick is to use the nose of the bar as much as possible. Hold the chainsaw above the level of the work so that only the rounded bar end comes in contact with the wood. Try drawing curves on the surface of the wood using the bar nose, starting at the point furthest from your body and drawing the saw towards you. You can make a controlled shallow cut which curves quite smoothly.

Move your whole body fluidly while maintaining a gentle but steady pressure on the bar. Keep the tip down so that most of the cutting is done on the curved end of the bar. It cuts fast because the chain passing over the curve offers more bite than on the flat side of the bar.

To cut more deeply and define the shape marked out by your original curved cut, repeat the cut moving the bar slightly away from the area you wish to preserve, and into the waste wood. Go deeper. Make further cuts, each time moving the bar slightly further into the waste wood and away from the original cut. If you don't widen the cut with the tip of the bar, the deeper cuts will start to erode the part you want to save.

You are cutting a curve with a straight, flat bar so there has to be some width for the bar to twist in. As the groove gets deeper the chain on the top of the nose may start to cut as well. At this point there could be a risk of kickback, but the movement towards you with constant steady pressure helps minimise this. Take special care though,

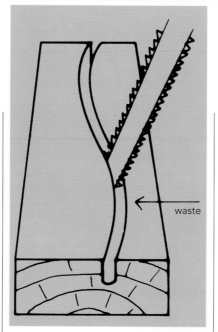

Cutting a deep curve with the tip of the bar, moving into the waste wood as the cut is widened on each stroke

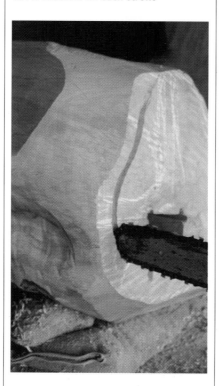

Above **The nose of the saw used to cut a curve. Subsequent cuts into the waste widen the cut**

Right **The cut is deepened and widened to allow the bar to twist within the hollow**

as you enter each cut, that the top of the nose does not contact the wood. Fluid sweeping movements are better than rigid over-controlled pressure.

With a powerful saw, this technique can be controlled, fluid and fast. In fact it comes close to being the equivalent for the sculptor of the free expression that painters such as Jackson Pollock experience as they trickle paint on the canvas.

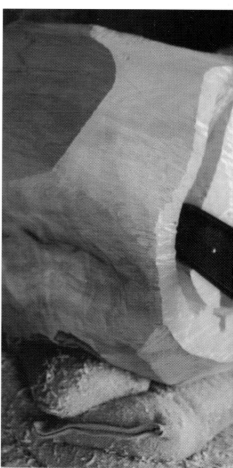

NIBBLING

When working within a hollow form or cavity, lack of space does not allow most of the previously described techniques to be performed properly. You need to expand the cavity gradually, using careful controlled cuts, so that the bar does not damage the surrounding work. Using this technique, the timber is all removed as chips or, as is often the case when working with the grain, as long thin ribbons.

The initial hollow must be large enough to accommodate the bar, at least in one direction. Such a cavity can be produced by nosing (described next) or with a drill and wood bits, using a gouge to remove the core. Often there will be little extra space, so control of the chainsaw is crucial.

Set the saw in motion first, then insert the bar into the cavity and make a cut towards what will eventually be its perimeter. If the work is arranged so that you are cutting downwards then gravity is working with you. Carefully raise the saw so as not to strike the top of the cavity, and make the next cut parallel to and immediately adjacent to the first.

With succeeding cuts a keyhole-shaped cavity is created. The key slot is expanded little by little, if possible turning the work from time to time so that you continue to cut downwards as you work. Ideally the bar should be at right angles to the developing perimeter, though this is not always feasible. With some chains the bar tends to jump off the cut, so having a suitable chain can make a great difference.

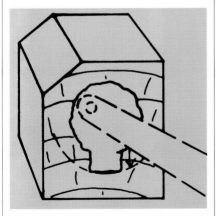

Nibbling to expand a cavity. Care must be taken to avoid kickback

This can be tense and demanding work, and also rather slow. Attention must be paid at all times to the position of the bar within the cavity so that the top of the nose is not allowed to strike the top of the cavity and cause kickback.

NOSING

Nosing, or boring, is a technique for creating very deep cavities or cutting holes through timber by pushing the nose of the bar straight into the wood. It is dangerous and hard on the saw, so I prefer not to use it. Some saw manufacturers apparently do not approve of it, though it is a widely used technique.

To start the cut, hold the saw with the nose down at an angle and cut a slot 10-20mm, about ½in deep. With the saw running in this slot, rotate the body of the saw so that the bar is now at right angles to the timber, maintaining steady firm pressure to force it deeper. If planning to cut right through the timber, know where the bar will emerge and plan your supports accordingly before commencing the cut.

Obviously the critical point is when the angle of the bar, including the top quadrant of the nose, will be in contact with the wood, and kickback is possible. Once the blade is deeper in the wood, control becomes easier. The initial slot should be deep enough to help hold the bar in position as it changes angle, and steady firm pressure is essential as the saw is rotated.

Needless to say, the timber should be very firmly supported when attempting this cut, which is not recommended for beginners. Using four such cuts arranged in a square, a section of wood can be removed to create a cavity, a technique often used in making post and rail fences.

SHAVING

Shaving is a useful technique for removing thin layers of timber from a surface with good control. It resembles

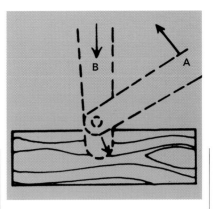

Nosing is not a technique for the beginner. At position 'A' the saw has created a slot ready for the whole saw to be rotated to the vertical position 'B' while maintaining firm downwards pressure to prevent kickback

floating except that the bar is not kept at 90° to the surface but instead lies flat. Generally it is more convenient to handle the saw with the blade vertical, so if possible turn the work so that the face to be shaved is also vertical.

The trick with shaving is to take only about half the thickness of the chain (the kerf) on each pass. If you take too much on any pass you will find that you are just sawing through the wood. By remaining on the surface the speed of cutting is greatly increased, control is easier, and the saw can follow around at least the broader curves. The surface produced can be so smooth that you can proceed directly to sanding.

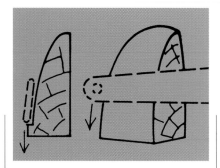

Shaving using the normal cutting edge of the bar. Less than the thickness of the chain is being removed at each pass

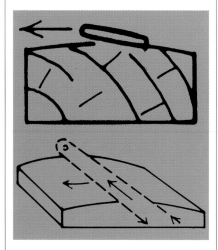

Shaving using the trailing edge of the bar, giving greater control of the depth of cut. Care must be taken to adjust to the saw's tendency to push towards the user

Normally the underside of the bar used for cutting is also used for shaving, but it is also possible to use the upper or trailing edge of the bar. Check the chain is not too slack on the bar first. Some caution is required as there will be a change in the forces operating, and the saw tends to push you away rather than pull you in to the cut. Again care is needed to ensure that the top quadrant of the nose does not dig in and cause kickback.

The bar itself lies flat on the surface being worked, and the saw slides across this surface, slightly angled so that it is the trailing edge that does the cutting. The effect is to limit the depth of cut to half the difference between the bar thickness and the cutter thickness, or kerf, a matter of only a millimetre or two.

Primal Event in progress: up to this stage, all shaping has been done with a chainsaw

The cutting is actually being done by the side of the cutting tooth. This is a most useful technique for the sculptor, but I suggest you experiment cautiously with it until experience gives you confidence.

IN SUMMARY

In practice, the eight techniques above are seldom so distinct when I am working. No doubt other people have developed different techniques, for the chainsaw is a versatile tool. The power of the saw, the hardness of the wood, and the type of chain fitted, will all affect the choice of technique. So too will simple laziness, for often it is more comfortable to continue plugging away with a technique that is working, however poorly, than to stop and realign the work or try out something new.

However, the techniques I describe do offer a range of options to expand the potential of your chainsaw so that it can be used safely and efficiently. ●

DON'T BE A BLOCKHEAD!

JOHN MIGNONE GIVES TIPS ON BLOCKING OUT AS HE CARVES A MAN'S HEAD

Although I started carving in the early 1980s I could not find the tools I thought I would need. Sharpening techniques also eluded me.

When I finally got started I floundered for two years, getting nowhere until I discovered people with art backgrounds did very well when they tried their hand at carving. I saw their first carvings were very good.

I realised carving was not so much the technical aspect of putting a tool to the wood as it was artistic vision and sight.

Then I came across a book entitled *Drawing on the Riqht Side of the Brain* by Betty Edwards. She reinforced what I had been thinking about: you need a certain perspective to carve well.

Drawing has helped develop this, and it has been essential since I enjoy carving faces and figures of people.

I have been told many of my busts have an English look to them. My work is a result of looking at pictures and carvings of people. I do not aim for a particular style, although I admit two of my favourite carvers are Ian Norbury and Ray Gonzalez, both from England.

For this project of a hooded man with a beard and moustache I drew a sketch of his front and side profiles. The bust, about half life size, was done from a block of basswood (*Tilia americana*) 180mm, 7in high x 145mm, 5¾in deep x 120mm, 4¾in wide.

I am most often asked about blocking out the basic features rather than refining them. This is why I will take the reader only so far on the face.

Though I show a finished bust and offer a front and side pattern, I would suggest dealing with such refinements as hair are subject to individual taste.

A beard, for example, can be rendered simply or very detailed. The same is true for the scalp hair, which I stylised to appear wavy with little if any detail.

Above **The finished bust.**
Left **The sketches of front and side profiles.**

PROFILES

Instead of using a bandsaw to establish the profiles in the wood I started by separating the face from the hood. The proportions were slightly larger than necessary to compensate for minor mistakes.

If you are carving a face you learn a lot more by starting off with a square block. What you learn is to block out the features in their correct positions. You cannot master this when you bandsaw the profiles.

The next step was drawing in a vertical centreline using a flexible ruler. This not only divided the face but also gave me an axis for the first part of the anatomy to be carved, the nose.

After drawing lines representing the top and bottom of the nose I began by cutting away wood from under it.

I recommend using a gouge instead of a knife. If you use a knife you end up with a sharp cut at the base of the nose. Faces are not like that. Instead there is a gentle curve where the nose blends into the upper lip. I used a 5mm, ³⁄₁₆in No 9 for the wood removal.

I then moved on to removing wood between the top of the nose and the brow line. Using a 35mm, 1⅜in No 2 gouge I started just below the line representing the top of the nose, working the tool across the plane of the face.

This is a large gouge for a small carving, but the larger the gouge the easier it is to remove wood. I do not waste time with small tools to hog off material.

I next worked on rounding the forehead into the sides of the face. If this figure did not have a beard I would have continued working down, rounding the chin at the same time.

This is part of a process that has me rounding the wood as often as possible. By doing this I am getting the features as close to where they should be as I can. I used a large fishtail, a 25mm, 1in No 5.

Blocking out the nose after a vertical centreline has been established and horizontal lines are drawn for the top and bottom of the nose.

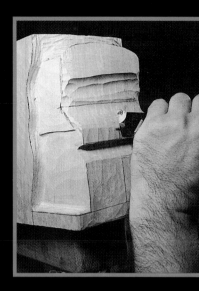

Establishing the brow and nose profile.

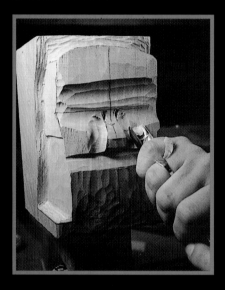

Removing wood from the sides of the nose.

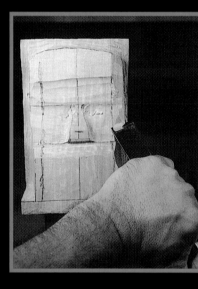

A human face is approximately four eye widths wide at the eye plane. Lines are drawn to represent the limits of that plane and where the face curves around to the sides of the head.

Creating a drooping piece of flesh that will give the face some age.

Giving emphasis to the cheek bones.

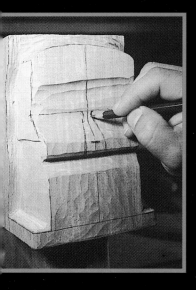

ating the sides of the nose.

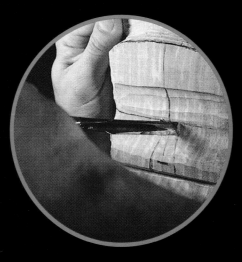

Creating the indentations on the sides of the nose requires pushing a gouge straight into the wood.

vering the area below the moustache.

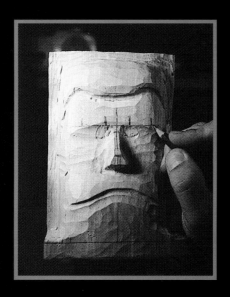

Establishing the width of the eyes.

ping the eye sockets.

Creating the lower lids by pushing a gouge straight into the wood.

EYE SOCKETS

I then chose an 18mm, ²³⁄₃₂in No 8 gouge to cut in where the eye sockets curve into the sides of the head. This attention to detail is something I see missing in many facial carvings. The eye socket areas are left too flat when in fact they curve around the head.

I used the same gouge to remove some wood above the brow line and deepen the top of the nose. I left extra wood for the hair that protruded from under the hood, knowing I could go back later and take more away.

I next needed to establish the sides of the nose. Taking a 10mm, ⅜in No 9 gouge and placing it at the bottom of the brow and top of the nose, I pushed it into the wood as far as it would go by hand. This created the indentations on either side of the nose.

I then used the 18mm, ²³⁄₃₂in No 8 gouge to remove wood on each side of the nose. Taking wood away from the base of the nose where it meets the lip is not as difficult as removing wood where the nose meets the brow.

When I got to the indentations which have to blend into the eye sockets, I had to make a slicing or skewing action to get a smooth cut.

The sides of the nose blend into the cheeks, leaving no sharp line or crease. Also be aware there is a muscle that extends from the top of the nose to the sides of the mouth. It follows the shape of a gentle curve.

HUMAN FACE

Besides making a nose too sharp looking, another common mistake I see is with the profile of the nose.

Nearly half a human nose is behind the upper lip. The mistake carvers make is in placing the nose so too much is sticking out from the face.

But because of the moustache on this bust, the tip of the nose will extend only a fraction beyond the front of the moustache.

I have read that as a rule of thumb

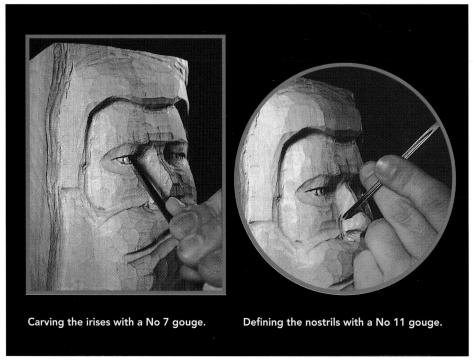

Carving the irises with a No 7 gouge.   Defining the nostrils with a No 11 gouge.

Photos by Roger Schroeder.

the human face is five eye widths across. I ran into a problem with that rule because my heads ending up looking too wide.

I now make the face four eye widths across the eye plane, which includes the sockets. Beyond the sockets the skull gradually enlarges to a fifth eye width at the area of the ears, but not including them.

Once I established the width of the face by making vertical lines on the wood, I cut back from those lines, removing wood and rounding the face. I used a 25mm, 1in No 2 fishtail gouge.

I did more work rounding the cheeks, shaping the nose, establishing the moustache and the hair line.

Making the nostrils takes some care because they have a deep crease as they merge with the face.

Instead of using a knife or V tool I took a 6mm, ¼in No 9 gouge and blocked out the nostrils. This created a softer look than another tool would have made.

Next I cut away some of the moustache to reveal more of the nose. I also cut in a line below the moustache to establish where it rested above the upper lip.

A common mistake that can surface later is to make the lower lip too far forward, giving the face a bulldog appearance. Make sure the lower lip is set farther back.

Next I went to work on the eye sockets. I drew pencil lines for the width of each eye as well as a centreline, and carved away wood from where the tops of the eye sockets were located.

I wanted this figure to appear nearing the end of middle age. To create this look I needed to make a piece of skin that drooped down and covered the top eyelid.

Using a 5mm, ³⁄₁₆in No 9 gouge, I made an S-shaped cut to represent this drooping skin. Since the skin overlapped the top eyelid, I had to lower the wood under it while keeping in mind a round eyeball was there. Another mistake carvers make is flattening the eyeballs.

EYEBALLS

After lowering the eyeball area with a 25mm, 1in No 5 fishtail gouge I needed to deepen the cheekbones. I took a 15mm, ⅝in No 8 gouge and removed wood from the sides of the head toward the nose. I also worked on the brow, putting more curvature into it.

I next went to work on the eyeballs. After using a 10mm, ³⁄₈in No 8 gouge to deepen the areas next to the nose, I made a cut under the eyeballs using a 10mm, ³⁄₈in No 9 gouge.

I then used a 10mm, ³⁄₈in No 5 gouge and made a straight-in cut to form the bottom eyelids. To further separate the eyelids, I used a sharp knife and pared away slivers of wood. While doing this I was conscious of maintaining the roundness of the eyeball.

An iris takes up about half the exposed eyeball. But it is not totally exposed because the upper and lower lids cover part of it.

If you were to show the entire iris the expression would appear shocked or frightened, not a look you want your bust to have.

I took a 6mm, ¼in No 7 gouge and cut in the shape of each iris, popping out thin slivers of wood in the process. Blocking out continued with more work on the nose. I flattened the bridge of the nose slightly using a 10mm, ³⁄₈in No 5 gouge. I held the gouge bevel up to make a convex cut.

I further outlined the nostrils using a 10mm, ³⁄₈in No 8 for the tops of the nostrils.

For the final shaping of the nostril crease I used a 2mm, ³⁄₃₂in No 11 gouge and outlined the area. ●

Drawing on the Right Side of the Brain by Betty Edwards, Perigee Books, published by The Putnam Publishing Group, 200 Madison Avenue, New York, NY 10016, USA. Price $13.95

John Mignone, 48, is a professional woodcarver, a classical musician and tree propagator who resides in East Meadow, Long Island, New York, USA. He and his father have been hardwood growers and propagators for 35 years. He has been carving professionally since 1990.

SHADOWLANDS

IN THE FIRST OF TWO ARTICLES, GRAHAM BULL STUDIES THE EFFECT OF LIGHT AND SHADE, AND HIGHLIGHTS THE IMPORTANCE OF SHADOW TO THE CARVER

The importance of shadow for the woodcarver can never be over-stated. Like most artistic skills, its effective use can be developed only by constant experimentation.

The easiest way to understand just how important shadow is, is to consider that whereas a painter has an infinite range of colours the woodcarver has only two, the colour of wood itself, and the dark of the shadow that can be carved into it.

True, shadows can be developed to reflect different degrees of darkness, but essentially we are dealing with one colour.

I will concentrate on relief carving, as it is here the concept of shadow creation is more easily understood.

If we strip the whole subject down to its bare elements, as unemotionally and analytically as possible, the only reason we carve wood is to decorate an otherwise boring surface. Before you accuse me of blasphemy, consider the statement from the position of the observer, not the carver.

To the non-woodie a piece of wood is just that, a piece of wood. A piece of wood becomes a beautiful carving only once we have covered it with a pleasing arrangement of shadows. You can see the carved design only by virtue of the shadows that compose it.

PHOTOGRAPHY

Photographers know shadow. It can enhance the natural colours in the picture, or interfere with them. Black and white photography in particular, trains the brain to interpret in black and white what the eye sees in colour, as an image made up of varying shades of grey.

This is the crux of the whole matter. To successfully develop shadow, you must start to see things differently, so from now on when you think relief carving, think shadow.

Every time you make a cut, ask yourself what kind of shadow it will make. Or better still, before you make a cut decide what shadow you want to make.

It is extremely important to consider the light you are carving by. If you don't use the right source, it will be impossible to see whether you are creating the right shadows or not.

The two most common forms of lighting are the fluorescent tube and the light bulb. Each is designed for a specific purpose:

The fluorescent tube is designed to produce lots of light in an economical form. It is for use in places where cheap, non directional and shadowless light is needed, places like offices and factories.

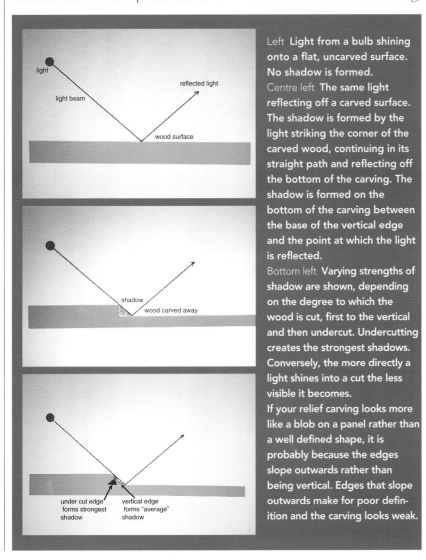

Left **Light from a bulb shining onto a flat, uncarved surface. No shadow is formed.**

Centre left **The same light reflecting off a carved surface. The shadow is formed by the light striking the corner of the carved wood, continuing in its straight path and reflecting off the bottom of the carving. The shadow is formed on the bottom of the carving between the base of the vertical edge and the point at which the light is reflected.**

Bottom left **Varying strengths of shadow are shown, depending on the degree to which the wood is cut, first to the vertical and then undercut. Undercutting creates the strongest shadows. Conversely, the more directly a light shines into a cut the less visible it becomes.**

If your relief carving looks more like a blob on a panel rather than a well defined shape, it is probably because the edges slope outwards rather than being vertical. Edges that slope outwards make for poor definition and the carving looks weak.

Top right **A relief pattern directly below a fluorescent tube. Note the poorly defined nature of the pattern.**

Centre right **The same pattern placed directly under an unshaded light bulb. Direct light from a filament tends to concentrate the light in a far more coherent fashion. Even the colours are truer.**

Bottom right **If the bare bulb is shaded to concentrate the light, and is moved to one side of the carving (in this case to the left), the density of the shadows increases, enhancing the visibility of features still further. The arrowed error is not visible in the first picture.**

Fluorescent light is deliberately diffuse, it doesn't throw shadows. It is therefore inappropriate for woodcarving or any activity, including woodturning and general woodwork, where you need to see everything you are creating, especially the mistakes!

If you have set up your workshop using fluorescent lighting, then my advice is to remove it, or at least don't use it for woodwork.

Strong cross lighting is better for woodcarving than overhead fluorescent lighting.

If you use fluorescent lighting and think you have done a wonderful job until you take your carving out into direct sunlight, where you suddenly see all sorts of mess, this is the reason. Natural direct sunlight creates shadow forming cross-lighting and that reveals all.

In fact in Sydney, Australia for example, the best lighting of all is the low sunlight of autumn, winter and spring mornings and afternoons when the deepest shadows are cast. In summer in the middle part of the day the sun is very much overhead, creating little cross lighting. If only we could stop the world going round!

EXPERIMENT

As we start to experiment with this shadow theory, we will discover the

way we can use different shadows for effect, right to the point where we start to create illusions with shadow, and make things look as they are not.

We will learn to tell lies with shadows and create all sorts of illusions such as depth where there is almost none, and the impression of curved surfaces that are really almost flat.

These things are very useful where you want to create decorative wall panels with timber only an inch or so thick, or the roundness of lily leaves on the flat of a chair back.

The more developed the up-front planning of our carvings, the more likely we will be to get good results for our efforts.

So for example, if we are to carve a surround for the fireplace in the lounge room, we should consider the kind of lighting that will be in use when the fire is being used. Is it a bulb in the ceiling, or a standard lamp off to one side, or both?

If we are carving a chair back in the kitchen, will the kitchen be in use during the day when the predominant light is through a window, or at night with an overhead fluorescent tube? Will a pediment on top of a wall cupboard be lit from above or from the bottom up?

A good way to assess lighting requirements is simply to move the carving from one room to another and note the changes in its appearance.

Once the lighting is sorted out, we can plan the overall carving. For example, if we are to carve a music stand to be used for on-stage performance, where the predominant lighting could be left, right, top or bottom of stage, or any combination of the whole lot at once, what better design for classical performances than the Byzantine rosette shown in the photograph?

No matter where the light is coming from, this pierced relief design will always show a multitude of shadow activity.

SURFACES

The planning process asks questions such as: Do I make a surface (such as the surfaces on the vines in the rosette) convex or concave? A convex surface will create one block of shadow when light falls across it, whereas a concavity will create two blocks of shadow across its surface.

If you want shadows dancing all over, then in this example go concave, as with the rosette.

Apart from the considerations of practicality, availability and workability of timber, the colour of the wood should be considered. Shadows are more easily seen on lighter wood than darker.

Avoid carving elaborate shadow detail on dark wood, and if you stain light wood dark, much of your hard work will disappear.

The light coloured oak (*Quercus spp*) carving from St Andrew's Cathedral at Inverness in Scotland has sufficient shadows created by carving against the light background to make the small figures easily visible. This photograph was taken with the available light at the time.

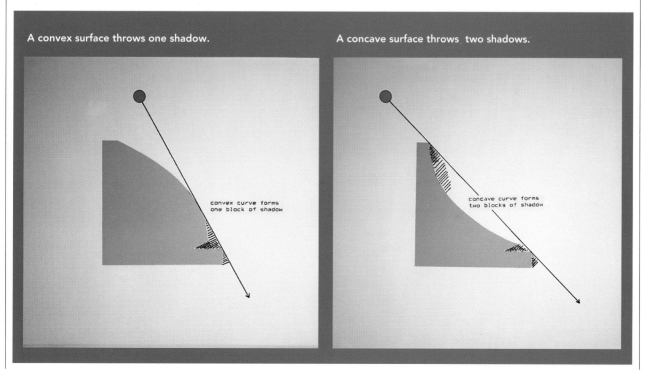

A convex surface throws one shadow.

convex curve forms one block of shadow

A concave surface throws two shadows.

concave curve forms two blocks of shadow

Right **A carved panel from St Andrew's Cathedral, Inverness, Scotland.**
Below **A darker carving from St Andrew's Cathedral, Sydney, Australia.**

A darker carved panel from St Andrew's Cathedral in Sydney, Australia, has less natural light, and the design carved in dark stained timber is really only visible in artificial light.

In this case, a spotlight was placed in such a way as to create a high shine on the high, flatter surfaces so they contrast to the darkness of the deeper curved surfaces, which reflect the same light at different angles so they appear dull. The detail of the carving is easily seen only by placing it in an 'unnatural' state.

Decor is also a consideration, so you cannot say one cathedral's carvings are better than the other. Nevertheless, these two examples show how the colour of the wood can make an enormous difference to a carving's visibility.

In the next article I will show how to create illusion with shadow, including depth and perspective. ●

Graham Bull is proprietor of the Whistlewood Studio and Craft Barn in Sydney, Australia. Self-taught, he has been a woodcarver for some 34 years and teaches carving in all its forms to about 100 people each year, from schoolchildren and hobbyists to professional woodworkers

SHADOWLANDS

PART TWO GRAHAM BULL CONCLUDES HIS WALK ON THE DARK SIDE OF CARVING TECHNIQUE

In the previous article I looked at some of the basic principles surrounding the subject of shadows. As you begin to develop these basic concepts, one of the most intriguing aspects of shadow work will begin to emerge, its ability to play tricks on the eye.

Carving a shadow line around a pattern separates it from the background. The stronger the shadow, the greater the appearance of depth

It is simply a matter of realising that the more we experiment, the more we can come up with. Sometimes if we want something to look like a particular thing, we need to carve it in exactly the opposite way to the true image.

How do we work out what to put where? It is all very well to say experiment, but there is a limit to how much time is available to do such things. Here are some hints and tips to add to your collection. You will be amazed at what you can get away with!

- A shadow line around the perimeter of a design will separate it from the background, increase visual intensity and apparent depth.
- A concave item set against a flat background will create a significant contrast and make it more obvious. A convex curve will do the opposite.
- A shadow line strategically placed in a carving will delineate one part from another, highlighting changes in angles, making them appear greater than is in fact the case.
- A little bit goes a long way. A small variation in the curvature of a surface will be interpreted and if necessary translated by the brain to conform to the memory perception of the item in real life. In other words, the brain will often fill in the blanks and see what the carver intended, even if it isn't real. This is particularly effective to the untrained eye of the casual observer.
- A flat surface will be very obvious in a carving of curves, because the surface will reflect light in a totally different direction from that of the surfaces surrounding it, and will tend not to cast shadows. So unless you want a surface to be very obvious, put a curve on it.

Remember, in nature there are no flat surfaces except in such things as crystals, so unless you want flat surfaces for effect, get rid of them. This applies especially to carving in the round.

PERSPECTIVE

The phenomenon of perspective is as fascinating and perplexing a topic as shadow, and as much fun to come to grips with.

There are many texts on the subject of perspective, particularly in art, technical drawing and architecture. But these are essentially pen on paper activities, using lines to make the perspective work. Woodcarving however, has to draw lines with shadows, so no shadow, no perspective!

By playing around with the infinite combinations of shape and shadow, you can create an infinite variety of perceived shapes. In fact perception is the crux of the matter.

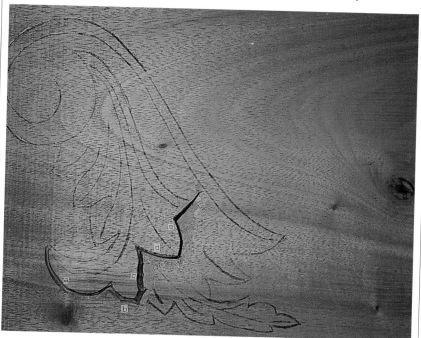

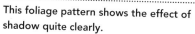

This foliage pattern shows the effect of shadow quite clearly.

a) The opening V tool cut.

b) The first gouge incision away from the outline of the pattern.

c) The outward sloping edge, casting virtually no shadow.

d) The shadow caused by the vertical edge.

e) The stronger shadow caused by undercutting.

The actual depth of the incision at d is identical to the depth at e (3mm, ⅛in), although e looks deeper. Shadow creates the illusion of depth.

Above left If shadow can be used to create the illusion of distance, then can it also be used to change the shape of things?

In the photograph the curl of this leaf looks round. The roundness of the curl is created by placing a strong shadow beneath it, that is under the edges, then by carving a strong elliptical curve along one edge and trailing the other edge away just enough to change the direction of the reflected light, while throwing a very faint, graduated shadow over the sloping surface.

You are not conscious of this graduated surface shadow, but it creates the illusion the curve is much greater than it really is.

Left A cross section of the leaf, highlighting the different curves and the undercuts around the edges. The curl in the leaf is created by carving a strong curve on one edge and placing a shadow under the other, which can also give it greater apparent depth.

Left Knave of Spades, a large carved panel adapted from a printed Swiss Alchemist's playing card series of the 17th century. In particular look at the village pump-stand on the left hand side.

Right A cross-section of the pump-stand carving. A combination of shadow lines and shadows over curved surfaces creates an illusion of depth and shape.

undercut

concave surface

surface slopes inwards

cross section of village pump stand

What we perceive pleases or displeases us. If we like the look of what we see, we are happy with it. If we don't we aren't. So whatever you do, if you create a pleasurable perception, you have succeeded in your endeavours.

Do not mistake perception for perfection, as often the more perfect the detail the less pleasurable the perception.

Remember the brain is able to, and will always interpret things, the way it wants them to be. It will fill in details that are not there, and will make up or alter shapes and perspectives to suit the overall images it expects to see.

If a certain shadow makes a carving look better, keep it, and try to work out why. The chances are that more shadows will make it look better still. ●

Graham Bull is proprietor of the Whistlewood Studio and Craft Barn in Sydney, Australia. Self-taught, he has been a woodcarver for some 34 years and teaches carving in all its forms to about 100 people each year, from schoolchildren and hobbyists to professional woodworkers

Above **Perspective:**
Terrace Lounge Room carved by Andrew Tarlinton, Sydney, Australia.

The dimensions of the carving are 350 x 300mm, 14 x 12in, and the depth is 12mm, ½in, in jelutong (*Dyera costulata*).

You automatically see the carving as a whole, which is the first secret to its success. It looks like the lounge room in a terrace. Whatever its inherent weaknesses as a carving, your brain accepts the subject for what it purports to be and in the first instance, glosses over any imperfections.

The overall depth of the lounge is 14mm, ⁹⁄₃₂in, although it looks significantly greater. Given normal ratios, if the length of the lounge is about 150mm, 6in, the depth of the carved lounge chair should be about 60mm, 2⅜in. Yet it is squashed into a depth about one sixth of that. Shadow has been used to change the perspective.

This is clear if you look at the arms of the chair. They are angled inwards so the back looks narrower than the front. The exaggerated angle of the arms increases the perception of distance and adds to the apparent depth of the chair.

To the brain the back of the chair appears further away. The use of shadow work around the cushions, underneath the chair and around the arms helps to create the illusion of depth.

The stairs demonstrate a different distortion of reality, giving the impression of a flight leading upwards. The first stair slopes at about 45°, the second at roughly 30°. Each step is undercut around its edges, creating shadow lines that distinguish each from the next.

The spiral effect is created by making each successive, wedge-shaped step narrower and more horizontal than the preceding one, so that each reflects light differently and the whole appears to recede upwards. The dark shadow on the third step gives the illusion of depth and makes it look longer than it really is, when it is actually less than half the length of the first step.

The wall with the curtains is similarly carved in perspective, with the skirting board and cornice converging on one another in the distance (which is 14mm, ⁹⁄₃₂in, in the carving).

The ceiling is carved at an angle that is all but vertical, that slopes just enough to throw a shadow over it to make it look flat. The important thing is that it is at a different angle from the walls, so it reflects light differently.

DIVIDE AND RULE

JIM COOPER SHOWS HOW TO MAKE A PAIR OF PROPORTIONAL DIVIDERS FOR SIZING UP A CARVING FROM A MAQUETTE

Many carvers like to work from a maquette (clay model of the finished piece), but it is not always feasible to make a full size one, especially if you are doing a large carving.

Making a small maquette will still be helpful in visualising the work, and will also give the opportunity to experiment with different shapes and positions to refine the design.

But there is the problem of how to use the small model to give accurate dimensions for the finished piece. You need a process to take information from the maquette to the workpiece, because it is difficult to do this well purely by eye, though of course working by eye will be a major part of the operation.

Even experienced carvers use a lot of information from the maquette. The creative work, or art, has gone into making it, and then a little science is needed to speed up the rest of the work.

Measurements can be taken with a tape or rule, but dividers are much more convenient. Each measurement will have to be multiplied by the enlargement ratio, which gets difficult if you are not using whole numbers. Using a pair of proportional dividers makes the whole job easier.

DIVIDERS

Dividers consist of two arms, both having points at each end. If the arms are pivoted as in a pair of scissors, the ratio of the gap at one end to that at the other will always be the same. The ratio will depend on where you put the pivot.

If you put the pivot in the centre points of both arms, the gaps at both ends will be the same. There is a ratio of

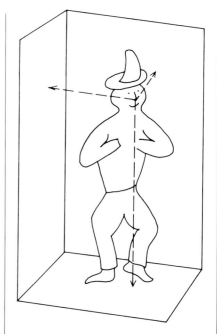

Finding a fixed reference point would require putting the maquette and workpiece in a corner and measuring three dimensions

one to one, shown as 1:1. If the arms are pivoted at one third along their lengths, the gap at one end will be twice the size of the smaller gap, a ratio of 2:1. This ratio will remain constant however wide apart you spread the arms.

You can buy dividers with a movable pivot point which can be locked anywhere along their length. Whole number ratio settings are marked and there is a guide pin which locates these for greater accuracy.

My metal dividers are 12in, 305mm long which means they are only suitable for small work, but you can make larger, less sophisticated wooden dividers quite easily.

The drawing shows the dimensions for various ratio settings, but these are not vital as for most carvers a constant setting is what is needed, rather than an exact whole number setting. Remember, though, if your instrument is not exact, do not mix measurement taking with another instrument.

I made another large set of

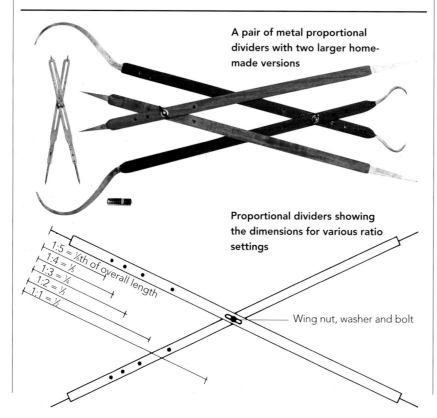

A pair of metal proportional dividers with two larger home-made versions

Proportional dividers showing the dimensions for various ratio settings

1:5 = 1/6 th of overall length
1:4 = 1/5
1:3 = 1/4
1:2 = 1/3
1:1 = 1/2

Wing nut, washer and bolt

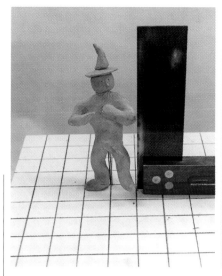

Extreme parts of the maquette are found with a square and marked on the base grid

Dimensions are taken from the grid and reference point with the small end of the dividers before being transferred to the large grid with the other end of the dividers

Above **The carving block is placed on the reference points on the large grid and vertical lines drawn with a square**
Below **Vertical measurements are taken and marked on the block using the dividers**

dividers using the ends of an old set of calliper dividers. If using curved ends like these, it is important to ensure the points are on the same centre line as the centre of the pivot.

MEASURING

To fix a point you will need three dimensions, one vertical and two horizontal, but you can only take these if you have somewhere from which to measure.

You could put the maquette in a corner which would give two walls and a floor from which to measure, but the workpiece would also need to be in a corner and the right distance away

An easier way is to use fixed reference points on a floor grid

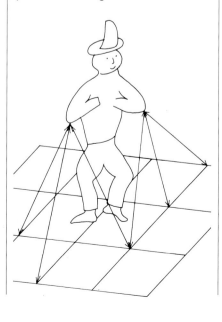

from the walls for it to work. In practice this would be difficult.

You can, however, take the vertical dimensions from the floor, a fixed plane, and the floor can also be used when taking measurements from fixed points by using a base grid and a square.

This method will give several critical points in the early stages of a carving, but as work progresses other methods must be found for finding dimensions of other points on the carving.

I have used a simple figure maquette as an example which I enlarged three times. Remember when enlarging, any errors will be multiplied by the same ratio, so it is important to be accurate.

First I drew a base grid and stood my modelling clay figure on it. I put location marks on the maquette so it could be accurately relocated in case it moved.

Then I used a square to locate three extreme points on the figure, the elbows and left foot, and mark them on the base.

I then drew a grid three times larger, using the proportional dividers to step off the grid, and put reference letters and numbers on the lines to match those on the smaller grid.

Using the small end of the dividers, I took the dimension from one point to a line on the small grid, then reversed the dividers and marked off the position on the large grid with the large end.

Each point had to be found by working from two grid lines at right angles to each other.

CARVING BLOCK

The next step was to locate the carving block on the marked extremity points on the large grid and draw vertical lines up the block from these points with a large square. The grid lines were also drawn up the block.

It was then possible to take vertical measurements with the dividers. First I marked the overall height, then one elbow and other key points. Note the points of the dividers must be kept in a vertical line.

I marked several positions to get the dimensions for the rim of the hat. When enough points had been marked I could join them up and remove waste areas.

As work continued it was necessary to keep checking back to the maquette in the same way. Calliper dividers were useful for checking dimensions across various parts of the figure and then adjustments could be made to the carving. Each time it was simply a case

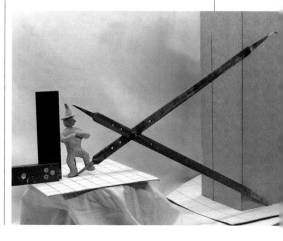

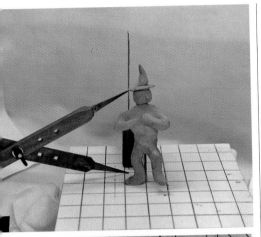

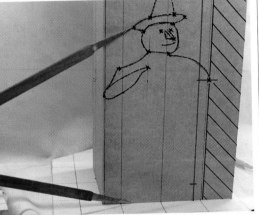

Top **Key points on the hat brim are measured with the dividers...**
Centre **...and transferred to the block. Grid lines are also marked vertically on the block**
Above **Calliper dividers are useful for taking measurements from the maquette**

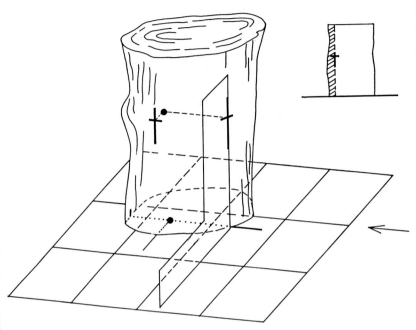

Above **Marking reference points on an irregular block. Extend lines away from the fixed reference points until a vertical line can be drawn with a square**

of reversing the proportional dividers to find the right enlarged dimension.

This method is fine if the blank is square and true, but the larger the work the less likely this is. You may even want to use a built up or laminated piece to give sufficient size without waste.

IRREGULAR SHAPES

When working on irregular shaped blocks the method is the same, but it becomes more difficult to apply. It then becomes a case of marking each point and cutting a little at a time as you go.

You may also have to extend lines away from critical points on the large grid until you can extend the lines vertically. Place the square on the grid where the extended line meets the edge of the block and mark the vertical in the area of the point. Then mark the height as described earlier. Waste can then be removed.

Even if you do not want to use the grid method for the transfer of dimensions, I am sure a set of proportional

dividers will be a worthwhile addition to your carving toolkit. They will also be useful for other jobs, such as enlarging a drawing, or even for picking up items that fall down the back of the workbench! ●

Jim Cooper, 51, has a degree in building and worked as a building and shopfitting manager. He started woodwork as a hobby in 1968 and has tried instrument making, turning and carving. He took up turning for a living during redundancy in the early 1980s, and in 1993 took a course in carpentry for historic building restoration. This led to restoration carving work, and he is also a part time college lecturer in carpentry and joinery.
A member of the BWA (Warwickshire region), Jim can be contacted for carving and turning commissions at 45 Bagnell Road, Kings Heath, Birmingham B13 0SJ.

ROUGH AND READY

WILLIAM GRAHAM EXPLAINS HOW A COPY CARVING MACHINE SAVES TIME AND HELPS HIS BUSINESS MAKE A PROFIT

Moneyreagh is a small village in Co. Down set among the rolling Castlereagh Hills. I have had my business here for 20 years. I learned woodcarving as a boy from an old wood and stone carver, who had worked for many years in London restoring the blitzed churches. Over the years, I have supplied many carved pieces for churches and public buildings.

I now find most of our work is for pubs and clubs around the province. Carving for fun is nice, but as a money making business it is difficult. People do not appreciate the time you spend on producing even the simplest item.

This is where the carving machine comes in. It almost eliminates the initial roughing out and sizing process, leaving you with the more pleasant finishing off.

For instance, all carvers find problems in getting the eyes and ears in the proper position and everything in proportion, or with multiple work, in achieving identical items.

I bought my machine some years ago. It is a four head Italian Bulleri, producing four exact clones from a single master, either in the round or flat.

SPEEDY SQUIRRELS

The procedure is extremely quick. For instance, I take a squirrel as the master and glue blocks of 3in, 75mm dried chestnut (*Aesculus hippocastanum*) together. This is left overnight to

....

The copy machine carves three squirrels simultaneously

harden. Any timber will do, some being better for different objects.

I tend to use lime (*Tilia vulgaris*) for finely detailed pieces, but we also buy many home grown supplies of sycamore (*Acer pseudoplatanus*), maple (*Acer campestre*), walnut (*Juglans regia*), beech (*Fagus sylvatica*), and cherry (*Prunus avium*).

The blocks, either two or four, depending on size, are loaded between centres on the lathe-type chucks. These revolve in either direction to offer up each face as required. We start with the largest cutter and go down in stages. The cutters work at a fast pace and soon the floor gets carpeted in chippings.

It is satisfying to see the objects take shape, as if by magic, and quite soon we can remove them from the machine for final finishing by hand.

CARVING TECHNIQUE

When the blank comes off the machine the full shape is there. All the major details are obvious such as eyes, fingers, toes and so on. The surface is sometimes woolly but this is reasonable for representing hair on animal figures.

We start by gouging in the main characteristics of the object. The big appealing eyes are carefully carved by removing the top layer of woolly timber, exposing the smooth surface below.

The lines around the eyes can be carved either with a parting or V tool or two opposing stabs with a slow gouge. Parting tools are difficult to sharpen and unless very sharp can cause serious damage. The fingers and toes are next, using the same technique of two opposing cuts with a small slow gouge.

We quickly remove the woolly surface and replace it with irregular tool marks to represent the animal's fur. This can be made more life-like by adding hair-like marks with a parting tool or the type of pyrography wire used with great success by decoy duck carvers.

By following this procedure we condense much of the work and can produce a presentable woodcarving in

Top **Some of the carvings produced by the copy machine after finishing by hand**
Above **Coat of arms carved by Philip Steele for Limavady Council Chambers**

Top **The different stages in carving a squirrel on the Bulleri copying machine**
Above **Operating the copy carving machine**

done in a big way in Europe where factories turn out roughed out carvings by the million.

Whole districts are turned into woodcarving centres with schools for carvers and all kind of small businesses finishing carvings for sale. With the tourist boom, I think there is room for the carver in Britain and wonder why so many wooden items are imported.

Someone carving for pleasure can take a lot of time putting their own skill to good effect, giving the piece their individuality and personality, so no two pieces look exactly the same.

There are those, like myself, who are slaves to father time and must decide how long can be expended on a carving to give a reasonable profit. I have rarely seen any carving book or article give any indication of the time spent on a piece of work. Of course this varies considerably depending on the level of skill and range of tools.

In our workshop we are faced with the old problem of making the job pay. If you consider the cost of materials, laminating blocks, overheads, wages and so on, carving becomes like any other commercial enterprise, figures on a balance sheet.

With time and training, surprising speed can be achieved by a skilled man and quite intricate pieces leave our workshop in reasonable time. A coat of arms carved in walnut, for instance, was completed by Philip Steele (once my apprentice and one of the best carvers around) in 50 hours.

The purists say the use of carving machines is cheating, but I don't see it that way. In early times joiners roamed the forests looking for a tree or branch growing in a certain shape to ease their burden of laboriously cutting the timber to shape.

Carving machines of various kinds have been in use for a long time, removing the initial waste wood and leaving the carver to show their skill. Why not try it yourself, you may get a pleasant surprise. ●

a short space of time. Most of these roughed out blocks are sold to woodcarvers so they can finish them, as we could not finish all we produce.

ENCOURAGING ENTERPRISE

One of our customers manufactures fine walking sticks with silver mounts. These are sold to collectors around the world and to stores like Harrods in London. We hand carve animal heads for some of his pieces.

Our carving business was set up with the help of L.E.D.U, a local enterprise agency helping small businesses to get established. The work we do is

William Graham began his career in wood with jewellery boxes for his sisters when aged eight. After serving as a joiner in a shipbuilding firm, he was taught by a carver who had worked on the rebuilding of London churches destroyed in the Second World War. After working as a joiner and carver in Belfast he built his own workshop 20 years ago and now specialises in carvings and shop fitting work.

You can contact Grace Joinery Works at 30 Ballykeel Road, Moneyreagh, Co. Down BT23 6BN
Tel: 01232 448281

Timber supplied by
Hasletts,
Fivemiletown, Co.Tyrone
and McGregor and Son,
Sydenham Road, Belfast

Carving Tools supplied by
McMaster Tools, Church Street, Belfast

ALLY OF THE DOLLS

AURIEL MIMS DISCUSSES THE INSPIRATION AND TECHNIQUES BEHIND HER NORFOLK DOLLS

I was rather taken aback when approached by *Woodcarving* magazine, in fact I blushed on the other end of the phone. I had been found out as a fraud.

With no professional training as a woodcarver, never even having seen a real woodcarver at work, and having found no better tool than my beloved Stanley knife with which to finish my work, how could I possibly write an article for professional woodcarvers?

However, I was assured readers covered a wide range of skill and experience and my unorthodox methods might be of interest to them, and perhaps provide a good laugh?

For my part I realised I had a unique chance to glean ideas and advice from the real McCoy. I would be a fool to turn down such an opportunity, so here goes.

I made my first carved wooden doll for our first child, Flora, when she was five. My husband and I were living in the wilds of Norfolk making a precarious living from our wooden toys which we sold weekly on Norwich market.

The doll which was admired by various friends, led to my making similar dolls, sometimes portrait dolls, and over 15 years a design developed.

Some of my dolls have found homes in the USA, Canada, Sweden, Switzerland, Japan and Egypt. I sometimes wonder what they can see from their windowsill or shelf, I would love to know.

....

Woodcarving is a major feature in the personality of each doll.

COMPONENTS

The carved wooden components: heads, hands, lower leg and feet, are painted and finished in beeswax. These are drilled and stitched to a soft cloth body and dressed in natural fabrics.

The principle of such a design is probably inspired by the Parisian dolls of the 19th century, whose porcelain head and shoulders, lower arm and hands, and lower legs were stitched onto a kid body, stuffed with sawdust. The adaptation to a soft cloth body and wood components is simple and obvious.

Without the complication of jointed limbs, the doll has much less chance of being broken, or of hurting a child, but can still mimic most natural poses.

It was coming across local Edwardian photos which inspired the launching of my Norfolk Dolls three years ago. The open innocence of the faces of the children in those photos fascinated me, and it is this quality

which I try to capture in my dolls, each of which is different.

My aim initially was to establish Norfolk Dolls as a name, by concentrating on the children. Adult characters would be added later, dolls representing the Edwardian village community, such as the blacksmith, joiner, shopkeeper, vicar and schoolteacher.

These characters I am starting to work on now, but these photographs illustrate the process of making my Norfolk Doll children.

The process starts with drawings inspired by old photographs. Sometimes I use clay if I have difficulty in moving from the photo to three dimensions.

When I have the right face I draw the head to scale (the dolls stand at 450–600mm, 18–20in tall), and cut a profile in paper which I draw onto a block of lime (*Tilia vulgaris*).

Boots, legs and hands are also marked out on lime, and are cut on a bandsaw, together with the head. Boys' hands are larger than girls' hands, and boots are different too. It is surprising how much character can be expressed in a boot.

Then comes the vice, chisel and mallet. I use a range of chisels and gouges, starting with the largest. There is something very satisfying about the hard physical work of this part of the process.

Then comes the whittling. I suppose my natural inclination in 3-D work is to model, and whittling has that quality.

This stage is a delicate teasing out of the personality of the little person, perhaps a quality in its mouth or dimples in the cheeks. The person is in there and a gentle meditative approach seems to allow it to emerge. I enjoy this stage, it is mysterious and seems to

Top **The good old Stanley knife.**
Above **It is surprising how much character can be expressed in a boot.**

....

involve a bit of magic.

I have scoured catalogues for a better tool with which to whittle than my beloved Stanley knife, but the one I wrote off for doesn't keep its edge, and when I'm sitting by the Rayburn whittling away, I don't fancy going out to the cold workshop to sharpen it, when it is so easy to simply change the blade.

EXTREMITIES

Feet and hands require less concentration and I often work these at Covent Garden market where I have a regular fortnightly Sunday stall.

People watch in morbid fascination, a look of horror on their faces, waiting I suspect, not for the emergence of a perfect foot, but for fingers to fly! But as yet, I still have all eight, and two thumbs. I do usually wear a leather thumb-stall.

The sanding and painting need no comment, and assembly and dressing are also outside the woodcarver's domain.

There is no doubt that wood, for me, has a special magic. To use any other material for my dolls would have no appeal for me.

It is strong yet gentle, feels alive in my hands, seems to enjoy being metamorphosed, and has a wicked sense of humour.

When a blemish resembling a spot appears on the end of the nose of a face you have laboured over devotedly, or a shake suddenly manifests, what can you do but smile and acknowledge that you'll never be the master and that to work with wood is a privilege, not a right. ●

Auriel Mims completed her Diploma in Art & Design in painting at Chelsea School of Art in the mid 1960s. She worked at Bethnal Green Museum of Childhood as a museum assistant, where her interest in dolls began. She launched her Norfolk Dolls series three years ago.
She can be contacted at
Wayside Cottage, Thwaite Common, Erpingham, Norfolk NR11 7QQ
Tel: 01263 761665

GOING WITH THE GRAIN

DAVID CLARK DESCRIBES THE PROBLEMS HE ENCOUNTERED WHEN CARVING SOME FIGURES IN OLD, SPLIT YEW

There was an old yew (*Taxus baccata*) stump about 760mm, 30in high in front of my garden rubbish heap, and in the summer of 1993 I asked a friend with a chainsaw to cut it down.

It made six logs of dubious quality, because it was rotten in the middle. But I thought I might turn some small bowls or lidded boxes out of them.

In the autumn of the following year I took a two-month break. I left behind the possibility of woodturning, but discovered there was a woodcarver's studio in the grounds at The Abbey, Sutton Courtenay.

Teddy Hutton was the resident woodcarver, and I took with me a few gouges and a handy mallet, and one of the logs.

The only woodcarving I had done before was a linear gothic crucifix in pencil cedar (*Juniperus virginiana*) when I was 18, and two strange pieces three years before, a head in limewood (*Tilia Vulgaris*) and a small yew figure. I had no developed techniques.

I thought woodcarving would involve a lot of tedious chisel and mallet work getting rid of surplus wood before getting down to the serious business of fine carving.

At the Abbey studio I saw the carving potential of the Arbortech and the Powerfile with its continuous sanding belt, and realised that such tedium was a thing of the past.

But the yew log remained in my room, the object of long contemplation. What was in it? I looked at it every day for two weeks and the gentle curve of the tree impressed itself upon me.

After a while I decided to make a start and clear away the rotten wood to see what was left.

The Arbortech is a fierce tool and it took me a while to learn how to control it. Eventually it became a fairly accurate carving tool in my hands, digging out hollows and quickly removing surplus wood.

The curve of the sapwood began to suggest an angel's wings and there seemed to be enough solid wood on the left of the log for a kneeling woman's form.

I had noticed the teacher of a creative relaxation workshop I had attended kneeling in just this position. At the time I had sketched her quickly in charcoal. Now, I took up a pencil and sketchbook and made a few quick outlines of possibilities.

Original design sketches.

The raw block of yew. It contained rotten areas and splits, and a vein of purple.

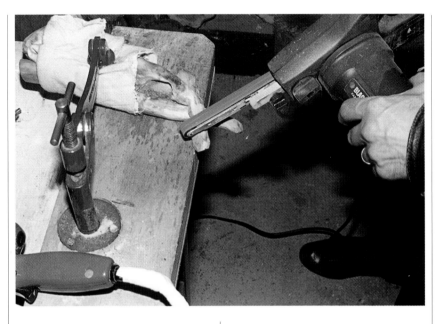

ANNUNCIATION

My next thought was this was big stuff. I could hardly attempt what was essentially an Annunciation theme with so little woodcarving experience. Surely, Tilman Riemenschneider did an apprenticeship and journeyman's work before tackling this sort of thing. But then another voice inside me said, risk it.

My excitement grew as the grain began to reveal itself. There was a vein of purple just inside the sapwood which was exposed as I chiselled out the shape of the wings at the back.

If I was careful this would colour the inside of the wings too, and the curling lines of the grain could suggest feathers.

With careful strokes of the chisel watching the grain all the time, I could play with those lines. And the dark closer grain suggested the fall of both the angel's and the woman's hair.

As I was cutting into the concave of the wing on the right side, tragedy struck. I knew there was a split, but hoped it would hold. Instead it widened.

Teddy Hutton, who was used to wood splitting, was undismayed. "Glue it", he said. So I poured ordinary

Using the Powerfile to shape a piece of yew root.

woodworker's adhesive into the crack and held it together with masking tape. With the other vertical marks in the wood, the split was virtually invisible.

Early last year, after displaying the piece in an exhibition, another split caused the wing to fall off. The same process proved effective.

PROPORTIONS

Another problem for me was proportion. The figures were taking shape nicely, but the woman's head was lumpish with its headcloth, and the angel's head was too big and square. I was terrified of taking off too much wood.

What should I do about noses and eyes and mouths? Yew splits notoriously easily. I had made the angel's face too flat for a proper nose and I considered the kneeling figure's face inaccessible.

I decided to risk being accused of copping out and to have the faces featureless, leaving more to the imagination and to the body language of the figures.

So I took up the Powerfile and removed the headcloth and was pleased with the simplicity of the result. Remember a face is always wedge-shaped, and I felt my own jaw to confirm it.

The belt sander brought about rapid transformation. I completed the angel's hairline, framing the face and his neckline with a small V-shaped gouge, taking care to sharpen it thoroughly first.

The angel's hip under his elbow remained a problem. There was too much of him. He must seem to have floated into the maiden's presence, and the lower part of his body must disappear.

Again my fear of taking off too much wood surfaced, but as I removed more and more, the pleasing inclination of the angel's body towards the maiden was emphasised and the wing looked lighter and more free.

Next I needed to dig out the space between the two figures. As I did so another stronger purple streak appeared in the grain under the

The finished figures in yew, 340mm, 13¼in high.

The purple streak can be seen down the back of the woman's figure and the split down the angel's wing.

The grain pattern was used to suggest feathers and hair. The purple streak can clearly be seen down the woman's back.

Rear of the figures, showing the grain pattern and splits in the wing.

left forearm of the angel. It delineated naturally a long loose sleeve, and needed only a little emphasis with the gouge at the opening.

When I dug out the stump six months later for more carving wood, I found a root crossing a rusty iron pipe which was drawing up the colour!

MESSAGE

Since this piece took so long in the making, what did it mean to me? It could be a fairly conventional Annunciation scene: the angel Gabriel bringing the message to Mary, "Fear not, Mary, for you have found favour with God. You shall conceive and bear a son, and you shall call him Jesus".

I also had other ideas: the guardian angel protecting, or comforting, the anima (soul), or simply a winged messenger bringing assurance of love to a young woman.

There was nothing in the carving to suggest this was the Annunciation, no Madonna lily beloved of medieval iconographers, no words engraved.

In an earlier sketch I had drawn a scroll and the incised lettering FEAR NOT across the lower body of the angel. In fact the interpretation sprang from my mind, built on past experience.

Finally, my break over, I brought the carving home. How should I finish it? I tried button polish at first and it produced a brilliant shine. Too much, I thought, and I sanded it off with fine sandpaper.

I next applied a little furniture polish and it took on the sort of matt shine I felt appropriate for the piece.

It looked rather squat on the level surface. Somehow it needed to be lifted on a contrasting material.

In the Leicestershire uplands there is a lot of slate lying about. So I selected a fine blue piece of the right thickness and took it down to my stonemason's yard, where they kindly ground flat the top and bottom of it.

I am a hoarder by nature and it took only a moment's foraging in my utility room to find a couple of old 100mm, 4in screws to fix the carving through the slate after drilling holes with a stonemason's drill.

Finally, I found this composition had slowly emerged from the wood itself. I felt I had gone with the grain in a deeper sense, and had a pleasing result which was good both to look at and to touch.

The finished angel and woman was 255 x 340mm high, 10 x 13¼in. ●

Powerfile available from
Black & Decker Ltd, Westpoint,
The Grove, Slough,
Berkshire SL1 1QQ.
Tel: 01753 511234.

Arbortech supplied in the UK by
BriMarc Associates,
8 Ladbroke Park, Millers Road,
Warwick CV34 5AE.
Tel: 01926 493389.

The Rev David Clark has been interested in the arts since childhood, but did not start carving until he was 18. He became a Church of England priest and was for 15 years industrial chaplain in Norwich. For the last 11 years he has been Team Rector in the parish of Oadby, Leicester. He is also a professional tenor. In the last eight years he has discovered woodturning and his mother-in-law's carving gouges.

SAFETY

Woodcarving should not be a dangerous activity, provided that sensible precautions are taken to avoid unnecessary risk.

Always ensure that work is securely held in a suitable clamp or other device, and that the workplace lighting is adequate.

Keep tools sharp; blunt tools are dangerous because they require more pressure and may behave unpredictably. Store them so that you, and others, cannot touch their cutting edges accidentally.

Be particular about disposing of shavings, finishing materials, oily rags, etc., which may be a fire hazard.

Do not work when your concentration is impaired by drugs, alcohol, or fatigue.

Do not remove safety guards from power tools; pay attention to electrical safety.

It is not safe to use a chainsaw without the protective clothing which is specially designed for this purpose, and attendance on a recognized training course is strongly recommended. Be aware that regulations governing chainsaw use are revised from time to time.

The safety advice in this book is intended for your guidance, but cannot cover every eventuality: the safe use of hand and power tools is the responsibility of the user. If you are unhappy with a particular technique or procedure, do not use it – there is always another way.

NOTES

Please note that names, addresses, prices etc. were correct at the time the articles were originally published, but may since have changed.

Although care has been taken to ensure that the metric measurements are true and accurate, they are only conversions from imperial; they have been rounded up or down to the nearest whole millimeter, or to the nearest convenient equivalent in cases where the imperial measurements themselves are only approximate. When following the projects, use either the metric or the imperial measurements; do not mix units.

INDEX

UPHOLSTERY

TOYMAKING

DOLLS' HOUSES AND MINIATURES

CRAFTS

VIDEOS

Drop-in and Pinstuffed Seats	*David James*
Stuffover Upholstery	*David James*
Elliptical Turning	*David Springett*
Woodturning Wizardry	*David Springett*
Turning Between Centres: The Basics	*Dennis White*
Turning Bowls	*Dennis White*
Boxes, Goblets and Screw Threads	*Dennis White*
Novelties and Projects	*Dennis White*
Classic Profiles	*Dennis White*
Twists and Advanced Turning	*Dennis White*
Sharpening the Professional Way	*Jim Kingshott*
Sharpening Turning & Carving Tools	*Jim Kingshott*
Bowl Turning	*John Jordan*
Hollow Turning	*John Jordan*
Woodturning: A Foundation Course	*Keith Rowley*
Carving a Figure: The Female Form	*Ray Gonzalez*
The Router: A Beginner's Guide	*Alan Goodsell*
The Scroll Saw: A Beginner's Guide	*John Burke*

MAGAZINES

WOODTURNING

WOODCARVING

FURNITURE & CABINETMAKING

THE ROUTER

WOODWORKING

THE DOLLS' HOUSE MAGAZINE

WATER GARDENING

OUTDOOR PHOTOGRAPHY

TRAVEL PHOTOGRAPHY

BLACK & WHITE PHOTOGRAPHY

BUSINESSMATTERS

The above represents a full list of all titles currently published or scheduled to be published.

All are available direct from the Publishers or through bookshops, newsagents and specialist retailers.

To place an order, or to obtain a complete catalogue, contact:

**GMC Publications,
Castle Place, 166 High Street, Lewes,
East Sussex BN7 1XU, United Kingdom
Tel: 01273 488005 Fax: 01273 478606**

E-mail: pubs@thegmcgroup.com

Orders by credit card are accepted